VIEW

<small>OF THE</small>

PAST AND PRESENT STATE

<small>OF THE</small>

ISLAND OF JAMAICA.

A

VIEW

OF THE

PAST AND PRESENT STATE

OF THE

ISLAND OF JAMAICA;

WITH

REMARKS

ON THE

MORAL AND PHYSICAL CONDITION

OF

THE SLAVES,

AND ON

THE ABOLITION OF SLAVERY IN THE COLONIES.

BY J. STEWART,

LATE OF JAMAICA.

NEGRO UNIVERSITIES PRESS
NEW YORK

Originally published in 1823
by Oliver & Boyd, Tweeddale-House

Reprinted 1969 by
Negro Universities Press
A DIVISION OF GREENWOOD PUBLISHING CORP.
NEW YORK

SBN 8371-2374-7

TO THE READER.

In the View here offered of the Past and Present State of the Island of Jamaica, the author has endeavoured to comprise every particular relating to it which appeared to him most worthy of attention,—avoiding as much as possible such minute and voluminous details as were incompatible with the limits of his work, and would not have materially contributed to its interest.

In such a work, a detailed history of the animal and vegetable productions of this important island, and, of course, of the West Indies generally, could not be expected; such a history (in part supplied by preceding publications) would in fact fill many volumes, and ought properly to be the subject of a distinct work, the province of the

zoologist and botanist.—He has, therefore, necessarily limited his notices on these subjects to
the most remarkable of each class of those productions. The historical, topographical, and
statistical notices, though concise, will be found
to embrace whatever is most interesting on those
subjects. Every particular of moment, relating
to the climate, diseases, soil, seasons, agriculture,
and commerce, has also been briefly noticed;
and such views are given of the government,
laws, and establishments, as will enable the
reader to form an accurate opinion of their more
important features. On the state of society—the
different classes of the free inhabitants—the
character, customs, and moral and physical condition of the slaves, and the means proposed of
improving their condition, as preliminary steps to
the gradual abolition of slavery, the author has
been more circumstantial—these being topics of
more particular interest, especially at the present
moment, and on which his long residence in
the island has enabled him to supply many important particulars.

In treating these last-mentioned subjects, the

author has been governed by the most perfect impartiality. Whatever differences of opinion may exist on some points which he discusses, as connected with those subjects, the accuracy and justness of his statements will at least be acknowledged. He has anxiously endeavoured to steer clear of all prejudices and party opinions. If, on the one hand, he conceives that the planters have, on some occasions, been unfairly accused by those who rather sought to vilify than convince them, he, on the other, thinks that their advocates are too prone to vindicate indiscriminately, and even hold up as faultless, whatever relates to the colonial system. The misrepresentations of the former originate in the partial and exaggerated statements of men who have visited the West Indies obviously for the purpose of noticing *only what was faulty*—and who, drawing sweeping conclusions from certain abuses and enormities they may have witnessed, exhibit a very unfair and distorted picture,—strengthening thereby those unqualified prejudices which have so assiduously been kept alive against the planters ;—while the latter, in their eagerness to repel the accusations of their opponents, are too frequently led into the opposite extreme of maintaining that there is nothing to amend in their system. This will sufficiently account for the irreconcilable discrepancies in many of the views laid before the public of the state of slavery in the colonies. From the conflicting statements—too often mixed up with revilings and abuse—of the colonists and anticolonists (as the former sometimes style the latter), it was hardly to be expected that any thing like an impartial view of the subject could be drawn.

Totally uninfluenced by such representations, the author has here given an unbiassed exposition of facts which have come within his view, accompanied by such opinions and remarks as his experience and judgment suggested. He has neither exaggerated nor palliated errors and abuses; and, while freely pointing out these, he has omitted no opportunity of bearing testimony to every humane and salutary improvement. To relate the truth, and nothing but the truth, has been his aim. He will not arrogantly pledge

himself that his book is free from errors—some
of which he is unconscious, may have crept
into the minuter commercial and other details;
but he trusts—should any exist—they will be
found of little moment, as far at least as regards
the more important matter. In short, he feels
confident that those who are best qualified to
form a correct opinion of his work will—whatever they may think of its literary merits—
award to it the higher credit of candour and
impartiality.

EDINBURGH, 1st July 1823.

CONTENTS.

xii

APPENDIX.

ERRATA.

P. 24, l. 16, *for* 18,000,000 *read* 20,000,000.   P. 99, l. 25, *for* brought
read bought.   P. 119, l. 20, *for* five *read* six.   P. 120, l. 17, *for* upwards of
read nearly.   P. 134, l. 23, *for* an order to all general officers, *read* a general order to all officers.   P. 143, l. 10, *for* of *read* of the.

VIEW OF JAMAICA.

VIEW

OF THE

PAST AND PRESENT STATE

OF THE

ISLAND OF JAMAICA.

CHAP. I.

GEOGRAPHICAL POSITION—HISTORY OF THE PRINCIPAL
EVENTS.

THE centre of the island of Jamaica is situated
in 18° 10′ 40″ north latitude, and in 77° 12′ 30″
west longitude, from London. It is 90 miles
west of St Domingo, about the same distance
south of Cuba, and 435 miles north of Cartha-
gena, on the continent of South America. It is
150 miles in length, and about 40 miles in its
mean breadth. Its name * is supposed to be de-

----

* The early Spanish historians wrote the name of this island
differently from the present spelling, viz. *Xaymaca.*

rived from a word in the language of the Aborigines, signifying *abounding in springs.*

This island was discovered by the great Columbus, in his second voyage to the New World, viz. in 1494, while coasting along the southern side of the island of Cuba. He made a landing, and took possession of the country with the usual formalities, but made no stay. In 1503, during his fourth and last voyage, he had, unexpectedly, an opportunity of knowing something more of Jamaica. Returning from Veragua to Hispaniola, he was compelled, by tempestuous weather, to put into one of its harbours, on the north side of the island, which, from this circumstance, still goes by the name of *Christopher's Cove.* Here his vessels got stranded, and he was in consequence detained for twelve months and four days—he and his people enduring inconceivable hardships and privations. The governor of Hispaniola, one of his most rancorous enemies, would not assist him, the Indians deserted him, * and his people revolted. From this extremity of distress he was at length happily relieved. This

---

* It is said that, while in Jamaica, Columbus, by predicting an eclipse of the sun, so impressed the Indians with the idea of his being a superior being, that they readily supplied him with provisions, and rendered him every other assistance in their power.

truly great man did not live long after this event. His health and strength were broken down by incessant toil, anxiety, and hardship; and that lofty and intrepid spirit, which had hitherto supported him through dangers and difficulties of no ordinary kind, at length sunk under the accumulated weight of bodily suffering, the persecutions of implacable enemies, and the ingratitude of his prince! Thus died one of the greatest of men, leaving behind him a name as splendid and imperishable as any which history records.

After the death of Columbus, his son Diego laid claim to the viceroyship of all the countries and islands discovered by his father. This the council of the Indies at Seville, before which he instituted a process against his sovereign, granted, together with a tenth part of all the gold and silver that might be found in those countries. But the king would not confirm to him more than the government and vice-admiralty of Hispaniola. He, however, persisted in his claim to the rights and authority that had been decreed him. But on his arrival in Hispaniola, he found that the king had invested in two other persons two separate governments, comprehending all the continent, and the island of Jamaica. This he considered as an unwarrantable infringement of his rights. He conceived, at least, that he was entitled to the privilege of nominating to the governments of Veragua and Jamaica.

Accordingly, he sent Don Juan de Esquivel with a small body of troops to secure Jamaica. This brave Castilian governed the infant colony with a humanity and moderation rare in these times of Spanish cruelty in the New World.* But he lived but a few years to dispense the blessings of a mild government to the natives; who, subsequently, were exterminated by the ferocious Spaniards, not one of their descendants being alive when the English conquered the island.

After the death of Diego Columbus, his honours and claims in the New World devolved on his eldest son, Don Lewis, who surrendered them to Charles V. for a grant of the province of Veragua and the island of Jamaica. Don Lewis died without issue; and his two brothers dying without male issue, their sister Isabella became

---

* " The affairs of Jamaica," (says Herrera), " went on prosperously, because Juan de Esquivel, having brought the natives to submission *without any effusion of blood*, they laboured in planting cotton, and raising other commodities, which yielded great profit."

Against the horrible barbarities perpetrated by the Spaniards on the unhappy aborigines of the New World, one virtuous Spaniard, Las Casas, (bishop of Chiapa), who witnessed them, indignantly raised his voice.

heiress of the Columbus family. By her marriage with the Count de Gelves, her rights devolved on the house of Braganza, in which they
continued till the year 1640, when they reverted
to the crown of Spain, in consequence of the
revolution by which the head of the Braganza
family was placed on the throne of Portugal.

The Spaniards built a town on the north side
of the island (near St Ann's Bay), called Seville,
and a village called Melilla, both of which they
afterwards abandoned; and St Jago de la Vega
(now Spanish Town) was subsequently founded
by Diego Columbus. Seville is reported to
have been destroyed, with its inhabitants, by the
Indians, in revenge for the cruelties exercised
on them by their merciless invaders.

The only articles which formed the export of
Jamaica at the time of its capture by the English
were cocoa, hog's lard, and hides; and the sale of
those articles, and the barter of their provisions
for such European commodities as they required,
constituted the only trade of the inhabitants.

The armament which wrested Jamaica from
the Spaniards (in 1655), was destined for another
enterprise, the conquest of Hispaniola; and to
the failure of that enterprise England is indebted
for this most important acquisition. So lightly,
however, did Oliver Cromwell appreciate this
conquest, and so displeased was he at the mis-

carriage of the actual object of the expedition, that the two commanders, Admiral Penn and General Venables, were sent by him, on their return home, to the Tower. It is, however, a curious fact, that Jamaica, at this time, produces a greater revenue to the mother country than the whole amount of the national revenue in the Protector's time. Jamaica was no doubt generally considered, at the period of its conquest, and for several years after, as far inferior in importance to either Cuba or Hispaniola; as in truth it would be at the present day, were those islands equally improved by cultivation. It was reserved for the enterprising industry and commercial spirit of the British to render Jamaica what it now is, the most highly cultivated and most productive colony in the American Archipelago. Thirty years ago, St Domingo (now Hayti) might have disputed with it that title; but that fine and fertile region became a prey to anarchy, a scene of misery and desolation,—the consequence of that sanguinary revolution which wrested it from its white possessors.*

In 1658, the Spaniards made an attempt to reconquer the island. They landed from Cuba with about two thousand infantry, at Rio Nuevo, a

---

* Hayti, now united into one republic, is at present in a more settled and prosperous state than formerly.

small harbour on the north side of the island, where they formed entrenchments. But they were defeated with great loss by the English, under Colonel D'Oyley, the lieutenant-governor, and finally driven from the island. After this defeat, the Spaniards made no effort of consequence to repossess themselves of Jamaica. But in 1694, Monsieur Du Casse, the governor of Hispaniola, made a descent on the island, and committed enormities disgraceful to the country whose troops he commanded. Not contented with plundering the defenceless inhabitants of the districts he ravaged, his soldiers burned the plantations, and even massacred many of the unfortunate persons who fell into their hands. At length he was defeated by the militia, and forced to embark precipitately with his dishonourable plunder.

From that time Jamaica has remained undisturbed by foreign enemies. It is well known that the French fleet, under Count de Grasse, was destined to make an attack on it in 1782. It is doubtful whether that formidable armament would have succeeded in making a conquest of the island, notwithstanding the inadequate force it had to repel such an attack; but happily the experiment was not tried, Admiral Rodney having intercepted and obtained over it a complete and glorious victory. The inhabitants, highly grateful for this important and well-timed service, paid the most splendid honours to the brave commander, who had thus rescued them in a moment of such imminent peril. The anniversary of this victory, (the 12th of April 1782), is celebrated by the most respectable of the inhabitants, and a statue and temple have been erected in Spanish Town in honour of the gallant admiral.

But though Jamaica has, since its possession by the English, been little molested by foreign enemies, there has arisen, at different times, within its own bosom, a foe more terrible than any external enemy—namely, the slaves ; and, at a later period, (viz. in 1795), a formidable tribe of the Maroons.

The first alarming insurrection of the slaves took pace in 1690 ; but the enormities committed were chiefly confined to the parish of Clarendon. In 1760 a most formidable insurrection of the Coromantees, one of the most ferocious of the African tribes, broke out in the parish of St Mary, and soon spread into other districts of the island. It appeared that the whole of that tribe throughout the island were accessary to that rebellion. A dreadful massacre of the defenceless whites, in various parts of the interior, ensued. The object of the insurgents was of course the total extermination of the whites. Happily, however, they were at length subdued, and some terrible examples were made of the most active of their leaders. Notwithstanding this severity, another insurrection was attempted in St Mary's only five years after, which, however, was disconcerted through the precipitation of the ringleaders. Happily for the whites, the insurgents wanted the skill and prudence to plan, combine, and direct their movements; they possessed a fearful odds of physical and numerical strength, but they knew not how to wield it.

Prior to the first insurrection, bodies of slaves had at different times absconded from their masters, and established themselves in the fastnesses of the woods; these became rallying points to other fugitive slaves :* at length they became so numerous and daring as to make incursions on the whites, carrying havoc and dismay wherever they went. This is the first origin of the Maroons. Under a bold and desperate leader, called Cudjoe, they at length bade defiance to the government, and carried on a regular warfare against it. Parties of whites were sent in pursuit of this banditti, and skirmishes often took place between them, with various success, but most commonly in favour of the Maroons, from

---

* There were also at this time fugitive negroes belonging to the Spaniards lurking in the woods.

their being more accustomed to traverse the mountainous woods, and better acquainted with the fastnesses and retreats they afforded. When hard pressed, and likely to be discomfited, they retired into these fastnesses ; from which they again issued, burning, and plundering, and massacring, with remorseless fury, wherever they directed their march

The white inhabitants being at length wearied and harassed by this savage warfare, and in continual danger from their barbarous enemies, and the government seeing no likelihood of being able to drive them from their haunts and compel them to surrender, a treaty was concluded with them by Governor Trelawny, by which they were declared free, and certain tracts of land were assigned to them. They were to be entirely subject to the laws and government of the whites; only, in petty cases, they might decide their own differences, subject, however, to the control of a white superintendent. It was also stipulated, that they should assist the whites in pursuing and reclaiming all runaway slaves, who might have fled into the woods, for each of whom, when brought in, they were to receive a stipulated reward. And, shocking to relate, the instructions not unfrequently were to bring in the fugitive slaves, *dead or alive ;* so that it was no unusual thing for a party of Maroons to take the

least troublesome method of earning their reward; namely, bringing in the head, instead of
the living body, of the unfortunate delinquent.
The Maroons were also to assist the whites in
all contests either with foreign or domestic enemies.

The Maroons continued peaceable until 1795,
when an unfortunate event occurred which
kindled an alarming and destructive rebellion.
Two Trelawny Town Maroons, (the most numerous and formidable tribe, or township, in the
island), were convicted by the magistrates of the
parish of St James of stealing a hog from a white
settler, and were sentenced for this crime to be
publicly whipped by the workhouse driver.
Their townsmen were indignant at this igno-
minious sentence: they said, that if the white
people had put their companions to death, they
would not have complained; but to disgrace and
degrade them by a punishment inflicted only on
slaves, was such an injury and insult to the whole
tribe as could only be atoned for by a retributive
vengeance.

At this time, too, they pretended to be ag-
grieved by other circumstances;—they wanted
more land, and they wanted a superintendent of
their own choosing. Lord Balcarras, the lieutenant-governor, would doubtless have listened
to any just complaints they might have made,

under other circumstances; but to grant demands
made in a tone of arrogant defiance was, he conceived, not sound policy. He therefore published a proclamation, demanding from them a
peaceable submission, and surrender of their
arms, under pain of being treated as rebels. Only
a few attended to this proclamation, and submitted; the rest continued refractory and in a
menacing attitude. Martial law was therefore
proclaimed, (August 1st 1795), the militia was
called out, and several regiments of regular troops
were instantly marched to the seat of war. The
intention was, by a prompt and general movement,
to surround the rebels in such a way as to cut
off the means of their retreat, and thus bring the
contest to a speedy termination. Those who expected such a result knew little of the Maroons;
as soon might they have arrested the eagle in his
flight as cut off the retreat of this agile and hardy
enemy.

The first signal of war was the disastrous over-
throw of Colonel Sandford's corps of light dragoons (the 20th regiment), reinforced by a party
of mounted militia, in all about four hundred
men, by an ambuscade of the Maroons, in a defile between the old and new Maroon towns.
This officer unfortunately pushed on farther than
his orders directed, and, through his temerity
and imprudence, perished, with thirty of his par-

ty, by a close and deadly fire from an unseen enemy. The affair was but of a few minutes, and had the courage of the insurgents been equal to their activity and skill as marksmen, it is probable that not one of the party would have escaped.

The next signal defeat of the whites was that of a detachment of the 83d regiment and a party of the Accompong-town Maroons, commanded by Colonel Fitch, wherein that officer, eight soldiers of the 83d, Captain Brisset of Fort Charlotte, and two of the friendly Maroons, were killed, and fourteen of the party wounded. It is here to be remarked, that the Accompong-town Maroons, not being implicated in the quarrel of the insurgent tribe, joined the whites, in virtue of the treaty made with their forefathers by Governor Trelawny. But they were at best a doubtful and unwilling ally; and after this defeat, they retired to their town, and refused to fight any more,—a resolution which the whites were not in a condition to oppose; glad, indeed, in the then posture of their affairs, to secure their neutrality.

The insurgent Maroons now formed themselves into different parties, each commanded by some daring and skilful captain, and attacked the whites at different points. Their policy was, not openly to face the parties of their adversaries, but to cut them off in detail. By means of their scouts and spies, they learnt the route of small detachments and escorts, which they ambushed and destroyed. On one occasion they killed every man of a detachment of regulars, convoying provisions to one of the posts. Their parties spread among the remoter settlements, where there were no troops stationed, reducing the buildings to ashes, and massacring the inhabitants,—too often under circumstances of the most savage barbarity. Terror and dismay now began to spread among the whites; great numbers of them had perished, while it was not distinctly ascertained that a single Maroon had fallen in action; such negroes as had been killed, in surprising their encampments, being fugitive slaves who had joined them, or been forced into their service, and made scouts and sentinels of. It was, in short, found that the whole military strength of the island was not a match for this handful of Maroons; and fearful auguries began to be entertained as to the issue of the contest. There was no prospect of bringing it to a speedy termination by the ordinary means of civilized warfare; the insurgents would become more audacious by success; there was a just apprehension that the other tribes of Maroons, tempted by the success of their brethren, would not long remain faithful to the whites; the dry season, when the crops begin, was approaching, at which time the insurgents would have it in their power to set the whole country in flames.* At this critical moment, the safety, and, probably, future ascendency of the whites, hung as it were upon a thread. They depended on the slaves remaining faithful and tranquil. They did remain faithful and peaceable, and their masters owe them an incalculable debt of gratitude for this their fidelity and good conduct. No symptoms of refactoriness or disobedience appeared, and a solitary white man, left in charge of a plantation, while his brother planters were performing the duty of soldiers, slept in safety amidst two, three, or four hundred slaves. The truth is, the slaves had a great dread of and aversion to the Maroons, and the impression on their minds was, that they would make far worse masters than their present owners. They could not forget, that at no distant period they, the Maroons, had become the willing and pitiless agents of cruel and oppressive white masters.

Notwithstanding this peaceable demeanour of

---

* During crop, the stubble of the cane fields, and even the grass, become so parched by the long droughts which usually prevail at that time, that, if fire were communicated to them, the plantations would inevitably be consumed by the flames, which spread with inconceivable fury and rapidity.

the slaves, the country was in a very alarming state, and the future appeared big with evil. The whole force of the island had been exerted hitherto to no purpose. In this state of affairs, Lord Balcarras, with the advice of his council, and the earnest recommendation of the principal inhabitants, resolved to send to the island of Cuba for blood-hounds, for the purpose of employing them against the rebellious Maroons— a new and terrible expedient, which nothing but dire necessity could have induced his lordship to have recourse to. His object was to terrify the Maroons into submission, by the introduction of these animals, and thus save the country, and put a stop to the horrible barbarities of those savages. He judged right as to the effect these canine allies would produce. The exaggerated accounts which some runaway slaves conveyed to the Maroons of the strength and ferocity of the dogs struck them with terror: in a short time after their introduction, a party of forty Maroons came in and surrendered themselves; and in two months after, (March 18th 1796), the whole surrendered, by capitulation, to General Walpole. The terms were, that their lives should be spared, and that they should be suffered to remain in the country, under the whites, as before. This last article the governor and assembly conceived to be highly impolitic, and they therefore refused to ratify it.* It was justly considered, that, though these people would remain for a time, from compulsion, apparently submissive and peaceable, they would yet brood over their hatred to the whites, and secretly meditate a future and signal vengeance, when some fit opportunity offered. They were, therefore, transported, at the expense of the island, to Nova Scotia, and subsequently, as the climate of that region was too cold for them, to Sierra Leon, in Africa.

This rebellion continued upwards of seven months, namely, from August 12th 1795, when the first action took place with Colonel Sandford's corps, till March 18th 1796. Although none of the other Maroons in the island joined in this rebellion, yet, as a measure of precaution, they were deprived of their arms.

The lieutenant-governor brought a considerable degree of odium upon himself by consenting to employ blood-hounds against the Maroons.

---

* The rejection of this article of the treaty led to a disagreeable rupture beetween General Walpole and the governor and assembly; the former viewing it as a dishonourable violation of the faith of treaties. Accordingly he declined accepting a sword, value 500 guineas, which the assembly voted him ; and, on his return to England, he laid a grave complaint before parliament of the conduct of the lieutenant-governor and assembly in this business.

A general outcry was raised in England, both in and out of parliament, against his lordship, on this occasion. Doubtless it was a proceeding which, unexplained, must have appeared, on the very face of it, not only highly objectionable, but heinous. It was not without the most grave deliberation, and after viewing the subject in all its bearings, that his lordship consented, at the earnest desire of the other two branches of the legislature, to send an accredited agent to Cuba to procure two hundred bloodhounds to be employed in this war. The intention was, as has been said, that they might, by the terror they inspired, induce the Maroons to come in and surrender themselves. This event their presence speedily brought about. Those who have ever traversed the wild and remote mountains of Jamaica, well know that they afford retreats where dogs cannot effectually be employed against such an enemy as the Maroons. This was sufficiently proved, for not a drop of blood was shed by these animals, excepting an unfortunate accident of one getting loose from its keeper, and severely injuring a female negro slave. They were muzzled, and held in couples by the Spanish chasseurs who attended them. By their keen scent they discovered the Maroon ambushes, and thus put the parties approaching them on their guard. From the moment of their arrival, the Maroons became exceedingly circumspect, and far less frequent in their murderous excursions. They became more solicitous about the safety of their women and children, and more attentive in guarding against surprises. The first party that came in declared that their surrender was solely owing to their dread of the Spanish dogs. Negroes are prone to exaggerate, and such of the slaves as had seen these animals, and afterwards joined the Maroons, gave to the latter a sufficiently appalling description of their size, their fierceness, their strength, their swiftness, and numbers. Thus, in short, was much bloodshed and barbarity, not to say the absolute destruction of the country, prevented by the introduction of those animals.*

During this rebellion, the white parties sometimes committed excesses which could answer no other end than to exasperate the Maroons,

---

* In addition to what has been said on the subject of the Spanish dogs, the question may be asked, whether a departure from the usages of civilized warfare be not justifiable against an enemy who tortures and puts to death the prisoners who fall into his hands? Doubtless it may, with reason, be said, that such an expedient savours too much of barbarity to be resorted to under any circumstances. Be this as it may, it must be gratifying to humanity to reflect, that, on this occasion, much evil was averted from one party, without injury to the other through the agency of these animals.

and render them more desperate and blood-thirsty. But on this, and some other topics connected with the Maroon rebellion, the author will take occasion to speak in giving an account of the character and habits of the Maroons.*

Since the termination of the Maroon rebellion, this island has remained undisturbed by either foreign or domestic enemies.

The constitution of Jamaica continued in a very unsettled state until 1728, when it was permanently settled by an agreement with the crown. During the first five years that the island was in possession of the English, an absolute military government existed. In 1660 the governor (Colonel D'Oyly) administered the government in conjunction with a council of twelve, chosen by the inhabitants. This was the first advance towards a representative system.

In 1663, the first general assembly was summoned by Sir Charles Littleton, then governor, and on the 20th of January 1664 they met. They exercised the right of adjourning themselves. Soon after the restoration, an arbitrary

---

* A more minute detail of the events of this rebellion than the author has here given, would neither suit the limits of his work nor be interesting to the reader. Those who seek for particular information on this subject, will find it in Dallas's " History of the Maroon Rebellion," in two volumes 8vo.

constitution was formed for the island, *as a punishment* for refusing a revenue to the crown of four and a half per cent. on the gross produce of the island; but it was indignantly rejected, " and ultimately (says Dr Colquhoun) abandoned by the parent state, without obtaining the impost which had been demanded, and the old privileges of the assembly were restored, and that of framing such laws for their internal government as the exigencies of the country required. Yet the sovereigns refused to confirm those privileges, which placed the affairs of Jamaica in a very unsettled state for fifty years, and greatly obstructed its progress towards improvement."

" The unhappy contest continued from the reign of Charles the Second to George the Second, when, in 1728, matters were compromised by an agreement, on the part of the assembly, to settle on the crown a perpetual revenue of £8000 a-year, on condition, first, That the quit-rents, then estimated at £1460 per annum, should form part of the sum; secondly, That the body of their laws should receive the royal assent; and, thirdly, That all such laws and statutes of England, as had at any time been esteemed, introduced, used, accepted, or received, as laws of the island, should be and continue laws of Jamaica for ever. This compromise matured the constitution of Jamaica."

Jamaica, since it has been in the hands of the English, has suffered not less from physical than political evils. It has been visited by earthquakes and hurricanes; and epidemical diseases almost as fatal in their ravages as the plague.

In 1692 an awful and destructive earthquake destroyed, within the space of three minutes, nine-tenths of the town of Port Royal, and the greater number of its inhabitants. This earthquake was felt over the whole island. On the north side 1000 acres of land, with its settlements and inhabitants, suddenly sunk. The anniversary of this awful catastrophe is still held in Jamaica as a day of fasting and humiliation. Since this signal and destructive visitation many earthquakes have been felt in Jamaica; one of which severely injured the town of Savanna la Mar: the rest were not attended with any serious consequences, though the shocks felt from some of them created the most lively apprehensions—as in that of 1802, at eleven o'clock at night, when, in an instant, the streets of the towns that felt it most sensibly were filled with people of all descriptions, who rushed out, naked, with wildness and dismay in their looks.

Since 1712 ten severe and destructive hurricanes are recorded, besides minor storms, which are of far more frequent occurrence. The misery and mischief which a hurricane, in the West Indies, brings with it, is inconceivable. The most tremendous one ever felt in Jamaica—at least since the English have been in possession of the island—was that of 1780. The loss of lives and property on that occasion was very great; and such was the calamitous and general distress that followed, that the British government felt it necessary to aid the sufferers. Since 1786, Jamaica has been, happily, exempt from what may properly be termed hurricanes, though it has experienced several tempests, attended by more or less injury, the severest of which was that of 1816.

With respect to the malignant fevers of this country, they have been so frequent and so fatal to the white population, that an account of them would fill many volumes. Of these, and other diseases of the country, something will be said in a future chapter.

The following particulars will show the progressive improvement of the cultivation, population, and commerce of Jamaica, for the last century and a half.

In 1673, there were in the island 7768 whites, and 9504 slaves. The chief products were cocoa, indigo, and hides. Sugar had just then been begun to be cultivated.

In 1722, the island produced 11,000 hogsheads of sugar.

In 1734, there were 7644 whites, 86,546 slaves, and 76,011 head of cattle, in the island.

In 1744, there were 9640 whites, 112,428 slaves, and 88,036 head of cattle; and the island produced 35,000 hogsheads of sugar, and 10,000 puncheons of rum.

In 1768, there were 17,000 whites, 166,914 slaves, and 135,773 head of cattle; and 55,761 hogsheads of sugar, and 15,551 puncheons of rum were produced.

In 1774, the island produced only 654,700 lbs. of coffee; and in 1790, 1,783,740 lbs.

At present there are in Jamaica about 350,000 slaves, 300,000 head of stock; and the annual average produce may be about 130,000 hogsheads of sugar, 60,000 puncheons of rum, and 18,000,000 lbs. of coffee, &c.

CHAP. II.

THE principal chain of mountains runs through the centre of the island, from east to west, along a considerable part of its extent. These are of various altitudes and degrees of acclivity. Some are lofty, broken, and abrupt; others of a lesser height and more gradual ascent, and spreading at their summits into an expanse of fine fertile country, beautifully varied with hill and dale, and interspersed with coffee, pimento, and other plantations, and grazing settlements, or *pens*. The loftiest and least accessible of the central mountains are the *Blue Mountains,* in the eastern part of the island, the highest peak of which is computed to be about 7000 feet above the level of the sea.

There is no island in the West Indies so diversified in its surface as Jamaica. Its mountains, its precipitous rocks, its countless hills, valleys, and glades—its lofty, rugged, and abrupt ascents—its deep ravines, caverns, and *cockpits**

---

* A level spot, surrounded and confined by lofty and abrupt mountains, into which a narrow defile leads.

—its thick-planted majestic woods—its numerous rivers, cascades, and mountain-streams, dashing through this wildness of nature—give to the interior a diversity and grandeur of appearance not to be found, perhaps, in any other island of similar extent. On descending towards the sea-shore, the scenery becomes less bold and stupendous, though still finely relieved by the varied surface of the country, by woods, fields, and luxuriant pastures of Guinea grass, beautifully shaded by the finest trees, displaying every tint of green. From the higher eminences is beheld the more level country below, covered with extensive cane-fields, intermixed with pastures, tufts of wood, and dwellings, stretching to the sea-shore, which is fringed with mangroves, and here and there enlivened with tufts and groves of cocoa-nut, palmeto, and cabbage trees.

No fossil remains of animals have been discovered in this island; but on the tops of some of the mountains, shells and other marine exuviæ have been found. The rocks are chiefly chalk, quartz, and limestone. Both in the interior and near the sea are numerous caverns, some of which are of considerable size, and contain many specimens of stalactites, particularly one in the parish of St Ann, which covers a large space of ground, and is intersected throughout by stalactite columns of various dimensions and shapes, like the massy pillars of a Gothic cathedral. Copper and lead are the only metals that have been ascertained to exist: no precious stones have been found. Mineralogical discoveries are not in fact made; the inhabitants find it more profitable to draw wealth from the surface of the earth, than explore its bowels for the precious metals; and researches of a purely scientific nature, after the rarities of the mineral kingdom, seldom engage any one's attention.

Jamaica is divided into three counties, Surry, Middlesex, and Cornwall, and these are subdivided into twenty-one parishes. It contains one city, Kingston, and thirty-three towns and villages. The principal of these are, St Jago de la Vega, Port Royal, Montego Bay, Falmouth, Savanna la Mar, Lucca, Morant Bay, Port Morant, Port Maria, Black River, and St Ann's Bay.

Kingston is a considerable city, and has a very great trade. Its population is about 30,000 persons of all descriptions. It is governed by a mayor, twelve aldermen, and twelve common councilmen, and has a town-guard and police. It contains some handsome private buildings in the West India style. It has two churches, one of the regular establishment, the other of the presbyterian persuasion. The latter is a handsome and spacious structure. It was erected

some years ago by the numerous and respectable
body of Presbyterians in Kingston, aided by occasional grants from the Assembly. Their pastor
is appointed by the church of Scotland. Prior
to the erection of this church, it was felt as a
great evil that there should be only one church
of the establishment in so populous a city. There
are some good institutions here for charitable
purposes, particularly the free school, the hospital, the lunatic asylum, and the asylum for
deserted negroes. The last-mentioned is of a
nature so benevolent and necessary, that none of
the parishes ought to be without one. This city
is so hot, and often so exceedingly unhealthy,
that most of the merchants have country resi-
dences in cool and elevated parts of the vicinity,
to which they retire when the business of the
day is over. The harbour is protected by a narrow slip of land, of which Port Royal forms the
extremity.

St Jago de la Vega, or Spanish Town, as it is
usually called, is the principal town of the parish
of St Catherine, and is the seat of government.
It is a small town, but the handsomest in the
island, from its being embellished with the King's
House (the residence of the governor), and the
public offices. The supreme court of judicature,
court of chancery, court of errors, &c. sit here.
It has a free school, poor-house, a charity for the

support of poor widows, and another for the support of poor maidens and distressed strangers.

Port Royal, the chief town of the parish of the same name, is chiefly remarkable for its harbour being the station for the men of war, for its naval arsenal, and its fortifications. The town of itself contained few good houses before the fire which, in 1815, almost totally consumed it; but it is now rebuilding in a better style. The bulk of the inhabitants are people of colour, and others, employed in supplying the navy with necessaries, and keeping houses of rendezvous for the seamen.

Montego Bay is the chief town and seaport of the parish of St James. It is, in consequence of its trade, a thriving and pretty populous town. It is, however, far inferior to what it once was, namely, prior to the fire which, in 1795, destroyed the greater part of it. In 1811 it again suffered severely from a similar calamity. The inhabitants at length saw, and have since in some measure remedied, the causes of these misfortunes. The houses being built chiefly of wood, that material fed and propagated the devouring element; and there was much danger from the low petty houses inhabited by free people of colour and negroes, scattered over every part of the town, where spirits were retailed, and scenes of inebriety perpetually occurred. Most of the houses that have been built since the last fire are formed chiefly of brick or stone. There is a neat church here, a free school is established, and a new jail has lately been erected. The Cornwall assize courts are held here.

The harbour of this town is exposed to great danger, from a heavy swell of the sea setting into it during the prevalence of the north winds. To remedy this evil, a breakwater was projected about thirty years ago, and a tonnage was levied on the shipping to defray the expense. Since then, immense sums of money have been literally buried in the sea, the work being still incomplete. The projectors began by sinking stones of various sizes in the line of the intended breakwater, which were often swept away by the violence of the waves, and were even at best a very unstable foundation for such a superstructure as was required. A prodigious waste of money and labour would have been saved by the simple and obvious measure of employing an able engineer, who, if the scheme had been practicable, would have marked out a plan for carrying it into execution in the most effectual and least expensive way.

Falmouth is the principal town and seaport of the parish of Trelawny. About thirty-five years ago it was an inconsiderable village; now it is larger and more populous than Montego Bay. This rapid rise it owes chiefly to its harbour, where a greater quantity of produce is shipped than from any other part of the island, Kingston excepted. This gives employment to about 15,000 tons of British shipping. There is a good church here, a very handsome and spacious court-house, a marine hospital, a neat jail, substantial and commodious barracks, and a free school. The inhabitants are supplied with water by means of a hydraulic machine. In 1808 a great part of this town was consumed by fire, but it has since been rebuilt in a better style.

In the other towns there is nothing that claims particular attention. Each of them has its church, its court-house, its free school, its jail, and its workhouse; and this comprehends all of any moment that can be said of them.

There is no country in the world better supplied than Jamaica with harbours and other shelters for shipping. There are thirty principal harbours, besides more than double that number of bays, creeks, and coves, capable of affording more or less shelter to vessels. The safest and most capacious of the harbours are those of Kingston, Old Harbour, Port Antonio, Port Morant, and Lucca.

Another great advantage this island possesses

is its numerous fine rivers,* and the multitude
of its rivulets and springs. Of the former there
is only one that is navigable for small craft, viz.
Black River, on which merchandize, &c. is
brought down and taken up a distance of about
thirty miles; but all of them are of great value
and importance, on account of the plantations
they irrigate, the numerous mills they turn, and
the beauty and interest they give to the country
through which they flow. Many of them form
beautiful cascades in their course (two of which,
in the parish of St Ann, are admired by every
traveller), and give an additional charm to the
picturesque and magnificent scenery along their
banks. It will appear surprising, that, in an
island of such limited extent as Jamaica, there
should be no less than forty rivers, varying in
their breadth from twenty to an hundred feet or
more. Most of these abound with the finest fish,
some account of which will be given in the proper place. The springs and rivulets, though numerous, are very unequally distributed. In some
parts of the island seven or eight may be counted
within the circuit of as many miles, while there

---

* Over some of these are built handsome and substantial
bridges—conveniences of which many parts of the island, some
years ago, stood much in need.

are other districts so far removed from water, that the inhabitants residing in them are obliged to have recourse to tanks and ponds.

The public roads are in general very good. They are superintended and kept in repair by *way-wardens*, as they are called, who are appointed by the vestries for the purpose. A parish-tax is levied to defray the expense. Since the Maroon rebellion, many new roads of communication have been opened by authority of the legislature, by whom suitable sums have been voted for completing them. The difficulty of traversing the country during that rebellion pointed out the expediency of these improvements; and, besides this public expediency, these new tracks operate to enhance the value of the lands in their neighbourhood, and to encourage settlers to cultivate them. Such is the rugged and unequal surface of many parts of the interior, that roads across the island cannot be made practicable for carriages. Along some of the public roads by the sea-side are planted rows of cocoa-nut trees, which intercept the piercing beams of a hot vertical sun, and have a pleasing rural appearance.

A variety of fruit and other trees appear scattered over the towns, and embosom the dwellings. The stately cabbage-tree, the cocoa-nut, the jasmine-tree, the orange, the shaddock, the umbrageous tamarind, and other tropical plants, adorn the premises and refresh the eye of the panting inhabitant. At a distance, and particularly from the sea, this mixture of tropical foliage has a picturesque and pleasing effect.

The houses are of various constructions. Some are built entirely of wood; but generally the lower story is of stone or brick, and the upper (for there are few houses of more than two stories) of wood. Some have a plain front, and others have piazzas below, and balconies, or virandoes, above. Sash-windows and jealousies are usually now intermixed; though in the more ancient houses, especially in the interior, the former are never found. A creole of former days, in building his country-house, had two principal objects in view, namely, stability against the shock of hurricanes, and security in the event of an insurrection of the slaves. Accordingly, the massy stone walls of the lower story of his house were perforated with loop-holes for musquetry; while the superstructure (of one story), surmounted with a considerably inclined roof, was formed of the most substantial hard timber. The first-named precaution is happily now not deemed necessary, security having kept pace with the introduction of a more humane system.

Jamaica contains, according to Mr Robertson's survey, 2,724,262 acres, of which there were in cultivation, in 1818,

	ACRES.
In sugar plantations......... 639,000	
In breeding farms, or pens,.....................280,000	
In coffee, pimento, ginger, cotton, &c.....181,000	
Total............1,100,000	

A considerable part of the uncultivated portion is, however, incapable of being turned to any account.

The soil is various: the kinds most common are, a stiff white or yellow clay, with a thin superstratum of vegetable mould; a deep rich black mould; a brick mould; a rich brown loam, intermixed with flint; loam without admixture; a light porous earth, intermixed with gravel and stones; marl thinly mixed with veins of vegetable mould. Of the adaptation of these soils to the different products of the country mention will be made under the head of agriculture.

In 1812, the number of the slaves in this island, according to the parochial returns, was 319,912; and in 1818, the number returned was 345,252. Part of this apparent increase is to be placed to the account of the registry act; persons who avoided giving in a true account of their slaves, before the passing of that act, in order to elude payment of the taxes, were at length compelled to render such returns, under pain of forfeiting their right to the slaves omitted. But there has also been a small natural increase.

The number of white inhabitants may be computed at 35,000;* and there may be about the same number of free persons of colour. But, as no regular census is taken of either of these classes, the precise number cannot be ascertained. The people of colour in a state of slavery are included in the slave population, of which they at present form about a tenth part.

---

* During the last century and a half, the whites, notwithstanding the great and constant emigration, have only increased about fivefold; while the slave population has been increased in a ratio of thirty-six to one.

CHAP. III.

THE climate of Jamaica is conformable to the latitude in which it is placed. The degrees of heat are various, according to the different periods of the year, and the various altitudes of the country. In July and August the heat often rises, in the hotter parts of the island, to 96 degrees of Fahrenheit, and is sometimes as high as 100; while in the months of December and January it seldom exceeds 75, and in the elevated parts of the interior it is sometimes as low as 55 : on one occasion, in the month of January, in a high and bleak part of the mountains, the author knew it to be as low as 48. There is in general a difference of about fifteen degrees between the temperature of the air of the higher parts of the island and that of the low country near the sea. It is cooler and more salubrious on the north side of the island than on the south. In this region, it has been kindly ordained by Providence, that the heat, which would otherwise be intolerable, and so destructive of human life as to render it almost uninhabitable, should be tempered by appropriate causes. While the inhabitant of the mountains enjoys a purer and more wholesome air than he who resides in the low lands near the ocean, the latter is comforted and refreshed by the daily sea-breeze, which periodically sets in, generally about nine o'clock in the morning. So peculiarly welcome is this friend of man, that the poor half-parched seaman, when he eyes the distant rippling of the ocean, and the dark-blue streak on its farthest verge indicative of its approach, hails it by the *healing* appellation of the *doctor*. Health sits perched on its wing, and gladness follows in its train. It is also observable, that, during the hottest time of the day, and in the most sultry months, a succession of light flying clouds continually pass over and intercept the sun's intense blaze. On travelling a few miles into the upland country, the inhabitant of the town, half-suffocated by heat and dust, enjoys an ineffably sweet relief. The very sight of the verdure and the foliage is refreshing to him : he gazes on the hills, the valleys, the tufts of trees around him, and inhales the breath of the balmy land-breeze which passes over him, with a keenness of delight inconceivable by any but those who have experienced such a change. He feels, in short, that he is transported into a region full of freshness and sweetness and beauty.

There is no striking variation of the seasons, excepting what is occasioned by the alternation of rainy and dry weather. The temperature of the air, as has already been said, is many degrees cooler during the winter months than in those of the summer; and in elevated and remote parts of the interior this difference is so sensibly felt, that the inhabitants sometimes have recourse to fires at the close of the day : it is, however, most perceptible in the mornings, before the dew is exhaled. On the highest peaks of the mountains snow was never known to have fallen; but hail has often been seen; generated in a colder region of the atmosphere, it, however, almost instantly dissolves on falling to the ground.

The rains do not always take place in the same months; and in different parts of the island there is a considerable variation in the time of their commencement. In the mountains they are earlier, more frequent, and more heavy, than in the low country. In the latter, one district will have rain a month or six weeks sooner or later than another not twenty miles distant from it. Sometimes what are called the spring rains do not set in till June, and even later; at other times, though not so frequently, they begin as early as March or April. This being the time for getting in the sugar crops on the north side of the island, these early rains are a considerable impediment. The roads being rutted and cut up, the planters find it a difficult task both to get home their canes and to forward their produce to the shipping places; besides the deficiency of fuel, occasioned by the want of opportunity to dry it, which to the sugar plantations is a primary concern, as without it the work of crop cannot be carried on. This will be better understood, when the reader is informed, that this fuel is the dried stems of the canes, after the juice is expressed. The spring rains usually last about two months, and sometimes longer. The autumnal or *fall rains*, as they are called by the planters, fall in October and November. These are essentially necessary to bring forward the young canes, which are generally planted at this season, in preference to the spring, as having a longer time to grow, and of course coming to greater perfection. The spring rains are by far the most violent. During the prevalence of these the air is most insufferably sultry. This intense heat, joined to a still and breezeless atmosphere, is a presage of the approaching torrent, which comes on with astonishing rapidity. The clouds hastily gather, and settle into a deep compact gloom, overshadowing the face of heaven, so lately cloudless and serene. A tremendous peal of thunder bursts from this dark cloud, and gives signal of the coming torrent: in a few minutes it descends in streams, of which no one can form an idea who has not witnessed such a scene. During its continuance, the firmament is rent with incessant peals of thunder, which are sometimes so frightfully loud as to resemble the close report of the heaviest artillery; while the quick and vivid flashes of lightning, threatening destruction as they shoot athwart the sky, are truly terrific. These rains, often for weeks together, set in regularly, and continue about the same length of time, namely, from two to three hours. Sometimes, however, very heavy rains will continue whole days and nights with little intermission. The autumnal rains are, as has been said, by no means so heavy as those of the spring, neither are they usually accompanied with thunder and lightning; but they are often attended by heavy gusts of wind from the north.

The rains—particularly those of the spring— before the heavier torrents have commenced, are frequently partial. It often happens, that, while the mountainous parts, which seldom suffer from want of rain, are visited by daily torrents, the low country is parched with excessive drought. Nay, the author has seen plantations severely suffering from drought, while others, divided from them only by a ridge of hills, were fa-voured by plenteous showers. These, passing along the one valley, never crossed over to the other; and this partial and tantalizing distribution of rain would sometimes continue for weeks. The dews which happily fall during droughts are a considerable help to vegetation.

It has been already remarked, that Jamaica has been fortunately exempt from the visitation of hurricanes since 1786, though it has experienced several storms or minor tempests. The following description will convey to the mind of the reader some idea of the violence of a West-India hurricane. It is taken from various accounts of the great hurricanes in Jamaica of 1780 and 1784, communicated by respectable eye-witnesses.

A hurricane is usually preceded by awful and certain prognostics. An unusual calm prevails; not a breath of wind is felt; the atmosphere is close and sultry, the clouds wild, broken, and perpetually and rapidly shifting; at length a deep and portentous gloom gradually settles and overspreads the hemisphere; the sun is enveloped in darkness; a deep, hollow, and murmuring sound is indistinctly heard, like the roaring of a distant cataract, or the howling of winds through remote woods; rapid and transient gusts of wind and rain speedily succeed; various birds of passage are seen hastily driving along the sky, or are thrown down by the violence of those gusts; even the cattle, grazing in the fields, as if instinctively aware of the approaching danger, withdraw to the adjacent thickets for shelter. The blasts soon become more impetuous; at one moment they rage with inconceivable fury, and the ensuing instant seem as it were suddenly to expire. In a few hours the hurricane reaches its acmé of violence—when all the winds of heaven, and from every point of the compass,* winged with destruction, seem let loose from their caverns. The largest trees are thrown prostrate, or shattered and stripped of their foliage; the provision-grounds are laid waste; the sugar-canes levelled to the earth, and, in the more exposed situations, torn up by the roots and wafted about like chaff. Many of the dwellings are blown down, or unroofed, and their inhabitants too often either buried in the ruins, or driven forth to perish unsheltered.

Nothing can be more appalling than the wild howling and threatening violence of a hurricane during the night, when the vivid and quickly-succeeding gleams of lightning, darting athwart the heavens, make " darkness visible," and heighten the horrors of the scene. Well might the witness of such a scene exclaim with King Lear,

---

* During a hurricane the wind rapidly shifts from one point to another.

" Let the great gods,
That keep this dreadful pother o'er our heads,
Find out their enemies now. Tremble, thou wretch,
That hast within thee undivulged crimes,
Unwhipt of justice!"

Nothing can be conceived more dismal than
the aspect of a country desolated by one of those
tropical blasts. The cane-fields appear as if a
roller had passed over them, and the woods as if
visited by some sudden blight; the rivers are
swollen and discoloured, and the level lands in-
undated by their overflowings, and by the torrents of rain that have fallen; numbers of the
dwellings are laid in ruins; the plantain-walks
(from which the inhabitants draw much of their
subsistence) are destroyed, and even the ground-
provisions, or various edible roots, do not entirely escape the general devastation. The
planter, in short, sees his crop destroyed; and,
what is far worse, he frequently beholds his
slaves perish around him for want of subsistence,
or by diseases brought upon them by improper
food, to which, in the extremity of hunger,
they resort. What adds to the horrors of such
a situation, is the long drought usually succeeding those visitations, by which the products of the earth spared by the tempest are
arrested in their growth, the vegetation being
dried up and suspended by the parching heat

and want of moisture. These accumulated
evils were never so severely felt as after the
great hurricane of 1780; at which time the
slaves were every day perishing in numbers,
partly by diseases (chiefly dysentery) produced
by unwholesome food, and partly by absolute
starvation. The lowest price of a barrel even of
old decayed flour was fourteen pounds Jamaica
currency—it was indeed a great favour to obtain
it at any price. A universal scarcity of other
provisions prevailed, and the miserable slaves
were compelled to feed on the wild-yam (a
bitter and unwholesome root), on half-ripe fruits,
and other wretched vegetables, which to their
craving appetites were yet sweet and gratifying.

At this time of general misery and privation,
there were some avaricious monopolizers, who,
regardless of the sufferings around them, kept
back their flour from the market, with a view of
obtaining a still higher price for it. A base avarice often defeats itself. One of these wretches
kept a considerable quantity of this article on
hand till the arrival of a fresh supply, which was
generously sold by the importer at a moderate
price; and the hoarded flour, being by this time
greatly injured by keeping, was sold by public
auction at about one-twentieth of the price its
sordid owner expected for it.

The most common diseases in Jamaica are,

malignant epidemic fever, commonly called yellow fever, common bilious fever, typhus fever, and intermittent fever, dysentery, pleurisy, and liver complaint. Pleurisy chiefly prevails among the slaves. Liver complaint, though common, is by no means so deadly a malady as it is in the east; a removal to a cold climate, in an early stage of the disorder, generally suffices to remove it: children are, however, often carried off by it. Dysentery is most prevalent and fatal among the negroes; it sometimes spreads over whole districts, and is contagious. Of this and other diseases to which the slaves are more peculiarly subject, some notice will be taken in treating of the slaves. Consumption is by no means a common disease. Of the chronic diseases, gout and rheumatism are very common; but very few cases of stone or gravel occur; they are diseases which are little known in the West Indies.

Of all the diseases of this country, the most violent and fatal is the malignant epidemic fever. Its ravages are at times as rapid and destructive as those of the plague. It is most fatal to new-comers; persons long resident in the island, and consequently inured to the climate, generally escape it, while hundreds of the former are perishing around them. It is attended by a highly inflammatory febrile affection of the whole system, with a particular determination to the head,

violent headache, nausea and irritation of the
stomach, restlessness, pain and weakness of the
spine, delirium, and an utter prostration of
strength. In two or three days, if the febrile
and inflammatory symptoms be not in some
measure subdued, the patient is cut off, though
a few may linger somewhat longer. Youth,
strength, the most robust frame, avail not in
withstanding this terrible foe; on these it operates most violently and rapidly. The remedies
generally adopted are powerful doses of calomel,
in the outset, and, afterwards, milder laxatives as
occasion requires; blisters applied to the back,
breast, neck, and sometimes head; sudorifics,
occasionally opiates, and, in the intermissions of
the fever, Peruvian bark mixed up in brandy
and water. Bleeding is seldom or never resorted
to. Some practitioners are advocates for the cold
affusion recommended by the late Dr Curry,
while others condemn it. There have been cases
where it has succeeded, but many more where it
has failed. Much certainly depends on the state
of the patient, and the crisis when it is used;
unseasonably applied, it may prove not only
injurious, but fatal. Unhappily, many of the
treatises that have been written on the nature
and treatment of this direful disease contain such
contradictory opinions as rather to perplex than
elucidate this most interesting subject. There is,

as may be supposed, an equal diversity of opinion among the practitioners—a thing not of rare occurrence among the gentlemen of the faculty ;—but it is much to be regretted that they should be so much at variance on a subject of such importance. Certain it is, that an effectual mode of combating this terrible scourge of the human race still remains a desideratum. It is at least to be hoped, from the collision of so many and such various opinions, that the precise truth, or something near it, may be elicited, and a treatment result which will no longer be involved in uncertainty or liable to objection.

There can be no doubt that terror and alarm have done much to assist the virulence and aggravate the ravages of this disease. The very apprehensions and forebodings which the presence of such a malady is calculated to produce in the mind of the unhappy patient, have no doubt operated fatally. Some years ago the yellow fever, as it was called, made its appearance in various parts of this island, and swept off great numbers. Consternation was spread in the vicinity of those parts where the disease most fatally prevailed. On this occasion, there were numerous instances of persons, apparently in perfect health, who were suddenly seized with fever, and in forty-eight hours afterwards were corpses. They lived on the same plantation with one who had recently died of yellow fever, or had attended the funeral of some who had fallen victims to it. A slight headache was the first symptom that alarmed them; soon after which a burning fever succeeded, and all its dreadful concomitants: the unhappy patient sunk into a deep despondency, and yielded in despair to its direful progress. On many plantations, every white person on them was swept off within the space of a few weeks.

In 1819 a malignant fever made dreadful ravages in Kingston and its vicinity, particularly among the troops. Of two regiments (the 50th and 92d), two-thirds were destroyed within the space of about two months; most of the officers and their families perished;* a panic seized the survivors; men who had faced death, on the field of battle, with unshrinking intrepidity, now dreaded the office of attending at the sick-bed of their comrades.† It would appear, that the instant the soldiers were seized with this fatal epi-

---

* One whole family, viz. Captain and Paymaster Montgomery of the 50th regiment, his son Major Montgomery, his son-in-law Major Rowe, and his daughter Mrs Rowe, were cut off within the space of a fortnight!

† Colonel Hill of the 50th, finding he could not prevail upon his soldiers to undertake this humane and necessary office, nobly set the example himself, and, grievous it is to add, fell a victim to his humanity.

demic they too generally gave themselves up as lost; and this unhappy despondency often fatally seconded the virulence of the disease. The miserable remnants of these regiments were subsequently, though too late, removed on board of ship for the benefit of the sea air, and the fever from this time gradually subsided. Had the troops, on the first appearance of the fever, been removed fifteen or twenty miles into the higher parts of the interior, it is probable that many lives would have been saved; for there, as has been said, the air is pure and comparatively cool; and it is an important fact, that in those parts malignant fever is almost totally unknown. During the several years that troops were stationed at Trelawny Maroon Town, they enjoyed as good health, and the mortality among them was as limited, as if they had been in the heart of England. It is true, there were no accommodations for the troops at Up-Park-camp so far back in the interior as has been mentioned; but barracks should now be established in a proper situation, as a resource against a similar calamity. Some remarks, published in Jamaica by the author, on occasion of this dreadful mortality, as they may be of some use to new comers in general, will be subjoined to this work.

Of the infectious influence of this disease there are various opinions. Some medical men de-

cidedly conceive it to be contagious, while others
are of a different opinion. Much may be said on
both sides of the question. That contagion exists
to a certain degree will hardly be denied. It
may, however, be communicated to some, while
others are exempt from it. Much depends on
the predisposition of the body to receive or resist
it. Medical men of some standing in the country
are seldom attacked by this disease from attending patients afflicted by it; but persons not inured to the climate, and with a predisposition of
body to receive disease, must necessarily be
affected by the morbid effluvia in the sick-room
of a patient under malignant fever, and probably,
in nine cases out of ten, catch the disease. But,
on the other hand, there is no proof that this
malady is so violently infectious as to be conveyed, like the plague, by contact, from one
country to another. It no doubt takes its rise
from a peculiar state of the atmosphere, which,
after long droughts, and especially in the neighbourhood of stagnant marshes, becomes impregnated with miasmata.

It is a curious fact, that the negroes and people of colour are not subject to the attacks of
this epidemic. While the malady is raging in
its greatest height among the whites, both of the
first-named classes may be perfectly healthy;
while, on the other hand, the whites may be

healthy when fever prevails among the negroes. The people of colour are by far the most healthy and hardy of the three classes.

Formerly there was a dreadful disease known in Jamaica, of the bowel kind, called the *dry belly-ache*, which used to carry off great numbers of the inhabitants of all classes, with a violence of pain and rapidity of progress truly terrible: in five or six hours, if relief was not given, the unhappy patient died. This appalling disease is now, happily, little known in the island. It would be curious to inquire to what cause or causes is owing the disappearance of so formidable an enemy. Doubtless it may in part be attributed to the atmosphere being less humid and better ventilated than during the time when the disease existed, from the inhabited parts of the island being now generally cleared of wood; but still more, perhaps, to the improved mode of living of the inhabitants. A medical practitioner, who had been many years in the island, professed to have been in possession of the only specific that ever had been discovered for this malady, for which he gave five hundred pounds to an old brown woman. He did not divulge his secret; and whether it died with him or not (for he is now no more) the author is unable to tell.

Vaccine inoculation has been introduced in

Jamaica, with most beneficial effect. There is in Kingston an institution for furthering the ends of this highly important discovery.

Health-officers are appointed at all the ports, whose duty it is to visit vessels from foreign parts, and report on the health of their crews.

CHAP. IV.

THE native vegetable productions of Jamaica, enriched with numerous acquisitions from other countries, form a great and interesting catalogue, to enumerate and describe which, systematically, would form a work of labour and bulk.* It is incompatible with the limits of a work like this to attempt more than to convey to the reader a general idea of the most remarkable productions of this island, which the author will here endeavour to do.

The forests of Jamaica abound with a great variety of the most valuable woods, fit for various purposes—as building, mill-work, wheel-making, cabinet-making, dying, and medicinal; as also many inferior kinds for the making of sugar-casks, shingles for houses, &c. The author has reckoned above fifty different species of the first-named description. Of these there are eight

---

* Some years ago a *Hortus Jamaicensis* was published in Jamaica. It is the most complete and scientific account of the vegetable productions of the island that has ever appeared.

species of extremely hard and heavy texture, susceptible of the highest polish, which are chiefly used for mill rollers and cogs, spokes for wheels, beams, &c. in building: they are too hard to be used in cabinet-work. Of these, the black and neesberry bully trees, the green-heart, the fiddle-wood, and rose-wood, grow to a great size. The iron-wood is remarkable for its iron-like hardness and weight (hence its name); but, resisting the best tools, it is of little other use than for rough posts for the negroes' houses: it does not grow to a great size. The most beautiful woods for ornamental cabinet-work are the mahogany, the bread-nut heart, and the satin-wood. The mahogany tree is one of the most elegant in the island; it grows to the height of from forty to fifty feet, and is adorned with a fine spreading dark-green foliage. There are not many of those trees now remaining in the island: being a profitable article of exportation, the greater number has been cut down for that purpose. The Jamaica mahogany is of a superior quality to that of Cuba or the Bay of Honduras. The bread-nut tree is in most parts of the island pretty abundant. This is both an ornamental and most useful tree: its wood is far more finely variegated than the mahogany, and is susceptible of a more brilliant polish; the leaves are a wholesome nutritious food for horses, mules, and sheep; and the kernels of the fruit afford an equally substantial diet to the negroes. This tree grows to a great height, and affords a fine shade to the cattle. But the tree that attains the greatest size (the *bombax* or cotton tree excepted) is the cedar: it sometimes measures upwards of thirty feet in girth near the root, and is of a proportionable height. One of these trees, cut some years ago on the south side of the island, produced, when sawed into plank, 30,000 superficial feet, which, at forty pounds currency per thousand feet, yielded the owner £1200. The cedar here is not of so fine a grain as that from the Levant. It is used chiefly in building, and for making vats, &c.

The black and green ebony, the yellow sanders, the lignum vitæ, the fustic, the logwood, &c. are too well known to require being described. The logwood tree forms a strong and beautiful hedge for the cane-fields, for which purpose it is generally used. The bitter-wood abounds here: it was at one time much used by the brewers as a substitute for hops, when there was a scarcity of that article, and sold at the enormous price of eighty pounds sterling per ton; but an equivalent duty having been laid on by government, it ceased to be an object of exportation. The cotton tree, though the largest of all the trees in the island, is of no other use than for making canoes, which are hollowed out from the trunks. This tree receives its name from a fine down which it bears in pods, though not at all of the same nature of the cotton wool, and convertible to no use but that of stuffing beds. One of the most useful trees in the island is the bamboo. This plant possesses advantages peculiar to itself: it may be reared on an indifferent soil; it arrives at its full growth in four or five years; and, when established, it renews itself, as it is cut down, by a continual succession of shoots, which in time form a thick cluster of many trees of various growths. Though not convertible into such numerous uses as its Chinese namesake, it being of a different species, it is calculated to supply many essential wants. It is split into wattles or hurdles for the dwellings of the negroes, used for rails for fences, cattle-pens, &c. and for hoops for sugar hogsheads, and formed by the slaves into a sort of canteens for carrying their water when they are travelling. It is most excellent fuel, a valuable object to such plantations as have little wood remaining; and its foliage affords both fodder and shade to the cattle. In short, this excellent plant, which Providence seems kindly to have placed within the planter's reach, so easily and quickly reared, and productive of so many benefits, should be cultivated, to a necessary extent, on every plantation where there is a scarcity of wood; though, strange to say, there are many where it is little attended to.

One of the most curious trees in this island is the mangrove. Its element is the ocean, along whose margin it grows, taking root in the sands, and shooting its numerous stems downwards, so as to form a thickly-planted natural palisado: the depth of water where it grows is sometimes from two to three feet, and its height from fifteen to twenty feet. Those parts of the stems which are below the water are often covered with a small species of oyster, which explains the paradox of *oysters growing upon trees*. The wood of this plant is hard, and, when large enough, makes excellent knees for boats; but it is chiefly used for fuel.

The pimento tree (bearing the fine aromatic spice of that name) grows to the height of from twenty to thirty feet, and is about two feet in circumference. Notwithstanding its small size, it is one of the most beautiful trees in the island; its foliage is a fine dark-green, which, when contrasted with the profusion of blossoms it throws out, has a most pleasing effect. The fragrant odours with which this tree perfumes the air when in blossom reminds the traveller of Arabia.

The coffee tree is a handsome plant, with a small dark-green leaf, and bearing a profusion of milk-white blossoms. It will shoot up to the

height of fifteen or twenty feet, if left to itself;
but by regular pruning it is kept within four or
five. This is one of those instances where nature
powerfully feels the aid of art: by proper train-
ing this plant is made to produce ten times more
fruit than it would do in its natural state. The
coffee-bean is covered with a pulp, which, when
ripe, assumes a fine crimson red: it is then fit
for gathering, which operation commences in
October.

The cocoa tree grows to the height of from
fifteen to twenty feet, and bears its nuts in pods.
For several years after the English were in possession of this island, cocoa was one of its principal productions; but after sugar began to be
cultivated, this article was gradually neglected,
and at the present time little more is raised than is
sufficient for the consumption of the inhabitants.

The oil-nut tree (*ricinus*), producing the castor
oil, grows to the height of twelve or fifteen feet,
and has a large indented leaf. It bears the nut
which produces the oil in clusters. The oil is
either what is called *cold drawn*, by pressing, or
extracted by boiling: by the former method a
purer and finer-flavoured oil is obtained than by
the latter. Of the castor oil manufactured here,
the greater part is consumed in the island, it
being universally used as a mild laxative medi-
cine.

One of the most stately and beautiful trees here is the cabbage tree,* a species of the palm, of which there are two kinds, the Barbadoes and the native cabbage tree, the former being the tallest and most elegant. Some are upwards of an hundred feet high. It is in general perfectly straight, and unencumbered with branches to within ten or twelve feet of the top. The branches are from twelve to fifteen feet in length, and in shape like those of the cocoa-nut tree.

The cocoa-nut tree is too well known to require description. Suffice it to say, that it grows in great luxuriance, and abounds in every part of the island. On some plantations groves of them are formed; and an oil is extracted from them, which is used in lighting the works during crop. They are also occasionally distributed among the slaves as an article of food.

The woods afford timber adapted to every purpose, excepting that of rum puncheons; no good substitute for the white oak, of which these

---

* So called from the fine white substance which forms the top of its stem, somewhat resembling the taste of that vegetable. The negroes often cut them down for the sake of this substance; but it is only such as they find in the remote woods that they sacrifice for so trifling a prize. Those growing in the open country are carefully preserved—it would indeed argue a strange want of taste, if so beautiful and ornamental a tree were not.

are formed, having been discovered. Yet very considerable quantities of pine timber, of all dimensions, are regularly imported from North America, and sold at prices below those of the native timber. This is owing partly to the high price of labour in Jamaica, but chiefly to the low country being almost denuded of timber trees, these abounding only in the remote and mountainous districts, from whence it is difficult and expensive to bring them, there being few roads in those parts adapted to the conveying of bulky timber. Many plantations, indeed, have by no means a sufficiency of wood contiguous to them, even for fuel for their distillery houses, and are consequently supplied with coals from England; which, by the bye, cost them less than fuel brought from their distant mountain lands. Much of this expense might be saved by a proper attention to the rearing of bamboos.

Among the various delicious fruits which this island yields in inexhaustible abundance, are the pine-apple or anana, the orange, the shaddock, the forbidden fruit, the pomegranate, the fig, the granedillo, the neesberry (resembling in taste a mellow ripe bergamot pear), the cashew apple, the kennip, the sapadillo (a luscious fruit growing spontaneously in the woods), the banana, the mamee (a wild fruit), the star-apple, the sweet-sop, the musk-melon and water-melon, the sweet-

lemon, the citron, the avagato-pear, &c.; besides
the exotics introduced within the last thirty or
forty years, viz. the mango (of which there are
several varieties), the chirimoya, the akee, the
jack-fruit, the bread-fruit, &c. some of which
are natives of India, and others of the islands
in the South Pacific Ocean. Very fine grapes
are also produced. All the exotic fruits thrive;
but the sago tree, cinnamon tree, nutmeg tree,
tea plant, cloves, &c. do not attain perfection;
the cinnamon tree has indeed been raised, with
some difficulty, more as an object of curiosity
than profit. Mangoes are become so common,
and are so plentiful in the season of bearing,
that the hogs are fed with them. The bread-
fruit is by no means so important an acquisition
as was expected. The negroes, who are good
judges of the substantial benefits of vegetable
production, regard this stranger with great apathy, except as a novelty: they prefer the cultivation of the more productive plantain. The
truth is, the bread-fruit is an insipid and not
very substantial food; add to which, that if a
hurricane were to sweep the trees to the ground,
as it certainly would, it would require four years
to bring them forward again to a state of bearing; whereas only one year is required for the
plantain. This latter fruit is gathered in for use
before it is ripe. It is then a very substantial

food; but with ripeness it acquires a sweet taste, and loses much of its nutritive quality. It is generally roasted, and used as a substitute for bread. One of the most remarkable fruits above enumerated is the avagato pear. Before being perfectly ripe, it is intolerably bitter to the taste; after which, however, it is so rich and luscious, but without any degree of sweetness, that it has, appropriately enough, been styled the *vegetable marrow* of the western world. It is, in short, when in full perfection, a very pleasant and wholesome food.

There are a great variety of wholesome and nutritious roots produced in this island—as the yam (*diascorea*), the yampy, the coco, the sweet and bitter cassada, the sweet potato, &c. Of the yam there are five species, the largest of which sometimes weighs from forty to fifty pounds. The sweet cassada is an extremely pleasant food; but the bitter sort is a deadly poison in its natural state, though perfectly harmless and wholesome when prepared in the usual way, namely, by reducing it to a pulp, expressing the juice (which contains the poison), drying the substance so as to form a sort of meal, and baking it into cakes. This is a tedious process; but as this plant is extremely hardy, flourishing in the poorest soil (a mixed gravelly one), and suffering far less from drought than any of the other edible roots, it is not deemed advisable to give it up, though there are some who think, and no doubt rationally, that the planters should extirpate this deleterious plant from their soil. Few accidents however happen from it.

As the roots, or ground-provisions, as they are here called, are not liable to sustain very serious injury from storms, there is a very judicious law, (which however is not so strictly attended to as it should be), by which the owners of all estates and other settlements are required to have ten acres of such provisions for every hundred slaves, over and above the negro-grounds and the plantain-walks. This is intended as a resource against that famine which has too frequently and fatally succeeded hurricanes, and the consequent destruction of the plantain-walks, and as a source of supply, in the meantime, for the poorer and more helpless of the slaves. So productive is the soil, when good, and the seasons regular, of the roots here mentioned, particularly the yam and coco, that the constant labour of one able negro would be competent to feed upwards of fifty. This may be easily conceived, by considering that, though a negro and his wife do not work above a tenth part of the year in their ground, yet the produce of that labour, if they are industrious, and the soil and seasons favourable, will maintain them and a family of four or five children, and leave a surplus for market.

Both maize (or Indian corn) and Guinea corn grow in great luxuriance in this island; and rice could be raised on the low and marshy lands, though it is not an object of attention. Indian corn is universally cultivated, and yields an incredible return.* In four months it is fit to be gathered in. Guinea corn is not raised in any great quantity on the north side of the island, but in some districts on the south side the slaves are chiefly subsisted on this grain, which is peculiarly calculated to endure the two greatest disadvantages to vegetable productions, poverty of soil and drought.

None of the European fruits arrive at perfection here, except grapes. A few tolerable strawberries are raised; and the apple-tree grows to a middling size, but bears a very inferior fruit, which, however, might be improved by engrafting. The peach is raised, but very rarely produces fruit. No other kinds succeed in any de-

---

* The author took three ears of Indian corn from one stem, the produce of one grain, on which there were 1940 grains. This, however, was a rare instance of great increase. The average increase may be about a thousandfold.

gree. Most of the European esculents are, however, raised with tolerable success, and, in the
mountainous districts, a few in as great perfection
as in England; as lettuce, different kinds of the
white cabbage, French beans, and a few others.
Potatoes, and the white pea, produce a good first
crop, but they degenerate if replanted with seed
from it; the former loses much of its flavour
even in a first planting. Turnips, leeks, rad-
dishes, carrots, celery, asparagus, &c. succeed
tolerably; but cauliflowers, artichokes, Windsor
beans, and onions, do not thrive in common;
though there is one district of the island—the
Liguanea mountains—where the first is cultivated with some success; and as to onions, the
want of them is not felt, there being abundance
of echallots, far surpassing them in flavour.* To
compensate, too, for the want or paucity of many
European esculents, the inhabitants are abundantly supplied with a variety of the finest indigenous esculents, almost throughout the whole
year: of these, the lima and the sugar bean
are the most highly prized; there are six or
seven species of pulse; the Indian kale and ca-
lalu (the last growing spontaneously in the fields),

* Considerable quantities of onions are, in their season,
brought here from North America, Madeira, &c.

are equal to spinage; the *ochra* and *chocho* are also greatly esteemed as wholesome and pleasant esculents.

But it is now time to say something of that important plant and grand staple of the country, the sugar-cane, whose uses are perhaps more numerous and valuable than those of any other plant whatever. It produces sugar, rum, molasses, excellent vinegar, fodder for cattle, thatching for the negroes' houses, and (from the burnt stems,) ashes, which serve either for manure, or as an ingredient in the cement used in building in the coppers, &c. The sugar-cane takes twelve months to ripen, if what is called a *ratoon* cane (that is, a product from the stock), and fourteen if a plant cane; but the former may be cut in dry years in the eleventh month. The Bourbon cane (so called from its being brought last from the isle of Bourbon, though originally a native of the Society Islands), was introduced into Jamaica about thirty years ago, on account of its great size, and consequent capacity to yield a far greater proportion of sugar than the cane before established in the island; which is now almost extinct, a few plantations only retaining the species. The Bourbon cane, when planted in a good soil, will grow to the height of twelve or fifteen feet in the stem, and seven or eight inches in girth, being double the size of the common cane, and yielding nearly twice the quantity of sugar, viz. from three to four tons per acre. As the soil, however, gets exhausted, the cane gradually diminishes in size and productiveness to from three to four feet in height, and about one hogshead per acre; after which the field is thrown up and replanted. The common cane had however its advantages; its juice was richer,—it yielded a heavier and more substantial sugar,—it exhausted the soil much less,—it suffered less from droughts, —and its leaves afforded a larger supply of fodder for the cattle, and of a more substantial kind; so that the planters were for some time doubtful of the benefit and expediency of the exchange. The plantations, upon the whole, have not produced, on an average, much more sugar than they did previously to the introduction of the Bourbon cane. This cane, requiring much more manure to *keep it in heart* than the old cane, it soon became necessary, after its establishment, to circumscribe the extent of field; but one important benefit arose from this—it abridged, in proportion, the labour of the slaves. A common error of some planters is, the keeping up of too great an extent of field; that is, for example, spreading over a field of two hundred acres a quantum of manure sufficient only for one hundred and fifty; though the latter field, duly manured, will yield as great a return as

the former only superficially so, besides the
benefit of fallowing and lessening the amount of
labour.

There are several varieties of the sugar-cane,
viz. the common cane of the island, the Bourbon
cane, the transparent cane, the ribbon cane, the
Batavian or purple cane, and the green stripe
cane. The Bourbon and transparent canes are
those chiefly cultivated; the ribbon cane is sometimes also planted on account of its hardy nature,
being more capable of enduring dry weather than
the other two, though it yields much less juice.
It is the most beautiful of all the species, being
finely variegated with alternate stripes of crimson and pale yellow, whence it takes its name.
The Batavian cane is in no estimation; it is the
least productive of all the species, and is therefore merely preserved as a variety.

The indigo is a small-leaved shrub of from
two to three feet high, which, on being macerated
and infused in water, yields the dye of that name.
It has not for many years past been much cultivated. Ginger is cultivated on some of the settlements, and forms an article of export. Tur-
meric, which resembles the ginger plant in the
structure of its leaves and its manner of bearing,
is very little attended to. The Indian arrow-
root, which produces the highly-prized flour of

that name, is an oblong-leaved plant, with roots somewhat resembling a carrot in shape, from which the flour is obtained by maceration, in the manner of starch. The greater part of what is raised is for home consumption, it being a most useful article in the plantation hospitals and for the negro infants. Cotton is not now so extensively cultivated as formerly: it was chiefly raised in the parish of Vere. Tobacco is almost exclusively cultivated by the slaves, for their own use: it is inferior in flavour to the Cuba tobacco.

Flowers are not cultivated in this island with the same success as in Great Britain; the same pains are not taken; it is considered by many as a useless, unprofitable employment. A few of the European flowers thrive; but the more delicate of these blooming children of a more temperate sky droop and die under the uncongenial heat of a tropical sun. The rose blushes forth with its native beauty, but diminished in size; but the Chinese rose, or what is here called the ever-blooming rose, flourishes in vigour and luxuriance, spreading forth numerous and healthy branches, and displaying, almost all the year, a profusion of flowers. The white rose does not succeed. The auricula, the polyanthus, the carnation, the gillyflower, the narcissus, the sweet-william, &c. have been tried

by some, and, with much care, have been raised
above the surface of the earth; but they soon
languished and died.* The variegated pink is
sometimes raised. Other hardier natives of
Europe thrive better; the different species of the
marygold, the flaring sunflower, the variegated
balsam, a species of the lily, and one or two
others, flourish in perennial vigour; and, to compensate for the absence of such as cannot be
raised, a variety of other flowers, indigenous to
the country, or brought hither from congenial
climes, is raised by those who have a taste as
florists. But it is in the lone retreats and distant recesses of the mountains and woods where
innumerable wild flowers and blossoms, of the
richest dyes and sweetest perfume, are to be
found: many of which, if transplanted into the
garden, would form its gayest ornaments.
Here, even in the midst of December, are
seen trees with both blossoms and fruit at once
suspended from their branches—the rivalship
of Flora and Pomona, so common in the torrid
zone :

---

* This may in some measure be owing to their being planted
in improper situations, and partly perhaps to a want of skill.
In the mountains, flowers and other plants have been raised,
which do not succeed in the low lands.

" Another Flora here, of bolder hues,
And richer sweets, beyond our garden's pride,
Plays o'er the fields, and showers, with sudden hand,
Exuberant spring."

The wild-rose tree and the jasmine-tree are, when in blossom, among the most beautiful of the flower-bearing trees. The former is a thick spreading plant, growing to the height of twelve or fifteen feet, and throwing out a profusion of flowers, resembling, in colour and shape, a full-blown rose. The latter is about the same height, and bears a blossom resembling the flower from which it takes its name: there are two species, the white and the red. One of the richest flowers in the West Indies is the blossom of the grinadilla: nothing can exceed the beauty and brightness of its tints. This plant is sometimes formed into arbours, entwined with the Arabian jessamine, the blossom of which resembles the double narcissus, only not so large, and yields an agreeable fragrance. There are several varieties of the jessamine, as well as of the indigenous lily; of the latter, the most remarkable is the lotus, or water-lily. The European honeysuckle is unknown here; but there are a number of flowers and blossoms very much resembling it. Most of the aromatic herbs, as thyme, sweet-marjorum, sage, balm, mint, &c. thrive tolerably well.

Few countries produce a greater variety of medicinal plants than Jamaica—of which an ample catalogue will be found in the Hortus published some years ago.

There is a public botanic garden in the island, containing a good collection of exotics from various regions.

CHAP. V.

THE wild hog, the rat, and the mouse, are the only wild quadrupeds in Jamaica. Formerly, it is said, the woods abounded with a species of the monkey, but none are now to be found. The wild hogs frequent the remote woods, subsisting on the fruits and roots with which they abound. They are much larger than the common kind, and exceedingly fierce, particularly the male: when beset by the largest dogs, he turns on them undismayed, and keeps them at bay, until shot by the huntsman. Hunting the wild boar was a favourite diversion both of the hardy active white creole of the interior and of the Maroons. It is not now so often practised, these animals having retired into the remote recesses of the woods, where it is difficult to come up with them: so that when their flesh is desired for what is called a *barbecue*, (considered as a great delicacy here, being the hog's flesh smoked with a certain odoriferous wood, which communicates to it a peculiar flavour), negroes are usually sent in pursuit of them, or the Maroons, who still pursue this diversion, bring it occasionally to the white settlers. It is uncertain whether the wild hog is an original inhabitant of Jamaica or a descendant of those which the first discoverers may have left there.

It may appear superfluous to say any thing of so common and well-known an animal as the rat; but the truth is, these animals are of no little importance in this island. In no country is there a creature so destructive of property as the rat is in Jamaica; their ravages are inconceivable. One year with another, it is supposed that they destroy at least about a twentieth part of the sugar-canes throughout the island, amounting to little short of £200,000 currency per annum. The sugar-cane is their favourite food; but they also prey upon the Indian corn, on all the fruits that are accessible to them, and on many of the roots. Some idea will be formed of the immense swarms of those destructive animals that infest this island from the fact, that on a single plantation thirty thousand were destroyed in one year. Traps of various kinds are set to catch them, poison is resorted to, and terriers, and sometimes ferrets, are employed to explore their haunts and root them out; still, however, their numbers remain undiminished, as far at least as can be judged by the ravages they commit. They are of a much larger size than the European rat, especially that kind of them called by the negroes *racoons*. On the experiment being tried of putting one of these and a cat together, the latter declined attacking it.

This island abounds with unnumbered tribes of the feathered race—to describe which, as a naturalist, would require volumes. Only a few of these are endowed with the gift of song; the most remarkable of which is what is called the nightingale, though it has no affinity to the bird of that name in Europe. It is a species of the mock-bird; it is somewhat larger than the thrush; the plumage is a mingled white and dark-brown. The compass, variety, and sweetness of its pipe are astonishing; the united song of the thrush, the blackbird, the linnet, and the canary, does not possess a greater variety than that of this single bird, which, if inhabiting the same region, might well be supposed to imitate the notes of all of them. It commences its song at the dawn of day, and continues it till a late hour of the evening, shunning the gloomy retreats of the forest, and delighting in the cultivated pastures and shaded spots in the vicinity of the dwellings of man—of whom it is perfectly fearless, and by whom it is regarded as a sort of sacred bird, which it would be barbarous to molest. It is too delicate for confinement in a cage; at least the art has not yet been discovered of reconciling it to this durance: the truth is, pains are seldom taken to domesticate these warblers. The banana-bird—a beautiful bird of the finch tribe—and a few other species, have their song, but there is little variety in it.

But, though Nature has not bestowed so melodious a pipe on the birds of this region, with the remarkable exception mentioned, as on the feathered inhabitants of more temperate climes, she has, as if to compensate for this deficiency, decked them out in the most gay and brilliant colours:

> " For Nature's hand,
> That with a sportive vanity has deck'd
> The plumy nations, here her gayest hues
> Profusely pours. But if she bid them shine
> Array'd in all the beauteous beams of day,
> Yet, frugal still, she humbles them in song."

These exquisite tints are peculiarly displayed in the humming-bird (of which there are four species), and in several birds of the finch tribe. In the mountains there is a much greater variety of the feathered tribe than in the low country: they find, in the thick shades of the forest, abundance of the berries and wood-seeds on which they feed, and which the cultivated country does not yield.

There are here no less than nine different species of the wild pigeon,* of which the ring-tail is the largest, being almost as large as the pheasant, while the smallest is about the size of the quail. The former is considered as one of the greatest delicacies of the island, at a certain season of the year (from October to February), when the wood-seeds on which it feeds are ripe; at which time it is extremely fat, and is eagerly sought for by all who are fond of good eating. It is remarkable that this bird becomes shy and solitary at this time, hiding itself in the most lonely retreats of the woods, as if conscious of impending danger in the vicinity of man; while at other times it is frequently seen in the skirts of the woods, and not at all shy. The sportsman has therefore to travel over rocks and through almost impervious woods before he gets to the haunts of the ringtail, at the only time when it is worth the pursuit. The next species in point of size is the blue pigeon: the bald-pate is so called from the crown of its head being of a milk white, while the rest of its plumage is of a dark

---

* The ringtail, the blue pigeon, the bald-pate, the white-belly, or white-breast, the mountain-witch, the partridge pigeon, the lapwing pigeon, the pea-dove, and the ground-dove. Of these, the ringtail, blue pigeon, white-breast, partridge, and mountain-witch, are shy and solitary birds.

bluish colour. The most beautiful species is the white-breast, the brilliant colours of whose neck vary as the bird changes its position.

There are four species of the parrot here, namely, the maccaw, the black-billed, and the yellow-billed green parrot, and the paroquet. The maccaw is become very scarce; but the other three species are exceedingly numerous, appearing in large flocks, being a gregarious bird, and rending the air with their cries. The parrots frequent the high woods, from which, when the seeds on which they feed are scarce, they often descend to prey on the plantain-walks, the fruit of which they greedily devour. The paroquets are also destructive to the plantains as well as to the fields of Indian corn.

There is a variety of aquatic birds here, as ducks (of which there are two species), teal, coots, divers, &c. The two first named are migratory; they annually arrive here in great numbers in October, and disappear in February : they chiefly come from the opposite shores of the continent. A smaller species are natives of the island. About the same time the crane and the white galding (of the heron kind) come over in flocks from the island of Cuba. The plover appears, too, about the same period in some districts. The snipe and the ortolan are also migratory. The latter much resembles the European bird of that name; it feeds on the seed of the guinea-grass, in the pastures of which they often appear in prodigious flocks. They are much esteemed by the lovers of good eating, being thought little inferior to the French ortolan, so highly prized in the London market. Besides the migratory snipe (which is equal in size and flavour to the European), there is a small species peculiar to the island. The quail is now become a very common bird, though about forty years ago it was not known: it was imported from North America.

From what has been here said, the reader will have some idea of the abundance and variety of game in this island; which, by the bye, every free person is at liberty to shoot, there being no game laws in existence here.

The most valuable bird in this island is the most forbidding in its appearance, and the most nauseous and disgusting in its habits, of any in it—namely, the black vulture, or carrion-crow. This animal seems a peculiar gift of Providence to the inhabitants, who, without its agency, would be desolated by pestilence. It eagerly and speedily devours all that putrid matter, which, if left unconsumed, would spread the seeds of disease and death through the atmosphere. So sensible are the inhabitants of the value of these birds, that there is a law against killing them.

There is another species of crow here, called the *gabbling-crow*, from its note resembling the rapid articulation of the human voice; but its habits are different from those of the carrion-crow : it is found only in the interior, and feeds on insects and small reptiles.

The sea around this island, and the rivers which water it, abound with various sorts of the finest fish. Of the former the calapavor, the mullet, the rock-fish, the baracoota, the grooper, the silk, the snapper, the jew-fish, are reckoned the best; and among the latter the fresh-water mullet, the snook, and the mud-fish. Nearly a hundred different species of sea and river fish might be enumerated that are caught and used by the inhabitants. There are times, however, when it is dangerous to eat of two or three kinds; the baracoota and the sprat, in particular, are sometimes highly deleterious, owing, it is supposed, to their feeding on some poisonous substance in the ocean, of the nature of copperas. To guard against this danger, a silver spoon is put into the vessel in which the fish is boiled; if it comes out of a dusky greenish colour the fish is unsound; if not, it may be safely ate. In richness and flavour the calapavor is almost equal to the salmon; and the mullet, which is something in shape and size like the trout, is greatly superior to that fish. The sea also produces the finest turtle, excellent lobsters, crabs, prawns, cockles, conques, and oysters; and the rivers, cray-fish and shrimps. One of the greatest natural curiosities in the West Indies is the land-crab, which cannot be properly classed with the tribe of shell-fish, being rather a so-journer on terra-firma, only visiting the sea once a year to wash off the spawn. They are seldom found more than three or four miles from the sea. They go out at night to feed, at which time the negroes, with torches, catch them. They run with great speed, holding up, at the same time, their claws in their defence, when assailed. When in spawn, they are prized as one of the greatest luxuries of the country. The green and hawks-bill turtle are found on the coasts. The flesh of the former only is esteem-ed, that of the latter being coarse and fishy; it yields, however, the shell so much prized in Europe, for which alone it is caught: that of the green turtle is of no value.

There are several species of the shark known in these seas. The white shark is the most com-mon, the largest, and most voracious. When goaded by hunger, he becomes utterly fearless, and will dart after his prey into the shallow water, in the view of numerous spectators. Those of the largest size are capable of devour-ing a man in a few minutes. When full-grown, he is about twenty feet long, and is armed with five rows of extremely sharp teeth. Few, however, are seen of that size, from ten to fifteen feet being the most usual size. In seizing his prey, he is obliged, from the formation of his mouth, to turn on his side; but this movement is performed with astonishing quickness. It is remarkable that a little fish, called by seamen the pilot-fish, usually attends this monster, and often swims close to his mouth, as if conscious of no danger. It is said this attendant directs the shark to his prey, as the jackall is supposed to direct the lion, and hence obtains the name of pilot; but this is merely hypothetical. Without repeating any of the horrible recitals the author has heard or read of the voracity of this terrible fish, he will content himself with mentioning one instance of which he was an eye-witness. A poor sailor, having, while ashore in Kingston, got inebriated in one of the grog-shops there, determined on swimming to the ship to which he belonged, though a boat was just at the time putting off to it. His shipmates used every argument to dissuade him from so mad an attempt, and even used force to get him into the boat; but all in vain—he jumped into the sea, but had not proceeded fifty yards from the shore before those in the boat, which was at some distance, heard a loud shriek; they instantly guessed what had happened, and rowed back with all haste to him. On approaching him, he uttered another piercing shriek, and was soon after taken into the boat, lifeless, and in a dreadfully mangled condition. A shark had bitten off one of his thighs, and soon after finished the murderous work by tearing out his entrails!

The baracoota is also a very voracious fish, but by no means so dangerous as the shark, on account of its inferior size, being seldom more than three feet in length. The conger-eel is both voracious and venomous in its bite; it is from five to seven feet in length, and of proportionable thickness: it may well be termed a sea snake; for, in its head, eyes, and teeth, it much resembles that reptile. It attacks persons in the water, and though the wound it inflicts is seldom deep, it is exceedingly difficult of cure.

Some of the largest of the rivers here contain alligators, some of which have been known to measure twelve feet in length. Persons who have read only exaggerated accounts of this animal, may conceive that it is terrible to the human species, both in the water and on land, of both of which elements it is an inhabitant. But the truth is, the alligator (of this island at least) is perfectly harmless to man. If, in bathing in the rivers which these animals frequent, a person should accidentally come in contact with one, instead of darting on him as his prey, he instantly plunges out of sight. All the harm, in short, which they usually do, is the destroying of the fish, and devouring the poultry and pigs that come in their way. The author has seen an alligator fastened with a chain about his neck, and fed upon fish, entrails, &c. which were occasionally thrown to him. He had been a mischievous plunderer of poultry in the neighbourhood, and was at last caught and secured. He became at length so far familiarized to the sight of his keepers as to devour in their presence whatever was given him.

There are three species of snake in Jamaica, viz. the yellow, the black, and the brown snake, the last being the smallest of the three. None of these are venomous in their bite, at least to a serious degree, instances having happened of negroes having been bitten by them without suffering any other consequence than a temporary pain, inflammation, and swelling of the part, and sometimes a slight degree of fever; to remove which, all that is necessary is a fomentation of the part with sweet oil, or warm lime-juice, and extracting the tooth of the animal if it has been left in the flesh. It is alleged by some that the bite of the brown snake is mortal; but no instance ever happened of its bite having produced death. Some of the yellow snakes are

from ten to twelve feet long, but the general
length is from six to eight. This animal is at
times exceedingly indolent and inoffensive;
when gorged with its periodical quantum of food,
and when coiled up and reposing itself, it will
permit a person to come up and touch it, without making an effort to move. Nay, some of
the African negroes have the boldness to stand
upon them for a short time while in this supine
state : they have a strange notion that this operation is a sovereign remedy for the bone-ache—a
painful disease to which they are subject. The
animal, under the pain of this extraordinary
pressure, writhes itself round, and soon dis-
lodges the intruder, but without any active exertion of resentment, and, on the removal of the
annoyance, it recomposes itself to rest. But
when hungry and in search of prey, and during
the season of pairing, it is more active and
irascible, but particularly at the latter time, when
it is not safe to disturb it. The strength of
this animal is incredible; the united exertions of
four or five able-bodied negroes cannot draw one
of large size from a place where it has got any
hold; so that one cannot, from this, altogether
discredit what is told of the monstrous serpents
of thirty feet long in India and Africa, which, it
is said, have been known to strangle the buffalo
and the tiger. There is something in the very

sight of a snake revolting to all other animals. We are startled if one unexpectedly comes in our way, though we may be aware there is no danger in his bite : horses and oxen start and snort if they see one near them, and dogs bark at them, but carefully keep aloof while they are in an attitude of defence. The black snake, when assailed by a dog, generally darts at his eyes; by which means the terriers, which never come in view of them without showing their antipathy, very frequently become blind. The domestic cat is terrified at the sight of the smallest-sized snake, and will not face it; though the wild cat, more fierce and daring, will probably not shun the encounter. A gentleman, a surveyor by profession, in traversing the woods, one day found the skeleton of a snake entwined round that of a cat; they had probably been fighting, and perished together in the conflict.

With respect to the power of fascination which it is said the snake possesses, the author never knew more than one instance that had the appearance of it. On riding along a road one day, he observed a little bird hopping, with a sort of circular and feeble motion, round a particular spot; he desired his servant to go and seize the little flutterer; but just as he had got to the spot, and was about to lay his hand on it, a large black snake darted from beneath the covert of the grass, and at the same instant the bird flew áway. That the snake has the power to a certain degree of fascinating human beings —in other words, electrifying them with terror, so as to deprive them of presence of mind (which is the only fascination to which any credit seems due), may be easily conceived. One of the largest size having got, during the night, through a jealousie, into a gentleman's bed-room, it crawled up into the bed, and, coiling itself on his body, fell soundly asleep. The gentleman soon after awakened, and, feeling something press heavily upon him, raised his head, and was electrified at the sight of the huge snake that lay upon him. He was so completely subdued by terror as to be utterly incapable of helping himself; he lay motionless, in a cold perspiration, not daring even to call for assistance. At length his negro servant, finding he did not come out at his accustomed time, suspected something was the matter, and went in to call him: on seeing the cause of his detention, he speedily relieved him by killing the animal.

The gallow-wasp is a very unsightly reptile; it is of the lizard species, but with a broader back and shorter tail: it seldom exceeds a foot in length. The bite of this animal was for some time thought to be venomous, and even mortal;

but that opinion is quite groundless. It is a shy and solitary creature, seldom being seen but in the loneliest retreats. Various species of the lizard abound here, among which the largest and most beautiful is the green lizard; it is about ten inches long; unlike the common lizard, its retreats are in trees, where it feeds on insects; like the camelion, it assumes various hues, as green, yellow, blue, and, when frightened, a dark-brownish colour. This creature is usually called the guano, though differing much from that animal, which is not a native of Jamaica, though abounding in the neighbouring island of Cuba.

Scorpions and centipedes are common here; but they do not multiply in such numbers as to be very troublesome to the inhabitants; at least they do not often come out from their hiding-places. Their sting is very severe, but not attended with other consequences than pain and inflammation of the part, which go off, after a time, by the application of proper fomentations. The pain from the sting of the wasp here is indeed almost equally severe as that inflicted by either of those animals. A far more troublesome insect than either of the foregoing is the cockroch (about the size of a large beetle), swarms of which infest every house, insinuating themselves into all parts of it, and into the furniture, and destroying the clothes they get among if not carefully attended to. During the rainy seasons, they issue out in swarms from their lurking-places in the houses, to the great annoyance of their inmates; though their bite is by no means keen, they have a very offensive smell. But the most annoying insect in the West Indies is the musquito. The evening and morning are the times when they are most numerous and troublesome in the houses; in the woods swarms of them are found at all times; but they shun the solar blaze, and are dispersed by high winds: they are found in the greatest numbers in the vicinity of marshes. They are provided with a proboscis for sucking the blood of those they assail, and the puncture they make is instantly and keenly felt, and raises a blister on the part. New-comers suffer far more severely from their attacks than those who have been some time in the country, as if there was something more inviting to them in the blood of the former. The numerous blisters they raise over the body occasion an incessant itchiness, which is peculiarly irksome; and the parts affected, but particularly the ankles and feet, are often swelled and inflamed to a great degree. When very numerous, a smoke is made in the houses, by which they are driven away. To guard against their annoyance in the night, the beds are hung with what are called musquito-nets, made of thin gauze. It is remarkable that the negroes, who cannot always afford this nocturnal defence, get into a mechanical habit of driving away these troublesome visitors, even while apparently wrapt in a profound sleep; the quick feeling of pain seemingly occasioning this unconscious movement of the hands.

The fire-fly is somewhat smaller than the cockroch; it is a harmless and cleanly insect; it is never seen during the day, but at night numbers issue out from their retreats, sport about in the air, and illumine the darkness by a vivid light which they emit from two glandular spots above their eyes. The light of one of these insects is, when held close, sufficient to enable a person to read. When the night is very dark, these animals have a lively and pleasing appearance. A still more splendid sight perhaps is the blaze of phosphoric light produced, on a dark night, by the countless myriads of glow-worms that spangle the bushes and trees around.

Bees are in great plenty in the woods; they hive in the hollow trunks of trees and in the cliffs of rocks; they find abundance of food in the profusion of blossoms and wild flowers, and the honey they produce is of an exquisitely fine flavour. They can easily be transferred into the hive by those who choose to be at the pains of attending to them, and they amply repay the trouble. Their most formidable enemies are the wasp, the cockroch, and the stinging black ant : the two first they may manage to repel; but the multitudinous race of ants, if they are suffered to have access to the hives, soon destroy the bees, or compel them to take flight.

CHAP. VI.

OXEN—HORSES—MULES—SHEEP—GOATS—HOGS—
POULTRY—DOMESTIC ANIMALS.

THE oxen in Jamaica are not so large as those in England, but capable of performing almost as much labour. Within the last thirty years they have been so greatly improved in size, by the occasional introduction of the English breed, that some have been killed that weighed, exclusive of offals, upwards of an hundred stone. The Spanish cattle imported from Cuba, &c. are of a much smaller size than those reared in the island, but they are generally more hardy. The oxen are employed in the waggons which bring down the produce to the wharfs, in carts, and in the plough, where that is used; for this last species of labour mules are too intractable, and horses would not bear the fatigue. The price of beef is at present 1s. 3d. currency per lb. No necessary of life has fluctuated more in Jamaica than this. The author remembers it once as low as 7½d. per lb., and at another time as high as 1s. 8d. There is often much wrangling between the inhabitants and the butchers about the price

of this article; but the latter, being usually supported by the planters, generally carry their
point; or rather the pen-keepers and butchers
combine together to fix what the price shall be—
not a very fair mode of deciding the matter,
these being the very persons who are interested
in maintaining as high a price as possible;—and
so jealous are they of this their prerogative, that
if a more conscientious individual among them
offers to sell at a lower rate, he is instantly hoot-
ed as an innovator. Strange that, though the
magistrates and vestries have the power of regulating the price of bread, they have no control
over that of beef, so that the buyer of that article
is obliged to take it at whatever price the seller
demands. The beef here, if the animal be not
too old and over-wrought, is sweet and savoury.

The horses bred in the island are middle-sized,
hardy, and active, well fitted for the saddle or
the harness, but unsuited to the cart or the
plough, in which they are never employed;
though were there a strong-boned breed in the
island, like the dray-horses in England, there is
no doubt they would be useful for either. But
the planters prefer oxen, because these will fetch
two-thirds of their original price after having
performed their period of service; and a certain
number of horned stock is required for the purpose of manure. The horses imported from

Cuba and the Spanish Main are smaller-sized than those reared in the country, but equally hardy. The English and North American horses, from being bred in so different a climate, are not so hardy, though, if kept in the stable, and carefully attended to, they thrive well; they shed their hair once a-year, after getting what is called their *winter-coat*. The breed of native horses has been greatly improved by the occasional introduction of high-bred blood horses from England. The race-horses here are beautiful animals, and almost equal in fleetness to the British racers. They are rode by negro jockeys, who acquire all the adroitness and *knowingness* of that description of men in other countries. It is lamentable to see the poor animals rode—as they are in most of the parishes—three and four mile heats at mid-day, under the intense heat of a vertical sun, in a climate like this, where an early hour of the morning would answer so much better. If the horse-masters are devoid of compassion for their generous and willing steeds, one would think that the risk of losing them, or at least rendering them useless, would have some weight with them. In all the parishes, races take place either annually or biennially. The price of a high-bred, thorough-broke native horse is sometimes as high as £140 currency; those of inferior kind from £30 to £70; and Spanish horses from £20 to £40: a native horse of the best description may be bought, unbroke, from the pens, at from ninety to an hundred pounds.

The mules in Jamaica are far more hardy than the horses: they undergo much greater fatigue, and require less sustenance and attention. They are consequently of great value to the planter, on account of the quantum of labour they perform on the plantations, where they are employed in the mills, and in conveying the sugar-canes to the works. But, along with this desirable quality of great strength and hardiness, the mule of the West Indies has a perverseness and stubbornness very difficult to subdue; few are taught to be so perfectly docile as to be equally fit for the saddle as a well-trained horse; yet the most stubborn are made to perform their work by the negroes, who have a wonderful knack in managing them. Great numbers of mules are bred upon the pens, and the Spaniards occasionally bring over additional supplies. The price of an unbroken native mule is from £35 to £40, and from £25 to £30 for a Spanish mule; but for a handsome saddle mule, free from vice, as high as an £100 will sometimes be given, so desirable is the rare union in this animal of gentleness with its natural capability of enduring fatigue. The mule here is not so large, at least not so long in the legs, as the Barbary mule; it is of a more round and compact make.

The sheep are very good, and the mutton excellent; it is 1s. 8d. per lb., being dearer than either beef or pork. Many of the sheep have no fleece, being covered with hair like goats. When well pastured and housed, they are very prolific. Goats thrive and increase with very little care, being much hardier than the sheep. They are such nimble and wandering animals, and so prone to trespass on the young canes, &c. that few planters keep them; but the small settlers raise great numbers, and every town and village abound with them: the brown people residing in these find their account in keeping as many as they can manage, for the purpose of supplying the inhabitants with milk; with four or five milch-goats, a brown woman can manage to support herself and family very comfortably: the milk they yield is sweet and much richer than cow's milk. These animals wander about in the roads, and in the woods and thickets, picking up a variety of food which sheep would not eat—as the leaves of various shrubs and trees, and even the bark of the latter, when nothing better comes in their way. The flesh of the young goats only is sweet and savoury: it sells at 1s. 3d. per lb.

All the foregoing animals feed chiefly on the Guinea grass; the natural grass is neither so luxuriant nor so fattening; they are also occasionally fed on the leaves of the bread-nut tree, which is nutritious and fattening, especially to sheep. Horses are occasionally fed on Indian corn, which is thought a still more substantial food for them than even oats.

Hogs are very plentiful; the climate is congenial to them; and the great variety of fruits, roots, and other vegetable productions with which the island abounds, enables the inhabitants to raise, at a small expense, great numbers of these animals. They are of a much smaller size than the English hog, short-legged, and chiefly black. Their flesh is far superior in sweetness and delicacy to the British, or North American pork, and can hardly be excelled by any in the world; and yet, strange as it may appear, the Irish pickled pork is sold to the negroes by the small retail dealers in provisions, at nearly double the price of the fresh pork of the country. This may in part be accounted for by the fondness of the negroes for whatever is highly-seasoned and calculated to give a zest to their vegetable broths. In the large towns fresh pork sells at from 1s. to 1s. 3d. per lb.; but in some of the less populous parts of the island it is sold as low as 10d. per lb.

Rabbits thrive here, and could be raised in

great numbers at little expense, were it possible to prevent the rats from destroying them; but these pernicious animals are great enemies to them, and it is difficult to devise means of preserving them from their attacks.

All kinds of poultry are raised here in the greatest abundance, excepting geese and the common duck, neither of which, with all the care that can be bestowed on them, multiply to such a degree as to render them profitable to their owners. But the Muscovy duck, the turkey, the Guinea fowl, and the common dunghill fowl, thrive and multiply wonderfully well. Of these, the last-mentioned is the most hardy and numerous race; they are as large and as fine-flavoured as those of the mother-country, and are more prolific. Besides the great numbers reared on the plantations for the use of the white people on them, and by every family living in the country, there are few slaves but have got their brood-hens in greater or less number, so that the markets are abundantly supplied with fowls almost throughout the year: a scarcity of Indian corn (on which they and the other poultry are fed), and the prodigious quantities which are brought up for the ships when they are about to sail for Europe, are the only circumstances which occasion a temporary diminution of this supply. Turkeys require somewhat more care in rearing.

The Muscovy duck is as hardy and prolific here as the common duck is in England. As to the Guinea fowl, it finds here a congenial climate; it is a wild and wandering sort of bird, that will not be confined to the discipline of a poultry-house, but lays its eggs in the thickets, where they are sure to be destroyed by rats or snakes if the owner does not in time discover the hidden treasure—which is no longer trusted to the improvident parent, but placed under a clucking hen, who hatches and rears the young strangers with as much care as if they were her own. This most prudent, careful, and useful of all the domestic birds, is also frequently employed to perform the same office for the turkey and the duck, neither of which is half so attentive a nurse.

Domestic pigeons thrive as well here as in England, provided they are kept from being molested by ants and other vermin; their great increase amply repays the trouble and expense of keeping them : they are fed, like the poultry, on Indian corn, of which they are very fond. Pea-fowls are raised, but more for ornament than use.

The prices of poultry, &c. are as follow :—A turkey-cock 26s. 8d.; a turkey-hen 13s. 4d. to 16s. 8d.; a goose 20s. (few of these are brought to market); a full-grown Muscovy duck 7s. 6d.;

a hen 3s. 9d. to 5s.; a capon 7s. 6d.; a pullet 2s. 6d.; a Guinea fowl 5s.; pigeons are usually sold at 2s. 6d. a pair. Eggs are 1s. 8d. a dozen, and when scarce 2s. 6d.

Dogs are very numerous in this island. With the exception of terriers (the breed of which is kept unmixed on the plantations, where they are employed in packs to hunt and destroy the rats), they are chiefly mongrels, or a mixed race from the different European species, blended with the Spanish blood-hound. The negroes are so exceedingly fond of dogs, that all who can afford to keep them have one or more in their possession. It is remarkable, that that most dreadful of all maladies, hydrophobia, is unknown here, at least the cases, if any happen, are very rare; the author has heard rumours of some having occurred, but no fact of the kind ever came within his knowledge, nor did he ever know of a case of actual canine madness. This appears to be a very curious fact. In Great Britain these animals are most subject to this malady in the hottest days of summer; in the West Indies they are exposed to a still more intense degree of heat, and yet they are exempt from it. Perhaps it may in some measure be owing to the much greater equality of temperature of the latter climate—to which these animals, like others, get inured.

This is the only hypothesis by which the author can account for this phenomenon.

Cats are very common; there is hardly a family without two or more of these favourite domestics, whose presence is absolutely necessary to prevent the dwellings from being overrun with rats: they have all the qualities of the European cat, but are of a smaller size.

CHAP. VII.

AGRICULTURE.

On most of the sugar plantations in Jamaica
there is a variety of soils, but some have a far
greater diversity than others. It is not unusual
to find, within the boundaries of one estate,
almost all the different soils of the country;
while others contain only two or three kinds.
The soils adapted to the sugar-cane are the various rich loams and moulds, and clay with a
superstratum of mould. The former are turned
up with the hoe, about four inches below the
surface of the earth, and formed into ridges,
called cane-holes—in the spaces between which
(four feet in breadth) the canes are planted. The
clay soil is usually turned up with the plough,
when it is suffered to remain six or more weeks
to *pulverise*, and then formed into cane-holes;
after which it is fit for planting. The softer
soils may be planted immediately after being
turned up; and this is rather an advantage than
otherwise to such soils. This *holing*, as it is
called, or digging of the land, is the most toil-
some work on a plantation, and the proprietors

therefore usually employ what are called jobbers to perform it—that is, men who have gangs of negroes whom they hire out to do any work of labour, for which they are either paid by the day or by the job, according to agreement. For digging cane-holes they get from eight to ten pounds per acre.

The manure generally made use of is that taken from the cattle-pens, after being properly prepared into a compost by the admixture of ashes, earth, &c. For the clay soils, ashes, marl, and sometimes lime, are used. Of the latter article the planters are indeed too sparing: though so admirably adapted for their cold argillaceous soils, there are few who ever think of having re course to it; no doubt deterred by the expense, not a conviction of its inefficacy. The manure is conveyed by the slaves in baskets, and from twelve to fourteen pounds weight is put into every cane-hole. An easier, and perhaps, for some soils, a still more effectual mode of enriching the fields to be planted, is what is called *penning* them over—that is, penning or folding the cattle on successive divisions of the land, until the whole field is gone over, at the rate of about 2000 head of cattle for one acre; the land being forthwith holed and planted on the removal of the pens. Three lengths of the top part of the cane, each having three, four, or more germs, are laid in each hole, with the germs placed sideways, and covered with a thin layer of earth. The lower and middle parts of the cane, when full-grown, do not produce shoots, so that nothing is lost; the top of the cane, which alone is fit for planting, being unfit for sugar. Good land, well manured, will produce four or five crops, when it is replanted. Very fertile land has been known to produce fifty or more crops, before the introduction of the Bourbon cane—that is, continued for fifty years to reproduce from the original stock; the field being occasionally manured, and supplied with fresh stocks or roots where any have decayed, soon after the field is reaped. This mode of cultivation is still pursued on plantations where the natural goodness of the soil will permit it. It is the best in many points of view : the land suffers less injury by not being turned up and exposed, and far less labour and expense are required in carrying it on. The returns of the land are various, according to the soil, seasons, manuring, and, on exhausted lands, the standing of the cane. A plant from a good soil, well manured, will yield four tons of sugar; while what is called a third rattoon, on an exhausted soil, will not produce half a ton. The magnitude of the crops of sugar estates depends so much on the seasons, that a plantation which, with favourable seasons, produces five hundred hogsheads, may not, if these should fail, yield one hundred.

The plough is not so generally in use here as it ought to be. It is true, the softer soils do not require it, and on very steep fields and stony land it cannot advantageously be used; but all the stiff soils require it: it facilitates the labour of holing, and breaks up the soil more effectually than the hoe alone.

In six or seven weeks after their being planted, the young cane plants have shot up to about the height of a foot, when they are weeded. They receive three or four subsequent weedings or cleanings, and, as the cane advances in height, the dry leaves are removed from it. Canes planted in November are fit for the mill in fourteen or fifteen months; if planted in May, they are usually cut the succeeding May. Canes reproduced from the stock require less time to come to maturity; and the labour of cleaning them is by no means so great as that of cleaning the plant canes, the ground having much fewer weeds, from being covered with the exuviæ of the cane.

The cane-land is divided into fields of various extent and shape, according to the nature of the ground. Intervals of about twenty feet are left between them, for the convenience of carriage; and they are enclosed and protected by stone walls, logwood hedges (much resembling the hawthorn), or mounds of earth planted with a prickly shrub called the penguin.

The harvest commences at different periods in different districts, the planters being mainly regulated in this by the seasons, or periods of rainy and dry weather. December, January, and February, are the usual times. The canes, when cut down, are tied up into bundles, and conveyed by carts and mules to the mill; where they are passed through iron cylinders, which press out the juice: this is conveyed to the boiling-house, where it is converted into sugar. The molasses is taken to the distilling-house, and, along with the scum from the vessels in which the sugar is boiled, made into rum. The stem of the cane, after being expressed, is dried, and used as fuel for boiling the sugar. The operations in the mill and the boiling-house go on both night and day, the negroes being formed into what are called *spells*, or divisions (two or three, according to their number), which relieve each other in the nocturnal part of the duty. The getting in of the crops lasts from three to four months. In the meantime, the sugar, when what is called cured, is sent in hogsheads, &c. to the wharfs, in waggons drawn by ten or twelve oxen.

The rugged and stony portions of the land are

covered with Guinea grass, a hardy plant that flourishes in such situations, requiring but little soil. The pastures thus formed are usually shaded by bread-nut, orange, fustic, and a variety of other ornamental trees, and form the most picturesque and beautiful of all the scenery of a plantation. This grass is a most important acquisition to the island. When once established in a congenial soil, it requires neither replanting nor supplying; and it so completely covers the ground, that few weeds grow up among it. It may be kept clean at the rate of 3s. 4d. an acre per annum; and if so kept, it will yield three and sometimes four cuttings, or as many grazings, in a year. All the grazing animals thrive on it. Jamaica is indebted to mere accident for this most valuable plant. A captain of a slave-ship having brought some of the seeds from Africa, for the purpose of feeding some birds, a few were thrown away, the birds having died: these produced so luxuriant a crop, that the planters eagerly set about propagating it, having previously ascertained its wholesome and nutritious quality. Such is the rapidity of its growth, that, at the commencement of the spring rains, after a long drought, it will, in the space of even a week, cover the most bare and arid pasture lands with a beautiful green sward, and in three weeks will have attained the height of four or five feet. Some years ago a species of grass was introduced here from the Bahamas, but it is not a great acquisition. It is extremely sweet and nourishing, but by no means productive, being a low creeping plant, seldom rising to more than three or four inches above the ground. It is so hardy, and tenacious of the soil of which it gets possession, that it is very difficult to extirpate it. It spreads its innumerable fibres in all directions so rapidly, that, if not carefully kept within bounds, it would get into the cane-fields, provision-grounds, &c. and become a pest. The planters have therefore rejected it, except as an ornament to the ground about their houses, its fine dark verdure and velvet-like softness forming a beautiful lawn. The Scotch grass grows with great luxuriance by the sides of rivers, and in other moist situations, where it sometimes attains the height of five or six feet; but it is not so substantial as the Guinea grass, and cannot be cultivated to any great extent. The indigenous grasses, of which there are many species, though wholesome, are far inferior to the Guinea grass, both in quality and productiveness. The grass fields receive no other culture than simple weeding occasionally, nor do they get any other manure than what falls from the stock that graze on them. All the manure that can be collected on the sugar plantations is reserved for the cane-fields.

A portion of the land is reserved for a plantain-walk and other provision-grounds. The plantain requires a good soil, and on such a soil it will flourish for any length of time; for it renders back to the soil fully as much as it withdraws from it, by the exuviæ it sheds, and its trunk, &c. when cut down, which form a perpetual succession of rich vegetable mould; so that a piece of good land laid out in plantain-walk continues to preserve all its original vigour and fertility. The trees, planted at twelve feet asunder, form in a few years into so many groups of five or six trees, and thus spread such a thick shade as to be impervious to the sun's rays. Few weeds therefore find entrance into a luxuriant plantain-walk; and thus it becomes, at a small expense, a source of plenty to its owner. But to endeavour to cultivate these trees on a poor soil is only a waste of time and labour. Yams, cocos, &c. are also raised; and a suitable portion of land is allotted to the slaves for provision-grounds. On many estates there is not a sufficiency of land suitable for provisions, or the seasons may not be favourable (the country, when stripped of wood, becoming more subject to drought); in which case the planters purchase a tract of mountain land, which supplies the property with both provisions and timber. To ensure an abundant supply of provisions to his slaves is to the planter an object beyond all others important: any inattention on this head would betray an equal want of humanity and sound policy.*

A sugar plantation producing two hundred hogsheads of sugar has usually about two hundred slaves, a hundred oxen, and fifty mules; but there is no fixing of any precise number of each as generally applicable. What are called laborious estates, that is, having much clay land, and planting much, require a greater proportion of able slaves than others, unless the land is *put in* (planted) by jobbers. The more distant an estate is from the shipping place, the more oxen of course are required to convey down the produce; and a property that has a water or a windmill does not require half the number of mules that it would with a cattle-mill only. Indeed, a plantation with a good water-mill, and easy-lying fields from which the canes may be carted, scarcely requires any mules.

* The raising of provisions is not sufficiently attended to by the planters in general, who annually expend large sums in the purchase of American provisions for their slaves, even when their produce is at the lowest ebb, and when additional portions of land and labour might so well be spared for that purpose.

The four great desiderata in settling a sugar plantation are, goodness of soil, easiness of access, convenience of distance from the shipping place, and a stream of water running through the premises. Although an estate may prove very productive without a union of all these advantages, it would be folly to settle upon a tract of land that possessed neither of them.

An estate producing 200 hogsheads of sugar, averaging 16 cwt., may be thus valued :—

500 acres of land, at £20 per acre, on an average,*..£10,000
    (Of which 150 acres, if the land be good, is sufficient for canes, the rest being in grass and provisions.)
200 slaves, averaging £100 each,..............20,000
140 horned stock, and 50 mules,................5,000
Buildings and utensils,............................8,000
_____

Jamaica currency,......£43,000

At least this is the current value of the different items, if purchased separately, the soil being

* Land in this island sells at various prices, according to quality and situation. Fertile land in a good situation will fetch £70 or £80 per acre; but in the remote mountains it may be bought for £5.

good, the property conveniently situated, and the slaves healthy and able; though many such estates, brought to the hammer through the distress of their owners, would not, in the present depreciated state of such property in the West Indies, bring even £30,000. On the capital here stated the owner *has at present hardly one per cent.** after all expenses are paid—such is the depreciated value of his produce. His rum, indeed, barely repays the expense of manufacturing it, and the value of the casks that contain it. Of all classes of persons holding property in the West Indies, the sugar planter, in short, is by far the severest sufferer; but as the interests of many classes of persons intimately depend on his prosperity, distress would necessarily be spread among these classes by his ruin.

The coffee planter is more fortunate than the sugar planter, having not half so large a capital at stake, and the commodity he cultivates fetching, though not a large, at least a saving price. About six or seven years ago, and for several years antecedent, this article had fallen so low in price, that the cultivators were nearly ruined, and many of the plantations were thrown up. One man, more wise and patient than others,

---

* In 1821. Of late sugar has borne a higher price.

kept his stock on hand, borrowing money on it and on his plantation in the meantime, until a sudden and extraordinary rise took place, *the price being more than quadrupled;* by which means he realized a considerable fortune. A coffee plantation does not require above half the number of slaves and stock that a sugar estate does, neither is the labour so severe. The soil best adapted for the coffee tree is a deep brown loam : the trees are planted at the distance of about six feet, and are carefully kept clean and pruned. The season for gathering the berries is from October to January. It is pulped, &c. and dried on terraced platforms, called barbecues.

The season for gathering the pimento is from August to October. The extremities of the branches bearing the spice are broken off when nearly of the full size, but green ; for if suffered to become ripe it loses its aromatic quality, and is of no use. It is then picked off from the stems, and dried in the sun, in the same manner as coffee. Jamaica is the only West India island which produces this spice in such abundance as to render it an important article of commerce.

The breeding farms, or pens, here, are conducted in much the same manner as the grazing farms are in England. On some horses and mules are bred, and on others oxen, or mules and oxen. From 1000 to 1500 acres of land are laid out into pastures of different extent, either of Guinea grass or natural grass, according as the land is suitable for the one or the other. The more there is of the former, the more valuable and productive the pen is. From forty to fifty slaves are sufficient to perform the work of the largest pen. This is a safe and profitable way of laying out capital; for though the profits of the sugar planter (who is the pen-keeper's principal customer) should diminish ever so much, still the price of cattle holds up. From inability to purchase, the sugar planter may, however, turn his attention to the rearing of his own stock; or, what is worse, he may purchase without the ability to pay.

Agriculture, though practically well understood in this island, is very little cultivated as a science. A society of gentlemen, calling themselves the " Cornwall Agricultural Society," some years ago, made a show of doing something in this way; but this society soon died a natural death, and left no memorial of its labours behind for the benefit of the public. There was either a disinclination to the toil of scientific study, or a want of talent, or both, which rendered the attempt of these agriculturists abortive. And yet, considering the great variety and value of the products of this island, there are few countries that present a more ample and interesting field for inquiry on this subject; and it will be acknowledged that there is much room for improvement in many matters connected with husbandry, as it is now practised in Jamaica.

The price of negro labour is from 2s. 6d. to 3s. per day for a field negro, and 5s. for a mechanic. The value of an able field slave is £180 currency, and of a mechanic £300.

CHAP. VIII.

COMMERCE—INTERNAL TRADE—COINS—TAXES, &c.

THE commerce of Jamaica may be classed under the following heads :—The trade with the mother country—which is far more considerable than all the other branches together; the trade with British North America; and the trade with the island of Cuba and other Spanish islands, the Spanish Main or Terra Firma, and other territories on the American continent formerly belonging to Spain.

That an idea may be formed of the magnitude of the exports from this island, summaries of these for two years, at distant periods, are here given :—

	Exported, from Sept. 30, 1801, to Sept. 30, 1802.	Exported, from Sept. 30, 1819, to Sept. 30, 1820.
Hogsheads of sugar (aver. 16 cwt.)	129,554	115,065
Tierces of ditto (averaging 11 cwt.)	45,405	11,322
Barrels of ditto,	2,403	2,474
Puncheons of rum,	45,632	45,361
Hogsheads of ditto,	2,073	1,783
Barrels of ditto,	473	566
Kegs of ditto,	205	
Casks of molasses,	366	252

	Exported, from Sept. 30, 1801, to Sept. 30, 1802.	Exported, from Sept. 30, 1819, to Sept. 30, 1820.
Casks of ginger,	23	1,159
Bags of ditto,	2,079	316
Casks of pimento,	791	673
Bags of ditto (averaging 112 lbs.)	7,793	12,880
Pounds of coffee,	17,961,923	22,127,444

Besides the articles enumerated in the foregoing accounts, Jamaica exports a considerable quantity of cotton wool, chiefly imported from the foreign islands, under the free-port law ; also indigo, cocoa, tortoise-shell, mahogany (mostly of foreign import), dye-woods, hides, and various other articles of minor importance.* Considerable quantities of bullion (chiefly dollars) were exported to Great Britain during the late war; but very little is now sent, the fall in the price rendering it an unprofitable remittance.

From the above statements, it appears that there has been nearly one-fourth less sugar shipped in the latter period than in the first, while there has been a considerable increase of coffee and pimento. The magnitude of the crops of all articles of produce, of course, greatly

---

* In 1816 the import into the united kingdom of some of the above-mentioned articles was as follows:—Cotton wool, 1,021,674 lbs.; cocoa, 260 cwt.; indigo, 32,011 lbs.; fustic, 21,080 tons; logwood, 9638 tons; mahogany, 1396 tons.

depends on the seasons; and these may be favourable to one commodity, and unfavourable to another. It does not follow, that because there has been a bad sugar crop, there should also be a bad coffee or pimento crop; for while seasonable rains may fall in the districts where the two latter are cultivated, the sugar plantations may be parched by excessive drought. The cultivation of coffee has been very greatly extended within the last twenty-five years,* owing to the high prices it bore in consequence of the revolution in St Domingo, by which a considerable supply was withdrawn from the market. At the period of Buonaparte's exclusion system, it fell, as has been said, so low as hardly to repay the expense of cultivation. For some years past it has maintained a steady and encouraging price. Sugar cultivation has also been extended within the last twenty-five years. The average crop of the five years preceding 1799 was only 83,000 hogsheads, which, however, was partly owing to unfavourable seasons; while the great increase which immediately followed was

---

* From 1774 to 1790 the export of coffee was nearly tripled; this was considered by Bryan Edwards as an extraordinary increase. What then would he have thought of the increase from the latter period up to the year 1820, which it appears, from the statements here quoted, has been in the proportion of twelve to one?

to be attributed in some measure to the then universal cultivation of the Bourbon cane, introduced some years before, which yielded an extraordinary return, though it has since fallen off in productiveness.

The annual exports to Great Britain and Ireland may amount, one year with another, to about five millions; and those to other parts to about £400,000.

In return for its commodities, Jamaica receives from Great Britain an annual supply of almost all her manufactures. The exclusive right which she claims of supplying this and the other islands with her products is one important source of her commercial and manufacturing prosperity. The annual amount of British manufactures imported into this island alone is upwards of two millions.[*] The imports from other parts (of lumber, provisions, cattle, &c.) amount to nearly a million currency. A portion of the goods received from Great Britain is for the supply of the Spanish American settlements, particularly of cotton and linen goods. The quantity of these manufactures, but especially the former, that passed through Jamaica to those settlements, during the war, was immense. Kingston became the entrepot for

---

[*] During the late war the amount of British imports was considerably above what it is at present.

this trade; and the return was chiefly in bullion, which was remitted by the merchants and agents there to their consignees in Great Britain. The island of Cuba, and all the Spanish settlements from the Floridas to the Oroonoko, were indeed chiefly supplied with these articles through this channel. But on the return of peace, this flourishing trade ceased in a great degree, and such a revulsion ensued, that cotton goods fell in the Kingston market to little more than half their former price—that is, considerably below prime cost. The trade has revived a little since; but the Spaniards are more sparing of their gold and silver, and prefer giving their own commodities in exchange for what they receive—namely, horses, mules, oxen, hides, tortoise-shell, fustic, mahogany, &c.

From British North America, Jamaica and the other islands receive lumber, salted cod-fish, salmon, mackerel, oil, tar, &c. and give in return sugar, rum, molasses, coffee, and pimento.

The tonnage of all vessels trading to and round this island, from the 29th September 1816 to the 29th September 1817, was as follows:—From Great Britain and Ireland, 101,365 tons; from North America, 56,411 tons; from the Spanish Main and neighbouring islands, 15,557 tons; droggers, 3109 tons; vessels trading under the free-port act, 13,121 tons. Of this shipping there is engaged in the Kingston trade a very large proportion, viz. From Great Britain and Ireland, 35,964 tons; from North America, 36,085 tons; from the Spanish Main and islands, 12,691 tons; droggers, 2032 tons; vessels trading under the free-port act, 10,391 tons.

It has been the policy of Great Britain to shut the ports of her colonial possessions to all flags but her own—with such exceptions only as necessity or expediency dictated,—with a view of possessing herself of the carrying trade, directing their products into her market, and supplying them with her manufactures. Among the deviations from this policy was the permission granted to the West India islands to draw provisions and lumber from the United States, imported in either British or American bottoms, for which they gave rum, molasses, &c. in return.* This trade was at all times highly beneficial to the islands, because they were supplied by it with articles of which they were perpetually and unavoidably in want, and found in it a ready and profitable vent for some of their own products. But these products having fallen to ruinously low prices in the British

---

* Permission, under the free-port act, is also given to Spanish vessels of a certain description, to import into Jamaica articles the growth and produce of their American and West Indian possessions.

and British North American markets (the only ones to which the islands had for a long time access), the renewal of the intercourse with the United States became absolutely necessary to enable the planters to carry on the cultivation of their estates. The suspension of this intercourse was owing, first, to the refusal, on the part of Great Britain, to allow this trade to be carried on in any other than her own bottoms; and, secondly, to the refusal of the United States to permit it on any other principle than that of a perfect reciprocity of advantages. The former was right in endeavouring to obtain for herself, if she could, the whole of the carrying trade in the proposed intercourse; the latter acted naturally and rationally in rejecting a proposition so incompatible with the principles on which two independent states ought to carry on a commercial intercourse. As a remedy for this disagreement of opinion, it was proposed by the British, that a port of entrepot should be established, into which the Americans should bring their cargoes, and take from thence West India produce brought hither in British bottoms; and New Providence was named as being the most central and convenient. But this proposal the Americans likewise refused to accede to. They said, that, by such an arrangement, a vast disproportion of the carrying trade would be thrown into the hands of the British. Nevertheless, considerable quantities of American flour and lumber found their way thither and into other ports, and were thence exported to the West Indies; and St Jago de Cuba, in the island of Cuba, became also a medium for conveying these articles to Jamaica. But this did not relieve the planters; the merchants by whom this trade was carried on charged considerable profits on those articles, and thus was the cost greatly enhanced to them, and they had not a sufficient vent for their rum and molasses. What the planters required—and which has since been granted by the British government—was permission to the Americans to bring their provisions and lumber direct to the islands, where they might be obtained at a moderate rate, in exchange for rum, molasses, &c. at the island current prices.*

From the island of Madeira Jamaica receives considerable supplies of wine, for which bills on England are paid. This trade is therefore only beneficial in so far as regards the profits of the importers.

The coasting trade of the island is carried on

* The renewal of the intercourse between the islands and the United States has not, it seems, been productive of all the good the planters expected from it. The Americans want money, not rum, for their commodities, and the planters have no money to give them.

by means of droggers, or small vessels of from fifty to seventy tons burden. It consists of exportations of all sorts of dry goods, Irish provisions, cod-fish, &c. from Kingston to all the outports, the droggers taking, as return cargoes, sugar, rum, pimento, and other produce. The houses in the commission line in Kingston supply the store-keepers at the other ports with the above-mentioned commodities as cheaply as they could import them, and sometimes much cheaper; for in the market of this emporium of the island, goods, but especially those of a perishable nature, rise and fall according to the supply in it. For example, butter may one week sell at 2s. 1d. per pound, from its being scarce, and on the following week fall to 1s. 6d., in consequence of the arrival of a large supply.

The store-keepers, or retail dealers in almost all sorts of goods, charge an immense profit on them. In selling goods on credit, they have a very simple process for ascertaining the price to be charged. They multiply the sterling cost by three, and this gives them the amount in currency they are to demand, being a profit of somewhat more than cent. per cent.; and yet their actual profits may not ultimately be fifty per cent., in consequence of bad debts, &c. They lay their account with not receiving payment for at least a third of the goods they sell in this way, and they indemnify themselves by charging accordingly ;—in other words, they make the honest customer pay for the deficiencies of the fraudulent one,—than which nothing can be conceived more repugnant to fairness and equity. When a customer of the latter description goes into a store to make purchases, he is not inquisitive as to prices, as he has already made up his mind *not to pay for what he takes,* or at least to pay for only a small part, by way of keeping up his credit and inducing the store-keeper to give him another supply of goods when he wants it. It is astonishing to what an extent credit is indiscriminately given to persons whose properties are overwhelmed with debt, or whose characters and actions do not promise a very conscientious regard to the just claims of their creditors. The cash price of goods is from thirty to forty per cent. below the credit price. All the commodities of the country have also their cash prices, being about ten per cent. below what are called the market prices. The latter are fixed by a sort of compromise between the planters and merchants; the former by the respective buyers and sellers, regulated, of course, by the quality of the commodity. A wharfinger's receipt for a puncheon of rum, a tierce of coffee, or a bag of pimento, endorsed by the payer, passes in payment as readily as a bill or draft would do; so that these articles become a sort of circulating medium, and it is not unusual for a puncheon of rum, or other commodity, to pass through twenty or more different hands, without ever being moved from the wharf-store where it was deposited by its original owner, into whose possession it may again ultimately return.

The time when the ships arrive from Great Britain is from October to May; and they continue to depart, as they get freighted, from April till the first day of August, after which day, and until the hurricane months are over (August, September, and October), ships and their cargoes sailing for Great Britain pay double insurance. During war the ships sail in large fleets, under convoy: there were usually three convoys appointed—in May, June, and July. The convoys consisted of a seventy-four gun ship, two frigates, and two or three sloops of war. But in the event of a future war with America, more than double that force will probably be required to protect our West-India fleets; for that power, by the possession of the Floridas, commands the gulf-stream through which our trade usually passes; the windward passage being only practicable for deep-laden ships when there is a strong weather-current in their favour. Could Great Britain persuade Spain to allow her to occupy the Havannah as a naval station, she would indeed have an equal command over the gulf-passage as the Americans.

The coins in circulation in this island are chiefly Spanish. There are also some Portuguese gold pieces, and guineas and sovereigns. The Spanish gold coins are doubloons, value 16 dollars, or £5 : 6 : 8 currency; half doubloons; pistoles, value 4 dollars, or £1 : 6 : 8; and half pistoles. The Portuguese gold coins are johannoes, and half and quarter johannoes, the full value of which are £5, 10s., £2, 15s., and £1 : 7 : 6; but there are few of these coins that are not deficient more or less in weight, according to which their value is regulated—as indeed that of all the other gold coins are, at the rate of 3d. per grain. Very few of the Spanish coins are deficient in weight. A few moidores and half moidores are in circulation, the full value of which are £2 and £1; but they are generally deficient in weight. Guineas and sovereigns are not common, though there is a premium of about 10 per cent. on them, a guinea of full weight passing for £1 : 12 : 6 currency, and sovereigns in proportion. The silver coins are dollars, value 6s. 8d., half dollars, quarter dollars, half quarter dollars or 10d. pieces, and 5d. pieces; also pisterines at 1s. 3d., and rials or bits at 7½d.; but these have become rare. Bri-

tish silver coins are not common, and generally
pass below their actual value, a crown piece passing only for a dollar, and the rest in proportion.

The quantity of coin in circulation is by no
means sufficient for the purposes of commerce,
and there are no banks; but receiver-general's
checks, which readily pass at par, assist to supply
the deficiency. Bills drawn payable in Great
Britain, at ninety days after sight, bear the enormous premium of 20 per cent.:* the premium
has gradually advanced, since the return of peace,
from 10 per cent. to its present amount. During
the war, British bills have sometimes been at,
and even below par. This great rise in the premium is partly owing to the reduced price of
bullion in the British market, and partly to the
low and fluctuating state of that market for
West-India produce. Bills on Kingston, at
twenty or thirty days sight, pass at the out-ports
at 2½ per cent. below par.

The principal taxes in this island are, the poll-
tax of 6s. 8d. for each slave, and 1s. 8d. for each
horse, mule, or head of horned stock; the defi-
ciency-tax, as it is called, being 20s. for each slave,
but with this proviso, that every able-bodied
man, whether proprietor or person employed by

---

* In 1822 the premium on bills was as high at one time, in
Kingston, as 22½ per cent. !

him, who does duty in the militia, saves to the amount of £50 of this tax annually: it is, in fact, intended to operate, not as a productive tax, but as a means of keeping up the effective strength of the white population; for no planter would prefer paying this tax to keeping an adequate number of white persons in his employ to cover it. Formerly the wife and children of a white man saved each as much of this tax as he himself did; but this regulation did not long exist. There is, also, a land-tax of 3d. per acre, and quit-rent of ½d. per acre; a stamp-tax; a tax of 20s. on each wheel of all carriages not used in agriculture or for the conveyance of goods; and a house-tax of 12 per cent. on the amount of the rent.

There are also parochial taxes, viz. 6s. 8d. for each slave, and 1s. 8d. for each horse, mule, or head of horned stock; a road-tax of 4s. 9d. for each slave, for keeping the highways in repair; a tax on trade, and one on transient importers of goods, of 2 per cent. on their invoices.

The imported articles on which duties are levied are wines, spirits, compounds or liqueurs, tea, tobacco, fermented liquors, refined sugar, coffee, cocoa, indigo, cotton, ginger; also on flour, and on cattle.

The annual receipts, proceeding from the taxes, &c. may be estimated at about £280,000.

CHAP. IX.

GOVERNMENT — LEGISLATURE — LAWS — PAROCHIAL
REGULATIONS—ECCLESIASTICAL ESTABLISHMENT.

THE government of Jamaica is the most lucrative in the gift of the crown, next to the lord-lieutenancy of Ireland and the governor-generalship of India. Including all fees and emoluments,* it is computed to yield about £10,000 per annum.

The governor, besides his legislative prerogatives, has the style and authority of captain-general, is chancellor and judge of the court of errors and of ordinary. He has the presentation to all vacant livings, appoints the magistrates, the members of council, the assistant judges, the masters of chancery, and various public officers; he grants all commissions in the militia, lays on martial law in times of emergency, grants letters of marque, and may respite, though he cannot pardon, criminals. He has, besides, other minor

---

* These are, 1st, the fees in chancery; 2d, the fees in the court of ordinary (a very lucrative source of revenue); 3d, share of customhouse seizures, being a third; 4th, sale of militia and other commissions; 5th, escheats.

powers and prerogatives in his twofold capacity of governor and chancellor.

The governor, or lieutenant-governor, may be either a military man or a civilian. During the last fifty years there have been a greater proportion of the former appointed to this government. In time of war a military governor must doubtless be the most efficient. The Duke of Manchester is at present governor. His government has been marked by a mildness and moderation which has procured him the gratitude and attachment of the inhabitants, at whose earnest desire he has been allowed to retain his government more than double the time that any of his predecessors possessed it; and in testimony of the high sense the assembly had of his mild and equitable government, they unanimously voted him, a few years ago, an addition to his salary of £3000 currency.*

It must appear somewhat irrational that a governor of a West-India colony, who may know nothing of law, should be required to perform the duties of a chancellor. It is not a very rea-

---

* This grant has since, it appears, been withdrawn, on account of the distress of the colony. At the time when it was made, there were many who thought that a superb piece of plate would accord equally well with the dignity of the governor, and be more compatible with the circumstances of the colony.

sonable hypothesis, that a man should possess, by intuition, that knowledge of law necessary to qualify him for so important a situation. There may be heaven-born poets, and even orators; but a heaven-born lawyer is not a very common character. It may be said that this untaught, unprofessional chancellor has the advice and assistance of the masters in chancery, who must of course be well acquainted both with the spirit and practice of that court; and that, in difficult cases, he may take the advice of the attorney-general or advocate-general. But a judge, called upon to decide in intricate cases of the utmost importance, where immense property is frequently at stake, should possess that knowledge and talent within himself which will enable him to decide with the most perfect discrimination. It is true, an appeal lies from the colonial courts of chancery to the lord chancellor of England, or to the king and council; but these appeals are attended with prodigious additional expense and delay, and they certainly would be far less frequent were professional men appointed to preside in those courts: there would be a confidence in the wisdom and propriety of their decisions which would obviate the necessity and discourage the desire for appeal.

When the governor has given his assent to a bill which has passed the assembly and council, it of course passes into a law; but he may, if doubtful of the wisdom or policy of a legislative measure, suspend his assent until he has submitted it to his Majesty, by whose orders he acts. The British legislature claims a right to legislate for the colonies; but this right the colonial legislatures do not recognise, in so far as their internal policy is concerned; and the imperial parliament wisely forbears from pressing this claim, or interfering with the colonial assemblies; for so jealous are the latter of all interference, that, in order to counteract it, they would refuse granting the supplies—a measure the house of assembly of Jamaica have often resorted to, when they conceived their privileges invaded by either the governors or the council. Even with their favourite, the Duke of Manchester, they had a bickering of this sort at the commencement of his government, on account of the refusal of Major-general Carmichael to lay before the house authenticated copies of certain proceedings taken before courts-martial, respecting a mutiny in the 2d West-India regiment,* and an order to all the general officers, who had sat in or attended such courts-martial, to give no evidence before the house touching their proceedings. The duke vindicated the conduct of the general; and the

---

* Consisting of negroes.

house of assembly, in consequence, refused to " proceed to any other business, until reparation should be made for this breach of its privileges." The house was consequently prorogued, and an account of the affair was forwarded to England, to be laid before his Majesty—by whom orders were subsequently transmitted, *that the documents and evidence required by the house of assembly should be laid before it.*

At the time when the slave-registry act was in agitation, it was supposed in the West Indies that the British legislature meant to establish and enforce the registration by its own authority; and such a measure was recommended by many persons in parliament. But ministers saw that it would produce much discontent and agitation in the colonies, as it would be a direct attempt to legislate for them; and they chose therefore to lay before the colonial assemblies the wish of the British legislature, in the shape of an injunction, that they should carry the registration into effect by their own authority. This was done, though not precisely to the extent desired.

The council consists of twelve, including the president, who is usually the chief justice: he is the person next in power and rank to the governor, in the event of whose death, should there be no commander of the forces, he assumes the supreme power, with the title of president, until the arrival of another governor or lieutenant-governor. The council form the aristocratic branch of the legislature, besides being the advisers of the first branch,—an anomaly certainly far from constitutional, and frequently the cause of much difficulty and delay in the public business, through the jealousy and bickerings that almost every session occur between them and the house of representatives.

The house of assembly consists of forty-five members, viz. two each for eighteen of the parishes, and three each for the remaining three, viz. Kingston, Port Royal, and St Catherine. Its sessions commence in October, and continue till about the 20th of December. It has a speaker, sergeant at arms, librarian, chaplain, and messenger. The members are chosen by the freeholders septennially. The debates are often animated and warm, but there is not much display of that powerful and commanding eloquence which is so often witnessed in the British senate. This may in some measure be owing to the topics being so far inferior in magnitude and interest to those discussed in the imperial parliament.

The English common law is in force in Jamaica, but many of the statute laws are not—for example, the game laws, poor laws, bankrupt laws, and most of those relating to the revenue.

An English statute law, to have force in Jamaica, must be re-enacted by the legislature there. Lord Ellenborough's highly salutary law, rendering the cutting, maiming, or shooting a person, with intent to kill, a capital offence, was actually not in force in this island till the year 1820, when it was *naturalized*, if the phrase may be used, by an act of the legislature. It never was thought of till then, and probably would not have been thought of to this day, had not one or two very atrocious cases of attempts to murder occurred, the most remarkable of which was the following:—A man was summoned into the office of the clerk of the peace at Lucca, to answer the complaint of a person who had some trifling demand against him. The magistrate decided in favour of the complainant, and, in consequence, the wretch drew a pair of pistols from his pocket, and discharged them at the magistrate and the clerk of the peace! Both were very severely wounded, but ultimately recovered; while the sanguinary miscreant found means, amidst the astonishment and confusion created by this murderous act, to escape. He was, however, some time afterwards taken, brought to trial, found guilty *only of a misdemeanour*, and sentenced to *eighteen months imprisonment* —for what, had Lord Ellenborough's act been in force, he would have justly forfeited his life.

The English bankruptcy laws are not, as has been said, in force here; but there is, in lieu, the " Insolvent Debtors' Act," by which a debtor, on making oath that he is possessed of no property, above bare necessaries, and delivering his books, if he has any, into the hands of the deputy-marshal, or sheriff's deputy, is, after remaining three months in jail, exonerated from all demands against him. Much fraud, as may easily be supposed, is practised under this law. Personal property is secreted or secured, false oaths taken, and books destroyed, in order to defraud the injured creditors; and it is not unusual to see a man, who has just claimed the benefit of the insolvent act, continuing to live in his usual style, and even obtaining credit from the store-keepers and others with whom he deals : he has in fact become more *independent* since he *so conveniently settled* with his creditors; and, though he has no pretensions to the vulgar virtue of honesty, he can yet confidently speak of his *sacred regard to honour!* The priority law, in this island, opens a door for more numerous and extensive frauds than any other relating to property. By this law, the demand of the creditor holding a prior judgment against his debtor must be first satisfied before any other judgment-debts are paid ; if the debtor dies, the prior creditor enters a caveat on his estate—is appointed administrator on it—and pays himself in full, if the estate will admit of it; and should there be a residue, it goes to satisfy the other creditors, according to the priority of their judgments. It, however, most frequently happens that the junior creditors get nothing, especially those whose demands are not on judgment. A creditor, holding a junior judgment, may issue his writ and levy on the property of his debtor, but this property can be replevined; the prior judgment stands as a barrier between him and the property of his debtor—it must first be satisfied; so that, by issuing and levying, he only harasses his debtor without benefit to himself. He may, however, buy up the prior judgment, or judgments, and thus obtain access to his debtor's property; or he may arrest his person, if he can; but this is seldom practicable, the debtor locking his gates, and keeping aloof from the gripe of the marshal's followers, or desperately defending himself if taken by surprise. It is not an unusual practice for dishonest persons to place their properties beyond the reach of their creditors by means of the priority law; such an one grants to a friend, in whom he can confide, an admission of judgment on a fictitious debt, of considerable amount, and by means of this document keeps at bay the *bona-fide* creditors; or, which is equally dishonourable, he conveys his property, by deed of gift, to his wife, or his children, before any judgments have been obtained against him; thus nullifying his present debts, and contracting others, which he may, or may not, pay, as he pleases. In the meantime, he coolly tells such of his creditors as may be a little too urgent, or may hint at an arrest, that it will be better for them to be patient and forbearing, and to trust to his *generosity;* for that, if they go to extremities with him, they will not get a farthing,—he having, at the worst, a very simple remedy at hand—namely, taking the benefit of the insolvent act. The man who thus defrauds, or keeps his creditors at bay, generally shields himself from censure, by professions of an intention to pay—*when he is able;* and so many examples, among all classes, of this mode of dealing exist, that those who are guilty of it do not appear to feel at all abashed; neither are they, strange as it may seem, treated with much less outward respect than if they had not been guilty of such unprincipled conduct. The only precaution the store-keeper, &c. can take to guard himself against this species of fraud, is to search the public records, and ascertain whether, in the first place, the property which his would-be debtor holds, is *his own or not;* or whether there are prior judgments against him to the amount of that property, should it not have been passed away by deed of gift or otherwise, or is not covered by mortgage; and, if not, to secure himself by taking early judgment on his account. Most of the people, of the description here mentioned, whether male or female, speak most knowingly on the subject of law, and make it their study to become acquainted with all its mysteries. So numerous are the common actions, or suits for debt, in the supreme and assize courts, that a whole day, during their sittings, is set apart for these only. In the petty courts, or courts of quarter-session, no debts above twenty pounds can be sued for; and all debts, of whatever amount, due by debtors not residing in the same parish as the creditor, can be sued for only in the assize-court of the county in which the latter resides.

By a law of the island, no person can leave it without advertising his intention three weeks before hand; in which case it is in the power of a creditor to stop him till his demand be satisfied; and if any master of a vessel takes him from the island without such public notice, he subjects himself to a heavy penalty. Persons intending to leave the island are legally obliged, besides thus publishing their intention, to take out a ticket, or passport, signed by the governor, from the secretary's office, for which they pay £1 : 6 : 3.

The consolidated slave-laws, or code of laws enacted chiefly for the protection of the slaves,* is a separate code, the result of a more enlightened and humane view of the duties of masters to their slaves, and of the necessity of enforcing the performance of those duties by positive enactments, which has been gradually gaining ground in the West Indies for the last thirty-five years—before which time the condition of the unhappy slave depended in a great measure on the will and pleasure of his master. These laws contain many excellent and humane provisions, which, were they duly carried into execution, would render the condition of the slaves as secure and comfortable as the state and nature of slavery would admit. But there are obstacles to the due execution of those laws which must first be removed ere they can have full efficiency; the principal of these is the absolute legal nullity of the evidence of a slave against a white man. But on this subject, and on the principal provisions of the slave-code, the author will enter more at large in treating of the slaves. All

---

* A portion of them relates to the right of property in slaves, as also to offences committed by them.

trials of slaves, even those for capital offences, are carried on in the petty courts, or quarter-sessions of the respective parishes. These trials are usually conducted with the most perfect regard to impartial justice, and generally with a leaning of mercy towards the delinquent. The court appoints counsel to conduct his defence. When a white man stands accused of the murder of a slave, he is tried in the supreme court, or either of assize-courts, according to the county in which the murder has been committed. Should he be convicted, he suffers the same penalty of the law as a slave would who had been convicted of killing a white man. The great difficulty is to bring home legal evidence against the former. In 1821 a white man shot a slave, employed along with others by a deputy-marshal to assist in making a levy of slaves belonging to this man, on a writ against him. The evidence of the other slaves so employed was nugatory; and the marshal's follower who headed them, having been convicted of perjury on a former occasion, his evidence was deemed inadmissible by the court. The culprit would accordingly have been acquitted for want of evidence, had it not been for the testimony *of two of his own witnesses* (his housekeeper and his daughter), who, in their cross examination, admitted the fact of his having shot the slave, under the impression of its being a justifiable act in defence of his property. On this evidence he was convicted and executed, though recommended to mercy by the jury. His housekeeper and daughter were free persons of colour,—a class of people whose evidence some years ago was inadmissible against the whites,—a disability since very properly removed by the legislature.

The supreme court of judicature holds its sittings in Spanish Town, three times a-year: its jurisdiction extends over the county of Middlesex. The chief justice presides in it, with whom are associated two or three assistant judges. Of the latter there are usually eight or ten appointed, who take it in turns to sit: they have a salary of £500 currency. The salary of the chief justice has been lately augmented by the legislature from four to six thousand pounds. There are two assize-courts, one for the county of Surrey, the other for the county of Cornwall. Like the supreme court, they sit every four months, but at different periods. For each of these there are eight assistant judges appointed, two or three of whom sit in turns with the chief justice: they receive no salaries. Neither them nor the assistant judges of the supreme court are regularly bred to the law; they are appointed by the governor from among the most respectable gentlemen of property in each county. This practice

of appointing unprofessional men as judges has
often and justly been complained of: it is not
to be supposed that such men are qualified to
decide in intricate cases of law. It has accordingly been proposed to substitute three professional gentlemen, selected from the bar, as puisne
judges, in room of the present assistant judges;
but this proposal has hitherto been over-ruled.
Men cannot easily be prevailed upon to give up
any portion of their dignities or emoluments
even where the good of the community demands
such a sacrifice. The predecessor of the present
chief justice (who was impeached and convicted
by the House of Assembly of misconduct and
malversation in his office, and was compelled in
consequence to *resign*) managed, by a species of
generalship peculiar to him, to lead some of his
brother judges into an acquiescence in strange
decisions, the precise nature of which they did
not at the moment fully comprehend. The present chief justice (an active, able, and upright
judge) has uniformly, since his appointment,
presided at both the assize-courts, and his decisions have given the highest satisfaction—at least
to all the disinterested part of the community;
for it is next to impossible that a judge should
please every one. But in the event of his being
unable to attend through indisposition, the
bench, in all the superior courts, must be left to

the assistant judges—respectable, well-meaning men, it is true, but certainly not qualified by education and study to preside in a superior court of law. Among the barristers there are some men of very considerable talent. There are from eighty to ninety attorneys usually practising in this island, a proof of the abundance of business in their line, and of the propensity of the inhabitants rather to go to law than settle their disputes on the plain principle of moral equity. It has been calculated that upwards of half a million of money is annually expended here in law, including chancery suits, notwithstanding that the fees and charges have lately been considerably reduced by the legislature.

In the court of chancery there are from twenty to thirty masters, and a registrar: there is besides an equal number of masters extraordinary, who do not practise in the court. There is also a court of errors, to which appeals lie from the courts of law, and of which the governor and council are the judges;—a court of ordinary, for the probate of wills and granting letters of administration, of which the governor is sole ordinary;—and a court of vice-admiralty, the judge of which is appointed by the crown.

The three most lucrative offices in Jamaica, connected with the law, are those of the secretary of the island, the provost-marshal-general, and the clerk (prothonotary) of the supreme court. They are held by patent from the crown, and the duties attached to them are performed by deputies,—the patentees residing in England, and farming out these their offices to the highest bidders. Bryon Edwards estimates the profits of the first to be upwards of £6000 Sterling; of the second £7000 Sterling; and of the third about £9000 currency, per annum. But since his time the emoluments of these offices must have greatly increased.

The secretary of the island is keeper of the public records; in his office authenticated copies of the laws are kept; and all deeds, wills, sales, and patents, as also certified accounts of the produce of estates in the charge of trustees, attorneys, and guardians of orphans, must be registered in it.

The provost-marshal-general is high-sheriff of the island, and in each of the parishes he has a deputy of his own nomination. This office was probably established under the military government, and thence derived its name.

The offices of registrar of the court of chancery, of receiver-general, or treasurer of the island, and of naval-officer, and collector of Kingston, are also situations of great emolument.

In the parochial courts of quarter-session the custos, or chief magistrate, presides, assisted by two of the other magistrates, who sit in rotation. They take cognisance of all common actions not exceeding twenty pounds,* and of actions of assault, and other breaches of the peace, within their respective jurisdictions. All offences committed by slaves belonging to the respective parishes are also, as has been said, tried by these courts; but petty offences are usually inquired into and punished by two magistrates, who sit in rotation for that purpose, and who also hear and redress all complaints of cruelty and oppression made by slaves against their masters or overseers. The due performance of this latter duty is often attended with much difficulty, however honestly and zealously the magistrates may wish to do justice to the complainants; for unless the latter can show marks of improper severity, their complaints are liable to be regarded as idle and frivolous, and, instead of redress, they may, as a *necessary* example, be punished for absconding from their work on false and frivolous pretences.

In each parish there is a vestry, composed of ten freeholders, chosen by their fellow-freeholders, who, with the custos, two other magistrates, and the rector, form a vestry, or council for the or-

---

* Debts not exceeding forty shillings may be determined before a justice of the peace.

dering and regulating of all matters appertaining to the parish.

The established religion of Jamaica is that of the church of England. Each parish has a rector and a curate. The rectors have a stipend of £420 currency, and a parsonage-house,* a very inadequate income for a clergyman in the West Indies, were there no other emoluments attached to the livings; but this stipend does not form a fourth part, and, in some parishes, not, perhaps, above an eighth part of the average income of the rectors. Their fees are the principal source of their incomes, which vary from about £1500 to £3000, and even upwards, according to the wealth and population of the respective parishes. Kingston may be regarded as the most productive rectory in the island, and next to it, St Catherine's, St Thomas in the East, St James's, and Trelawny. The fees arise from marriages, baptisms, and funerals; also permission to erect monuments in the church, &c. The fees for marrying and baptizing, as fixed by law, are very moderate; and if the parties choose to have these solemnities performed in the church, the rector is not entitled to demand more than the legal fees. But this is seldom done, except by the poorest persons: it is not considered as liberal

---

* A few have also glebes, of more or less value.

or genteel : the rector is usually sent for, and then it is understood that his fee shall be in proportion to the rank and wealth of the parties, and the distance he may have to travel when so summoned. No precise sum is fixed, the amount greatly depending on the liberality of the parties; but few would choose to be considered as less liberal, on such occasions, than their neighbours, and the rectors therefore have not often occasion to complain of not being well paid for their trouble. Three doubloons (£16 currency) for a marriage, baptism, or funeral, is the usual fee given; but opulent persons usually give considerably more. These enormous fees, or rather *free gifts,* have all the privilege and permanency which long-standing usages usually attain. There are no tithes here. The stipends of the clergy are paid from the public funds.

The curates were appointed a few years ago by an act of the legislature. Their salary is £500 currency; but they have no other emolument from their curacies. The ostensible object of their appointment was, that they should preach to and instruct the slaves in the Christian religion—an object, which, from whatsoever cause, has been rendered in a great measure abortive. Either the curates are lukewarm in the cause, or the planters do not wish the time and attention of their slaves to be occupied by religious discussions,—or, which is most probable, both of these causes have operated to render the intentions of the legislature nugatory. As it is, the curates have dwindled into mere assistants to the rectors, who were, before their appointment, fully able to perform all their clerical duties. By a law of some standing in the island, the rectors are required to set apart two hours of every Sunday to the religious instruction of the slaves; but this law is very little attended to:* the truth is, that, however willing the rectors might be to perform this duty, very few of the slaves have it in their power to attend church; they are either in attendance on their owners, or their time is occupied in a necessary attention to their own affairs; for Sunday is not a day of rest and relaxation to the plantation slave; he must work on that day, or starve.

It has long been a subject of just complaint that the clerical office in Jamaica has been accessible to men disqualified both by education and previous habits to fill it. It was a sort of

---

* A few praiseworthy examples might be mentioned of clergymen who cheerfully and even zealously devoted themselves to the duty of instructing the slaves, as far as lay in their power. Among these, the Rev. Mr Trew, rector of St Thomas in the East, seconded by the worthy custos of that parish, was the most zealous and diligent.

dernier resort to men who had not succeeded in other professions, or who thought it a more thriving one than that which they pursued: hence it was not unusual to see a quondam merchant, a military officer, or even an overseer of a plantation, who had the necessary interest, ordained to the ministry here. This degradation of the clerical office, by the admission into it of men who had no other end in view than to better their situation, has no doubt contributed, among other causes, to encourage that immorality and disregard of religion so generally prevalent among all classes. Of late years, however, a better order of men has been introduced into the ministry: some young men, regularly educated in the universities, have been appointed to vacant curacies, and others will no doubt follow, should they be encouraged by the prospect of a preferment, in turn, to the vacant rectories: thus they will form a source of supply of fit and proper persons for the ministry—men who will act from a paramount sense of duty, —not be influenced in the performance of it by time-serving views of interest and convenience.

There is an ecclesiastical court here, for exercising ecclesiastical jurisdiction and control: it is composed of three of the rectors, viz. those of Kingston, Port Royal, and St Andrews, or St

Catherine's, a registrar, and apparitor. The bishop of London is the diocesan.

There is a fund for the benefit of the widows and orphans of clergymen, which is supported by a contribution of ten per cent. from the stipends of the rectors.

There is in Kingston a Presbyterian church. It was established, about seven years ago, by the Presbyterian inhabitants of that city, who are numerous, opulent, and respectable, assisted by some grants from the assembly. This establishment is recognised as a branch of the church of Scotland, and its pastors are appointed by the presbytery of Edinburgh. Some narrow-minded persons in the assembly opposed any grants of the public money being voted in aid of this church, on the grounds of its *not being recognised by the constitution*, and its having no better claim to such support than other dissenting establishments: they forgot that the Presbyterian is the established religion of an integral part of the British empire, and that the British legislature sanctions and assists three Presbyterian establishments in India. The fact is, that the establishment in Kingston had become absolutely necessary; for, from the greatly increased population of that city, the parish-church had become insufficient to contain the inhabitants; and that circumstance, and the natural desire which men have to worship their Creator after the manner of their forefathers, suggested to the Presbyterian inhabitants the propriety of building a church for themselves.

There is a Roman Catholic chapel in Kingston, several meeting-houses belonging to Methodists, Moravians, Anabaptists, &c. and a Jewish synagogue.

CHAP. X.

NAVAL AND MILITARY ESTABLISHMENTS—MILITIA—
POST-OFFICE, AND PACKETS.

In war-time the naval establishment of Jamaica is considerable. It usually consists of three line-of-battle ships, four or five frigates, and eight or ten gun-brigs and smaller cruisers, commanded by an admiral. In peace the establishment is reduced to one or two frigates, and six or seven smaller vessels. These have been employed, since the last peace, in protecting the trade to the Spanish and Independent settlements on the American continent, against the numerous piratical vessels which have infested the Atlantic during the contest between Old Spain and her revolted colonies. In the event of a war with the United States, the British government will probably find it necessary to double her naval force on the Jamaica station, for the protection of its trade, in consequence of the former power having, by the possession of the Floridas, obtained the command of the gulf passage, and the rapid and formidable increase of her navy. A strong squadron will at least be required to escort the Jamaica trade beyond the Bahamas. It is probable indeed that America looks forward to the ultimate possession of the British West-India islands as a certain event. There is, however, no cause for apprehending such an event, while the inhabitants themselves have no desire to change masters.

Port Royal harbour is the station for the men of war; and here there is a dock-yard, store-houses, and conveniences for careening ships.

The number of regular troops usually stationed here in war time is about three thousand, and in peace about two thousand, which last number the island supports. In this number are included about two hundred artillerists. The governor, if a military man, is commander in chief of the forces; if not, a commander in chief is appointed, who, in the absence or on the death of the governor, becomes, *pro tempore*, lieutenant-governor. The head-quarters of the troops are at Up-Park Camp, in the vicinity of Kingston. One regiment is usually stationed on the north side of the island, the head-quarters of which are at Falmouth. Formerly the head-quarters of the regiments stationed in the county of Cornwall was the site of Trelawny Maroon Town, one of the most healthy spots in the island, which however has been given up, probably on account of the great expense attending the conveyance of provisions and stores thither,—an object surely more than counterbalanced by the preservation of the troops from disease.

Besides the white troops employed in the West Indies in war-time, there were eight West-India regiments, composed of negro soldiers, commanded by regular white officers. The embodying and employing of such a corps in the West Indies is considered by the inhabitants, and doubtless with much reason, as an impolitic step. The more perfect these troops may become in their discipline, the more dangerous and formidable they would be in case of defection (and examples have occurred to prove that their fidelity is not to be implicitly relied on) in a country to which they are attached by passions and affections not easily eradicated—not certainly operating in favour of their quondam masters and managers, but those of their own colour—their fellow-bondsmen, their friends, their relatives, their connexions. When a detachment of black soldiers was seen guarding and conveying some white deserters, pinioned and in a miserable plight, to head-quarters, it was regarded by the inhabitants as a novel and revolting sight; though, if white soldiers had guarded the delinquents, it would have excited no sensation.

There are some excellent fortifications in this island, the principal of which are the fortifications at Port Royal, Fort Augusta, and the fort called the Twelve Apostles. But many of the forts at the out-ports are neglected, and suffered to fall into a state of dilapidation and decay.

There is here a tolerably well-disciplined militia, and it is pretty numerous, considering the limited white population. From eight to ten thousand effective men (including about two thousand free people of colour and blacks enrolled with the whites) might, upon an emergency, be brought into the field.* Each parish has its regiment of foot, and one or two troops of horse. To each of the regiments are attached two field-pieces and a company of artillery. The officers are, as has been said, appointed by the governor, on the recommendation of the colonels; and so numerous are the candidates for commissions, that it is not unusual to see a battalion of about three hundred men have about fifty commissioned officers attached to it, besides nearly an equal number of non-commissioned officers; that is, one commissioned and one non-commissioned officer to every seven men. Among the former there are usually one colonel, two lieutenant-colonels, and two or more majors. The legal qualifications for a commission are two years

* The number in 1816 was 8900; at present it is somewhat more.

service in the ranks, and a certain income; but these regulations are not always attended to. In the recommendations to commissions much depends on petty local interests and connexions—on the favour and affection of the colonels, or their friends: without such interest or favour, merit and long services are rarely of any weight in such appointments. There may be exceptions; but this is the general system. The governor, who is the sole granter of commissions, has no power of discriminating as to the justness of the claims of those who apply for them; he has only to confirm the nomination of the colonels. The granting of commissions in the militia is a source of considerable emolument to the governor's secretary; the prices are as follow—commission of a general £30; of a colonel £21; of a lieutenant-colonel £15, 15s.; of a major £12, 10s.; of a captain £8, 5s.; of a lieutenant £5, 10s.; of an ensign, adjutant, and quarter-master, £3, 5s. &c.

The cavalry is tolerably well mounted, but it would be found far less effective in actual service than the infantry. Neither the men nor the horses are sufficiently well-trained to face a well-disciplined enemy; and the Maroon war showed, that, in an active warfare carried on in the interior, they were of little other use than the carrying of despatches. A few years ago a motion was made in the House of Assembly for reducing the troops of horse; but it was over-ruled.

The Jamaica militia differs in several respects from the militia of the mother-country. It is not raised by ballot, and no man can avoid the duty of serving by procuring a substitute; but every male between the age of sixteen and sixty, if not incapacitated by accident or infirmity, or exempted by official situation, or some convenient sinecure, is obliged to enrol himself in it. The regiments cannot be put on permanent duty except by the laying on of martial law: the regular routine of their duty, by the militia law, is attending drill once a month, and field-inspections once a quarter. When on permanent duty the militia receives pay * and rations. Arms and accoutrements are furnished by government, but the men must find their own regimentals. Mutiny and desertion, during martial law, are punishable with death, but ordinary offences by fines and imprisonment.

Three inspecting major-generals (one for each county) are appointed, from amongst the oldest militia colonels, to review and inspect, once a-year, the horse and foot militia,—each regiment and troop in its respective parish. Sir Eyre

* 2s. 6d. currency a day.

Coote, when lieutenant-governor of Jamaica, appointed regular officers to superintend the military affairs of the counties; and both he and Sir George Nugent, as well as Lieutenant-general Morrison, personally inspected the militia during their respective governments. They saw and judged with the eyes of experienced soldiers, and accordingly suggested many alterations and improvements which would never have occurred to an unmilitary general; and a marked and rapid improvement of the militia took place in consequence of this attention to it. But the militia generals do not like the interference of regular officers with their commands; they view it as an invasion of their rights; the title and authority of general have irresistible charms to them, with whatever trouble and difficulty its duties may be attended. Such indeed is the fondness for dignified situations and high-sounding titles, that one man sometimes holds the different situations of major-general of militia, assistant-judge of the grand court, and custos rotulorum and chief judge of the court of common-pleas, *without being either a soldier or a lawyer.*

As a safeguard against the danger of intrusting military commands, in actual service, to men ignorant of the science of tactics and its practical details, a scale of regular and colonial rank is very properly established during martial law.

According to this scale, a lieutenant-colonel of the line takes the colonial rank of major-general, and the command of the troops, both regular and militia, of the district; a major takes the rank of brigadier-general, and a captain, of lieutenant-colonel, &c. All this is highly necessary. A militia general, who has never made military tactics his particular study, nor has seen other service than that of the parade, though he might make a tolerable shift to wade through the duty of a review, would prove but an awkward leader on the day of battle. An experienced captain of regulars would certainly be a far more safe and able commander. A small mistake in the evolutions of a battalion may be easily rectified by a little consultation on the parade; but, in the face of an enemy, it is not quite so trifling an affair. The soldier will always follow with alacrity and confidence the officer who, he knows, will direct him with skill and promptitude; while, led by one who knows his duty but by halves, he can feel none of that inspiring confidence,— conscious that his mistakes, his demurs, and delays, must produce inevitable discomfiture and disgrace. Besides, it usually happens, that, by the time a militia officer arrives at the rank of general, he is too far advanced in years to be fit for the duties of active service: yet it is by no means uncommon to see men on the verge of seventy *volunteering* their services (for the law allows them to retire at sixty) as major-generals and colonels of regiments,—so fond are they of the " pomp, pride, and glorious circumstance of war." The veteran, who has seen the actual tug and turmoil of war, is glad, when honour will permit him, to repose under the shade of his laurels. Not so those parade warriors—they have no thought of retiring ; and should a considerate governor, in consequence of their superannuation, decline their further gratuitous services, it would be regarded as an inexpiable affront.

In Kingston, and in several of the parishes, the militia regiments are, very properly, under arms by dawn of day, and their duty is over by about nine o'clock, when the sun begins to be oppressively hot; but, in other parishes, instead of this humane regulation, the regiments are drilled during the very hottest time of the day, viz. from nine to twelve, to the endangering of the health, if not the lives, of the men.

During the existence of martial law, in actual warfare, or where the invasion of an enemy is expected, commissioners are appointed in the different parishes for regulating and furnishing necessaries for the troops: they consist of the most opulent and respectable of the old inhabitants, who are authorised to make requisitions of slaves, mules, oxen, and carts, from the plantations, for the transporting of baggage and provisions for the army—to purchase such provisions, and to impress whatever else may be promptly and unavoidably required.

The uniform, arms, and accoutrements of the militia, are much the same as those of the regulars, only that hats are worn instead of caps by the battalion companies. During the Maroon war this was found to be a most unwieldy and inconvenient mode of equipment, and it was accordingly exchanged for one in the style of that of a rifleman. In a hot climate the equipment ought to be as light and convenient as possible : on the parade it may be very well to prefer the gaudy and gorgeous to the useful; but the veteran who has seen some hard campaigns learns to appreciate the latter. At present some of the militia regiments have rifle companies attached to them; but if half of the militia were converted into sharp-shooters, it would become a far more effective corps. It is well known how terrible an enemy the American riflemen were in the war of independence; and America—at least that part of it which became the theatre of war, —is not half so much intersected with woods, mountains, rocks, and ravines, as Jamaica. Such indeed is the topographical nature of this country, that, though an enemy might be in possession of the towns, and even the fortifications, the interior could easily be defended against a very superior force. Nature affords innumerable situations here that may be deemed impregnable, without the assistance of art or the efforts of labour.

Though regular troops must be much more effective than the militia here, in a contest with an external and regular foe, yet in a warfare like that with the Maroons, the latter are better adapted than any troops of the line: they are more accustomed to the country and inured to the climate; they are more in the habit of traversing the woods, and more familiarized to the haunts and recesses they afford. Regular troops are taught to face danger without flinching or seeking for refuge from it; but this very bravery, or rather steadiness, which is the soul of discipline, in warring with a civilized foe, often proved the destruction of parties of regular soldiers, who were sent to watch the motions of the Maroons, or drive them from their haunts; while in their extreme caution and art of concealment consisted the principal generalship of these savages. The militia were more cautious; on marching through dangerous defiles, where they apprehended an ambuscade, they stole guardedly along, having recourse, like their barbarous adversaries, as occasion required, to the natural defences of rocks and trees. During this contest, a body of armed slaves, called *black-shot,* usually attended the expeditions of the whites: they behaved with great fidelity, and were exceedingly useful, as an advance-guard, in scouring the woods and discovering the retreats of the Maroons.

The post in this island is by no means so well regulated as in the mother-country. A mail arrives but once a-week from Kingston at the different parts of the island, Spanish Town excepted. It is conveyed on a mule, the post-man (a negro slave) riding another, at the average rate of about seventy miles in the twenty-four hours. This very slow travelling is in a great measure owing to the delays in forwarding the mail at the intermediate post-offices: the more of these there are between any two places, the longer the post is in performing the journey. As the mules which convey the post are in general well-trained, accidents seldom occur, and very few instances of attempts to rob the mail have been known, though the post-men go quite unarmed; but it is sometimes placed in jeopardy by the swelling of the rivers in consequence of heavy rains. There are forty post-offices throughout the island, besides the general post-office. The rate of postage is 1s. 3d. and 7½d., according to the distance, for single letters.

The letters from Great Britain are conveyed, monthly, by the packets: these are fast-sailing ship-rigged vessels, of from two to three hundred tons burthen, well armed and manned, especially in war-time. They have been known to run the passage direct to Jamaica in twenty-four days. A master of a packet is entitled to one hundred guineas if he arrives in Jamaica on or before the twentieth of each month. All foreign post-letters for Jamaica, as well as those from the British possessions, must pass through the general post-office of Great Britain.

CHAP. XI.

THE white inhabitants of Jamaica consist of
creoles, or natives of the country, and Europeans.
There may be about three of the former to two
of the latter. Formerly there was a marked
difference in the habits, manners, and mode of
life of those two classes, but that no longer generally exists. The primitive creolian customs and
manners are fast disappearing, being superseded
by the more polished manners of European life.
Even within the last fifteen or twenty years a
very considerable improvement has taken place
in the state of society here. This is owing in a
great measure to the now universally prevailing
practice of sending the children of both sexes to
Great Britain for their education. All who can
afford it must now give their children the benefit of this education. Formerly it was very different; a creole mother could not think of parting with her offspring—it seemed to her as if it
was a parting for ever; neither could she appreciate the advantages or perceive the necessity of
removing her child to a distant country to be in-

structed;—and, accordingly, it was brought up at home, too frequently in ignorance and un-limited indulgence. The advantages of a British education appeared at length so obvious, that parents became anxious that their children should possess them, at whatever hazard, or expense. Thus was laid the foundation of a great improvement in the minds and manners of the more opulent classes. The creole of the old school is now rarely to be met with, except among the lower orders. It has become more the fashion for gentlemen to improve their minds by study, and for ladies to practise the accomplishments peculiar to their sex : conversation has assumed a more refined tone, and the mode of life has become more rational and less dissipated. These improvements are of course chiefly confined to the genteeler families, whose members have had the advantage of a liberal education ; though others, who have not had such advantage, have at least made some progress in improvement by an endeavour to emulate their superiors.

There are obstacles, however, in this country, which must necessarily operate to keep down the state of society far below that improvement of which it would otherwise be capable. These partly grow out of and are inseparably connected with a state of slavery, but more especially arise from the gross immorality which too generally prevails among all ranks.

Wherever slavery exists, there must be many things attending it unfavourable to the improvement of the minds and manners of a people : arbitrary habits are acquired, irritation and violent passions are engendered—partly, indeed, by the perverseness of the slaves,—and the feelings are gradually blunted by the constant exercise of a too unrestrained power, and the scenes to which it is continually giving birth. There are unquestionably men of superior minds, incapable of abusing a power which fortune has given them over the happiness of their fellow-mortals, and who rather feel a pleasure in promoting their comforts—it is only to be wished that such characters were less rare. But this cannot be expected. Human nature is shaped and governed by the force of early habits and of example. The very children, in some families, are so used to see or hear the negro servants whipped, for the offences they commit, that it becomes a sort of *amusement* to them. It unfortunately happens that the females, as well as the males, are too apt to contract domineering and harsh ideas with respect to their slaves—ideas ill suited to the native softness and humanity of the female heart,—so that the severe and arbitrary mistress will not unfrequently be combined with the affectionate wife, the tender mother, and agreeable companion—such is the effect of early habits and accustomed prejudices, suffering qualities so anomalous to exist in the same breast. A young lady, while yet a child, has a little negress of her own age pointed out to her as one destined to be her future waiting-maid; her infant mind cannot conceive the harm of a little vexatious tyranny over this sable being, who is her property; and thus are arbitrary ideas gradually engrafted in her nature. The growth of this unamiable propensity is not sufficiently guarded against and corrected by the parents, who are too fond and indulgent to check these indications of *spirit* in their darlings; while, should the little black retaliate the ill usage she meets, she is immediately chastised for her *impertinence*. The more ignorant of the natives do not appear to be sensible that there is any impropriety in suffering their children to be witnesses of a most improper spectacle—the punishment of the slaves. The chastisement may have been justly inflicted; but why should the pliant mind of unhackneyed youth be thus early hardened and contaminated by witnessing such scenes? Such inflictions may in time be viewed with a sort of savage gratification; in the males it may produce brutality of mind; and

in the females, to say the least of it, an insensi-
bility of human misery, and a cold contemplation
of its distresses—qualities little in unison with
the female character, of which humanity and
compassion should ever form a part, for without
these, beauty, wit, and accomplishment would
lose half their charms. Such is the power of
habit over the heart, that the woman accustomed
to the exercise of severity soon loses all the natural softness of her sex. Nothing was more
common formerly than for white mistresses not
only to order their slaves to be punished, but
personally to see that the punishment was duly
inflicted! It must, however, in justice to the
white females of Jamaica of the present day, be
remarked, that such characters are now very rare,
except among the most low and ignorant; and
the author can with truth say, that he has known
ladies who were as kind, attentive, and indulgent
to their slaves, as their relative situations would
admit. The mistress of a family, where there
is a crowd of black and brown servants, has a
more difficult and painful duty to perform than
can well be conceived; they are often so refractory, vicious, and indolent, that, in managing
such a household, she is perhaps, in effect, a
greater slave than any of them. There is something in their manner, their behaviour, their language, and, not unfrequently their dress, which,

to one not accustomed to such attendants, must appear exceedingly disgusting. To the master, or mistress, whose pride is gratified by a numerous train of slaves around them, who know how to *manage* them, and who are accustomed to their ways, all this is pleasant enough; but to those who have been used to decent and orderly attendants, who require not the stimulus of the lash, such a barbarous retinue would be intolerable.

But even if slavery and its attendant abuses did not exist here, no great additional improvement in the state of society could be expected, while the most gross and open licentiousness continues, as at present, to prevail among all ranks of the whites. The males, of course, are here exclusively meant; for, as to the white females, it must be said, to their honour, that they are in general unexceptionably correct in their conduct: so particular are they on this point of character, that the white female who misconducts herself falls instantly, from her grade in society, below even that of the women of colour, in whose vocabulary of virtues chastity has no place. Every unmarried white man, and of every class, has his black or his brown mistress, with whom he lives openly; and of so little consequence is this thought, that his white female friends and relations think it no breach of decorum to visit his house, partake of his hospitality, fondle his children, and converse with his *housekeeper*—as if that conduct, which they regarded as disgraceful in their own class, was not so in the female of colour. The example of a few ladies of a juster way of thinking has little weight in discountenancing this levelling sort of familiarity. But the most striking proof of the low estimate of moral and religious obligation here is the fact, that the man who lives in open adultery,—that is, who keeps his brown or black mistress, in the very face of his wife and family and of the community, has generally as much outward respect shown him, and is as much countenanced, visited, and received into company, especially if he be a man of some weight and influence in the community, as if he had been guilty of no breach of decency or dereliction of moral duty! This profligacy is, however, less common than it was formerly; for among the old creoles, a brown or sable favourite, and sometimes even a haram of these *ladies*, was considered as an indispensable appendage to the establishment of a married man. In no country, however, are examples of female infidelity more rare than in Jamaica. The wedded fair, with whatever lack of patience she bears the insults of an unfaithful partner, has too lively a sense of the enormity of his crime to resent it by retaliation.

If a gentleman pays his addresses to a lady, it is not thought necessary, as a homage to her delicacy, to get rid, *a priori,* of his illicit establishment, nor is the lady so *unreasonable* as to expect such a sacrifice; the brown lady remains in the house till within a few days of the marriage, and, if she is of an accommodating disposition, even assists in making preparations for the reception of the bride; in which case there may be a tolerable good understanding between them, and the wife may even condescend to take in good part the occasional calls, inquiries, and proffered services of the ex-favourite, and make suitable returns of kindness to her and her children. Nothing is more common than for the brown mistress of a white man to apply to a respectable married lady to become godmother to her female infant,—a request which is not often refused, though the sponsor must be well aware that this child is destined, from the way in which she is brought up, to follow the footsteps of her mother. But it is thought to be only a form, and the kind-hearted white lady could hardly refuse so slight a favour to a *decent, well-behaved* brown woman, who would consider such refusal as a most grievous affront, for they do not consider the sponsorship of one of their own class as at all desirable or creditable.

These semi-barbarous customs and practices,

as they may well be called, will sufficiently show that this is not the happiest country in the world for a virtuous and well-educated female. The young ladies who are sent early in life to Great Britain to be educated readily perceive this, on their return, and often think with a sigh on the happier and more civilized country they have quitted. This alienation of attachment for their homes, and even their friends, the parents dread as one of the evils of an elegant and accomplished education in England, and not perhaps without reason; for a young lady, so educated, cannot help feeling dissatisfied and disgusted with many things she sees around her; and, however a sense of duty may dispose her to act, she must see, and be too prone to despise, the inferiority even of her nearest relatives. There are few females, so situated, that would not consider a permission to live in Great Britain, instead of Jamaica, as the greatest boon on earth.

The white females of the West Indies are generally rather of a more slender form than the European women. Their complexion, which they are peculiarly careful to preserve, is either a pure white or brunette, with but little or none of the bloom of the rose, which, to a stranger, has rather a sickly appearance at first, though that impression gradually wears off. Their features are sweet and regular—their eyes rather expressive

than sparkling—their voices soft and pleasing—
and their whole air and looks tender, gentle, and
feminine. With the appearance of languor and
indolence, they are active and animated on occasion, particularly when dancing, an amusement
of which they are particularly fond, and in which
they display a natural ease, gracefulness, and
agility, which surprise and delight a stranger.
They are fond of music, and there are few who
have not an intuitive taste for it, and fine voices.
They are accused of excessive indolence; and
outré examples of this are given by those whose
object is to exhibit them to ridicule. These ex-
aggerations, like all others of a national description, savour more of caricature than truth. The
heat of the climate, joined to the still habits of a
sedentary life, naturally beget a languor, listlessness, and disposition to self-indulgence, to which
the females of more northern climates are strangers. The daily loll in bed, before dinner, is so
gratifying a relaxation, that it has become almost as necessary as their nightly repose.

To sum up, in few words, the character of the
creole ladies,—they are so excessively fond of
pleasure and amusements, that they would be
glad if the whole texture of human life were
formed of nothing else; balls in particular are
their great delight: they are averse to whatever
requires much mental or bodily exertion, dancing

excepted; reading they do not care much about, except to fill up an idle hour; and diligence, industry, and economy, cannot be said to be among the number of their virtues. They are modest and decorous in their behaviour, and, when animated, sprightly and agreeable; they are obliging, generous, and hospitable (the latter virtue may be said to be proverbial of the creoles of both sexes), and, above all, scrupulously correct, as has been said, in their conduct. In short, they are, on the whole, formed to become affectionate wives, tender mothers, and warm-hearted friends. There is, of course, a great difference in manners and conversation, between the females who have received a genteel education in Great Britain, and those who have not had that advantage. The domestic education of the latter, or rather habits, and the scenes that are perpetually passing before them, have the effect, by giving a peculiar turn to their minds, of rendering them far inferior to their more favoured country-women—unless, indeed, that effect should be counteracted by the care and instruction of a judicious, well-informed mother.

The low, ignorant creole men are, generally, indolent, extravagant, unprincipled in their dealings, and depraved in their habits; in the two last of which qualities they are indeed rivalled by many of the Europeans of the same class.

But the creole gentleman, who has received a liberal education in Great Britain, is in no material respect different from the well-educated gentleman of any other country.

The Europeans who are settled in Jamaica come to it with one invariable view—that of making or mending their fortunes. Some few, after obtaining this end, continue in the island, purchase property, marry, and have families—in short, are domesticated as fixed inhabitants of the country. Such men, attached by a new train of connexions and endearments, seldom desire to return to their native country, to which, and to their relatives there, they become in time perfectly indifferent, and as great strangers as they at one time were to this their second home. Another class continue fixed in the country by less reputable attachments, which have, however, the effect, in time, of weaning them from every hope and wish for home, and of a more happy and respectable course of life. But by far the greater number—certainly not less than four-fifths—fall victims to disease before they have realized a sufficiency; while only a favoured few (perhaps not more than five or six in a hundred) ever return to their native country with a fortune, or competency.

When Europeans first arrive in the island, they are placed, according to their views, talents, and inclinations, either in the planting line, as *book-keepers;* in the mercantile line as clerks; or, if of any profession or trade, in a subordinate situation under others of such profession or trade; till, by proofs of their merit, their industry, and abilities, they obtain more independent and responsible situations. Much of their success depends on the interest and assistance of an able friend or friends, without whom a young man of merit may toil for many years to very little purpose.

As a great many low uneducated men come to Jamaica from Europe, it is observed, that such characters, when still further brutalized by the wretched habits they fall into here, are more dissolute in their lives, shameful in their excesses, and more unfeeling towards the slaves, than the lowest and most ignorant of the native whites. It is but justice to say, that, at the present day, when a respectable proprietor, or his agent, discovers such characters in his employ, he immediately dismisses them. Formerly men of this description were too common on the plantations; a robust frame, capable of enduring fatigue and hardship, was all that was sought for; education, moral habits, a humane disposition, were qualifications that never were inquired after, nor at all deemed necessary: the most riotous debauchery prevailed on the estates,

and excesses were often committed of which a
well-regulated mind can form no conception.
What sort of managers of the poor slaves such
men must have been may easily be conceived.
But a great change has happily taken place in
the West Indies. Men of this description meet
now with no encouragement; the planters in
general have become solicitous to procure a better order of men as superintendents on their
estates; and it is, at present, by no means unusual to see young men in the planting line who
have received the most respectable education,
and are of genteel and reputable connexions.
But, even with these advantages, men who enter
into this line are too prone to contract depraved
habits from the example and conversation of
those with whom they are too often obliged to
associate. They are indeed not in a situation to
foster and maintain the principles and opinions
in which they have been educated. The Sabbath is as any other day to them—not a day of
rest and religious observance, but one made up
of a mixture of toil and amusement; and
when they look around and see the universal
licentiousness that prevails, they are too apt to
lose the sense of moral distinctions. Doubtless,
too, there is in the very nature of slavery, in its
mildest form, something unfavourable to the cultivation of moral feeling. Men may be restrain-

ed—and they are here restrained—by very good
and well-intentioned laws, from exercising acts
of cruelty and oppression on the slaves, but still
harsh ideas and arbitrary habits, which may find
innumerable petty occasions of venting themselves, grow up, wherever slavery exists, in minds
where principle has not taken a deep hold. There
are no doubt humane and enlightened men in
the West Indies, who do all in their power to
render the condition of their slaves as easy and
comfortable as it can be made; but it is not
every proprietor or agent who deserves this
eulogium.

In the towns a more genteel society is to be
found than on the plantations; but the state of
morals is much the same;—and, as to the respect
paid to religion, it will be sufficient to say, that,
with a very few exceptions, the congregations in
the churches consist usually of a few white ladies, and a respectable proportion of free people
of colour and blacks.

CHAP. XII.

VARIOUS CLASSES AND PROFESSIONS.

In giving an account of the different classes and professions in this island, it is proper to begin with the planters, or proprietors of estates, who are by far the most opulent and important, and without whom, indeed, there would be little employment for any other. Under the general name of planters are included proprietors, attorneys, overseers, and book-keepers. Almost all the great proprietors reside in Great Britain, leaving their estates to the care and management of agents, or attorneys, as they are here called. This is much to be regretted. Many of them are men of liberal education and enlightened minds, which cannot always be said of their agents. By their presence and personal exertions the condition and treatment of their slaves would naturally be improved. It is true, they may forward instructions to that effect; but these instructions may or may not be carried into effect. None can have so lively an interest in the comfort and preservation of his slaves as a proprietor himself: this to him must be a primary object;

to his agent the making of a large crop may be, and often is, the principal concern. But the luxuries and pleasures of the British capital have seductions that outweigh the sense of duty and the calls of interest. The immense revenues thus spent, if diffused over the country from which they are drawn, would be important accessions to its wealth and prosperity. Most of the less opulent proprietors wisely reside in the island on their estates. Indeed so trifling are the net proceeds arising from sugar plantations at the present day, that they have no choice: to live in England, in the style to which they have been accustomed, would be ruinous. The lowest class of land proprietors are the inferior settlers, who either have a small pen, or a coffee or pimento walk, and who occasionally hire their slaves on the plantations, or to repair the public roads.

The attorney employed by the non-resident proprietor has the whole management of his estates and other concerns intrusted to him by power of attorney. He may be a resident proprietor, a merchant, a lawyer, a medical man, or an old experienced overseer who has given proofs of ability and diligence in his quondam situation. Some proprietors appoint two attorneys, one to manage their mercantile, law, and other concerns, the other a professional planter, to superintend the agricultural duties of their plantations. These agents have a joint power, and mutually share the emoluments of their agency. An attorney has sometimes fifteen or twenty estates, belonging to different proprietors, under his sole care. Some of these may be an hundred miles distant from one another; in which case, the attorney employs a sub-agent to overlook the management of the remote estates, he himself paying them a visit once a-year. The attorney who has the management of so many properties is in the way of rapidly realizing a great fortune: his emoluments are considerable, being a commission of five per cent. on all sales and purchases (the crop being valued at the existing current prices), though some are employed at a certain salary. Besides this, they have the privilege of residing, if they choose, on one of the properties, where they may live in splendour at no other expense than that of their wine. In a few years they may become opulent proprietors themselves— perhaps get into their hands some of the estates of their less active constituents, who will not take the trouble of managing their own properties. But the latter are beginning to be somewhat wiser: many now go upon the plan of allowing a stipulated salary to their attorneys, and no perquisite beyond that, and of confining them to the management of their estates only. They became sensible that it was safer to give a fixed

salary than a per centage on the crops; for in
the latter case there was a motive for making
great crops, at whatever expense of slaves or
stock, which fell solely on the proprietor. Formerly, when slaves could be easily replaced,
much oppression and a great waste of life was
occasioned by what was called the pushing system—that is, extracting from the soil as much
as possible by an over-working of the slaves.
The proprietors also begin to see that the attorney, who has more than six or eight plantations
to manage, cannot possibly do justice to the
whole by his personal attentions; many therefore restrict them to a certain number, and watch
over their proceedings by the minutest inquiries,
and by the instructions they occasionally forward.
But there is still a great latitude for abuses in
the management of estates in chancery, and there
are generally not a few in that unfortunate pre-
dicament. The chancellor appoints the receiver—
perhaps a man he never saw, and knows nothing
about,—and the property committed to his charge
is faithfully and honestly managed, or otherwise,
according to the character of the man. Sworn
accounts of the crops, and the disposal of them,
&c. are regularly rendered in to the chancellor;
but there are other important matters of which
he has no official information. The capabilities
of the estate, and the economy and judiciousness

of its management, are not inquired into; and accordingly there have been instances of estates so *managed* by an adroit receiver, that, instead of improving so as to pay off the demands against them, they have been involved deeper in debt, until at length they have been brought to the hammer, and the receiver, who had become a principal creditor, became the purchaser.

At the present day there are only a few of what are called great attorneys in the island—that is, having from fifteen to twenty estates under their charge (either as receivers or attorneys), producing a revenue of from eight to ten thousand pounds, without risk or deduction—an income far beyond that of the generality of the proprietors. These men will not condescend to take charge of a property on any other terms than those they have been accustomed to; but men who have yet their fortunes to make are contented to receive a moderate salary, not exceeding the half which their agency would produce if they were allowed the customary commissions.

The duty of an overseer consists in superintending the planting or farming concerns of the estate, ordering the proper work to be done, and seeing that it is duly executed. Under his control and direction, but qualified by the authority of the attorney or proprietor, are the book-keepers and tradesmen on the estate. The negroes, stock, fields, buildings, and utensils, are committed to his management and care. If an overseer be a man of education and feeling, and that feeling has not been extinguished by habits certainly not calculated to soften the heart or improve the manners, he has it in his power to impart much good in his situation. He may soften the hardships of the slaves, and render their toils more easy; he may hear and redress their complaints, settle their disputes, compose their quarrels, and repress their violence and injustice to each other. It would be a happy circumstance for the slaves if such characters were more common than they are among this class of persons; but the chief ambition of too many is rather who shall make the largest crops, the finest quality of sugar, &c. than who shall govern the slaves placed under their care with the greatest moderation and humanity. Nor are there wanting attorneys, who, anxious to outdo their predecessors in the magnitude of the crops, and thereby forward their own interests and reputation, too often act as a stimulus, instead of a restraint, on this impolitic and unfeeling zeal of the overseers, by perpetually reminding them of the quantum of produce and of work they expect—without, perhaps, duly proportioning either to the efficient strength of hands on the properties, or weighing in their minds the impolicy and inhumanity of purchasing a few additional hogsheads of sugar at the expense of the health and comfort of the slaves. They have no wish, of course, that the slaves should be ill treated; they merely want large crops, and that accordingly becomes a primary object with the overseer.

If an overseer, by his judicious management, succeeds in obtaining the confidence and good opinion of the proprietor he serves, he may in time be employed by him as his attorney.

But before a young man, following the profession of a planter, is employed as an overseer, he has to pass through the probationary situation of a *book-keeper*—a misplaced appellation, as one who had never seen an account-book in his life may yet be a very expert *book-keeper*. Of all situations in the country, this perhaps is the least enviable. A book-keeper is a sort of voluntary slave, who condemns himself for a term of years, on a paltry salary, seldom more than sufficient to support him decently in clothes, to a dull, cheerless, drudging life, in hopes he will one day become an overseer. This situation he usually obtains in five or six years; though, if he has no friend to assist him, he may continue toiling many years longer as a book-keeper. He follows the slaves, while at work, in a scorching sun by day, and at night, in crop-time, is deprived of a material portion of his natural rest, by being obliged, in his turn (generally every other night), to sit up and watch in the boiling-house, scarcely daring to give one moment to repose—to soften his fatigue and sooth his solitary labours with broken and unquiet slumbers :*—still he starts at the thought of the surly frown, the harsh censure of his overseer,—unless, perhaps, he has the good fortune to live under one of a humane and liberal disposition. If he has no acquaintance with any decent white families in the neighbourhood (which is generally the case), he is totally precluded from all intercourse with virtuous female society. The professional planter, indeed, whether overseer or book-keeper, is in a manner forced, however contrary to his inclinations, to a life of celibacy, unless he is fortunate enough to realize an independency, and at the same time preserve himself from being entangled in less reputable connexions; for, while still dependent, he would, by preferring the more honourable conjugal state, run the risk of bringing difficulty and want on his wife and children, few attorneys being disposed to employ a man with such an *encumbrance*. A brown woman, with three or four children, would be no material ob-

---

* Some explorers very humanely dispense with this nocturnal duty of the book-keepers on their estates.

jection, but a wife, with or without a family, is an insuperable one. There may be a few, but only a few, who think and act otherwise. This wretched policy is indeed unaccountable, particularly when it is considered, that by natural course it inevitably leads, or contributes to lead, to an order of things in the colonies very different from the present. Perhaps this narrow and illiberal policy would be less countenanced, were the great proprietors to reside in the island; for, having a great stake in the country, they would naturally look forward with solicitude to future probable events. Theirs is a permanent interest; their agents probably have no other view than speedily to realize fortunes and return with them to Europe.

But to return to the book-keeper. The man, placed in this situation, who has received but little education, who has been accustomed from his earliest years to a rustic and drudging life—who, in short, has directed the plough, or wielded the pitchfork, in his native country, is not so much to be sympathized with; he perhaps feels no hardship in the exchange. But the young man who has been liberally educated, and brought up in a sphere of life above the common, will find many things in this line little congenial to his taste and feelings. Let this unhackneyed youth be traced from his first departure from his native country. Previous to his crossing the Atlantic, he is terrified and alarmed by exaggerated accounts of the intolerable heat of the climate, the unwholesomeness of the atmosphere, the fatal ravages of the yellow fever, the savage and treacherous disposition of the negroes, and the *huge serpents and other venomous reptiles* with which the country is infested. But he is at the same time instigated and encouraged by happier representations.—He is told of the riches with which it abounds, the facility with which these may be acquired—in short, the prospect of realizing in a few years, in this land of promise, the fortune of a nabob. Full of hope and bright anticipations, he is eager to be freed from parental authority and academic thraldom, that he may enter on the golden enterprise. A very brief experience dispels the illusion, and shews him the fallacy of his hopes. He finds himself placed in a line of life where, to his first conception, every thing wears the appearance of barbarity and slavish oppression. He sees the slaves assembled in gangs in the fields, and kept to their work by the terror of whips, borne by black drivers—certainly not the most gentle of human kind; and he is prone, at times, to assimilate his own situation with that of his enslaved fellow-creatures. He contemplates the profession with a species of horror, and considers himself as doomed to a kind of banishment and bondage. This first impression is natural to a young mind, unaccustomed to such scenes of life, and before his minuter observation can contemplate the reverse of the medal, and discover in the condition of the negro slave many comforts and ameliorations which he could not for some time think compatible with such a situation. It is a novel scene to him; and the despondent state of his mind leads him to the most sombre conclusions,—casting a dark shade on every thing around him, and tincturing every feeling and thought with gloom, dislike, and suspicion. He seems to himself a forlorn and destitute being, placed in a situation he loathes, and in a sort of dependence on persons he despises—while a vast ocean separates him from friends, relatives, and the companions of his youth! Fortunate it will be for him, if, thus situated, he should possess strength of mind, and consolations and resources within himself, to support him under his hardships and mortifications —if, bereft, as he thus in a great measure is, of the sweets of social intercourse, his mind should have imbibed a taste for literary pleasures.— By reading, his leisure and solitary hours may be cheered and consoled, though he has little time to devote to that recreation : even Sunday, allotted by Heaven as a day of rest to man, he cannot altogether call his own ; and it would be unpardonable to allow books to interfere with the business of the estate. In short, if he has the misfortune of being placed under a harsh, vulgar, and unfeeling overseer—if he has no resource in friends, or in any other profession—if he wants that strength of mind and literary taste abovementioned—he is too apt to lose that pride and energy of character which ought to accompany us through life, and to contract low depraved habits, while his heart, thus isolated from all that is formed to inspire it with nobler feelings, becomes seared with a reckless apathy.

Some respectable and considerate employers have greatly improved the situation of this class of persons on their estates by many additional comforts ; and, provided they continue to be sober and industrious, they are promoted to be overseers by seniority, these situations being reserved for those only who have served an apprenticeship in the employment. The salary of a book-keeper is from £50 to £80 per annum ; that of an overseer from £140 to £200, and on some of the larger plantations £300 is allowed.

With respect to the mechanics on the plantations (carpenters, masons, coopers, &c.), their situation and prospects are more encouraging than those of the book-keepers, inasmuch as they receive, immediately on their being employed, salaries nearly equal to those of the overseers, and have the prospect of soon saving a few hundred pounds, and setting up for themselves. Add to which, that there is so constant a demand for their services, that nothing but the most glaring misconduct can occasion them to be long out of employment. The profession of a master coppersmith and plumber, if he has ten or twelve slaves brought up to the business, and a white or brown journeyman to attend them, is one of the most lucrative in the island; as, even with that small establishment, and constant employment, he may make from £3000 to £4000 per annum, provided he gets paid by all those who employ him—*a very rare and singular piece of good fortune.*

On the plantations there are in general very good hospitals, or, as they are here preposterously called, *hot-houses*, for the sick slaves. The surgeon is either employed by a proprietor of two, three, or more estates, to attend the hospitals of these alone—in which case he usually resides on one of them, and visits the hospitals every day; or (which is the most common way) he practises for a number of estates belonging to different persons, besides the smaller settlements in the neighbourhood. A medical man, with only one assistant, has sometimes the practice of fifteen or more estates, which, with the smaller properties, may contain a population of about four thousand—by far too extensive a practice for only two medical attendants; so that the hospitals, instead of being attended daily, are not visited oftener than twice or thrice a-week, especially on the remoter properties. At a sickly period, therefore, strict medical attention to all the patients must become utterly impracticable, and the loss of many valuable slaves may ensue. The obvious remedy for this evil is the limiting or proportioning the extent of practice to the number of the practitioners, and, if necessary, increasing their emoluments accordingly. Besides this extensive plantation practice, a surgeon has his *white practice*, which is generally more lucrative than the black. For his attendance on the slaves he is allowed 6s. 8d. per head for every slave, sick or well, and the proprietor furnishes the medicines. For every visit to a white patient the charge is £1 : 6 : 8 : this is reasonable enough, but the charge for medicines is enormous, being about 2000 per cent. on the prime cost!

Some of those who set up as medical men in Jamaica are not the most competent that could be desired.—Dispensing with the customary formalities of college lectures, hospital attendance, and diplomas, they set up as healers of disorders, with no other pretensions than having served a few years apprenticeship to an apothecary, or performed one or two voyages on board of an African trader as assistant *surgeon*. There are at present, however, many able practitioners in the island, though very few of them are regularly-bred physicians. A practitioner here unites the functions of physician, surgeon, and apothecary; he prescribes, performs operations, and compounds his own medicines.

In the medical profession, as in others in this island, success depends more on certain fortuitous circumstances than on either eminent talent or industry, though doubtless these contribute essentially to it. The death or resignation of a medical employer, or the favour of an able patron, may at once place a young man in a respectable practice, yielding from £2000 to £3000 per annum—a very comfortable transition from the drudgery of a humble assistant at £140 per annum. In this last situation the majority of the profession have to toil for an uncertain period, until some lucky event casts up. Two young men of equal education, talents, and industry in this profession, may have very different fortunes: one may gain a handsome independence in ten or twelve years, while the other, after a thirty years toil, may not have acquired more than a sufficiency.—So much for the different result of different fortunes, chances, and, it may be said, different casts of character; some men having a happier talent than others for pushing their way through life. In short, it may be said of the individuals of this profession in Jamaica, that some are overpaid, others have no more than a fair reward for their labours, while many have by no means even that reward. It is too much the fashion to throw a vast practice into the hands of one man, to the injury of others of his brethren who may be equally deserving.

The profession of the law is perhaps the most lucrative of any in Jamaica; but then the chance in favour of young adventurers in it is perhaps less than in the medical profession. A few old established houses in Spanish Town, each consisting of three or more attorneys, engross the bulk of the law business in the superior courts, and their revenues are very considerable; while the greater number have not more than moderate incomes, and a few, whose practice is chiefly in the petty courts, have barely sufficient to support themselves and families genteelly. Here again we see the influence of a name, of interest, friends, and connexions. An attorney, and a master of chancery (who, by the bye, may mutually accommodate each other in various ways), with a good established run of business, is in the high road to wealth, while their less fortunate brethren must lag far behind. The barrister, who unites a knowledge of law to a bold and powerful style of eloquence, and has acquired a name by his success in the courts, is, of course, in great request by the attorneys and their clients, and is in a fair way of acquiring wealth as well as eminence in his profession; but there are gentlemen at the bar here, sound lawyers, but no orators, whose business is far less encouraging than that of the attorney with even a moderate share of business. With all their superior education and legal acquirements, they are thrown into the back-ground, with respect to pecuniary advantages, by that branch of the profession, the members of which are but as pioneers to prepare the ground over which they are to proceed; and they are in a great measure dependent on that order for most of the briefs that are put into their hands. A few years ago, a reduction was made by the legislature of the fees and charges of the masters in chancery and attorneys at law, as well as of the fees of the courts.

The merchants and store-keepers have already been spoken of, and little need be added to what has been said of them. The former may be classed into *dry-good* merchants, provision merchants, and lumber merchants, though one man sometimes deals in all those articles. The retail

store-keeper's shop, or *store*, as it is called, contains a strange medley of all sorts of articles. In
one part of it may be a customer bargaining for
a cheese, a ham, a pound of tea, or a dozen of
wine or porter; in another, a gentleman may be
fitting himself with a pair of boots or a hat, or
cheapening a saddle; while a party of ladies,
elsewhere, are trying on bonnets, gloves, &c.
selecting ribbons, laces, and other fancy articles,
or culling some valuable articles of jewellery.

A considerable share of the retail trade is en-
grossed by the Jews, of whom there are a considerable number in this island. They sell at more
moderate prices than the Christian dealers, but
their goods are generally of an inferior description.

The vendue-masters, as they are called, are the
same as the auctioneers in Great Britain: goods
are placed in their hands to be sold either for
what they will fetch at public auction, or for a
certain price fixed by the owner. Their profits
are five per cent. on all sales.

Wharfingers are persons who keep public
wharfs for the shipment and storage of goods.
The rates of wharfage are fixed by law, and a
wharfinger is answerable for the goods, or for
any damage they may sustain, while under his
custody.

A jobber is one who, having, as a planter,

acquired a gang of forty, fifty, or more slaves, and a mountain settlement, retires from the planting line, and devotes his attention to his slaves, whom he hires out to perform work on the plantations.

The business of a surveyor is a lucrative one, where he has abundant employment; but it is laborious, and attended with many hardships. When traversing the remote and trackless woods, he is compelled, at times, to submit to a savage sort of life: he has to clamber over rocks and precipices, at the hazard of his life; he is exposed to the inclemencies of the weather, the damps of the woods, the vicissitudes of heat, cold, and fatigue; he eats his solitary and unsavoury meal on the barren rock, and at night he reposes on a temporary hurdle formed of the boughs of trees, surrounded by swarms of mosquitoes, and in danger of sickness.

There is very good encouragement in this island for saddlers, watchmakers, and tailors, who, if expert at their business, may realize a handsome competency in half the time which a planter can do.

CHAP. XIII.

EDUCATION—LITERATURE—AMUSEMENTS—ENTER-
TAINMENTS—TRAVELLING.

ONE of the most important wants in Jamaica is that of proper seminaries for the instruction of youth of the better class, who are on that account sent to Great Britain to be educated. In Kingston, and in some of the parishes, there are tolerably good public foundations, where the elements of education and some of the languages are taught, and in every parish there is a free school; but no parent, with the means of giving his son a British education, would think of placing him in these seminaries. The masters are generally inferior in talents and attainments to those who are at the head of the public schools in England; there is not that discipline and order maintained in the former as in the latter, and if there were, it would be a cause of perpetual discontent to the indulgent parents, many of whom would rather that their children should remain for ever in ignorance, than be subjected to any thing in the shape of correction. The usual plan is, to give the male children the elements of instruc-

tion in the island, and then send them to Great
Britain to have their education finished; but the
females are usually sent at five or six years of
age, there being only one seminary in the island
(in Kingston) where young ladies can receive
any thing like an accomplished education, and
even there it cannot be expected that their minds
and manners can be so well formed as in a well-
conducted seminary in Great Britain.

It is remarked of the children of the West
Indies, that they exhibit a quickness of understanding and capacity to learn at an earlier period of life than the children of colder climates.
This remark may be partly true, and some, perhaps, would be for assigning this phenomenon
to a mere physical cause; they would be for
ascribing it to the maturing influence of the
climate, and would probably say, that, like its
native fruits, or the beauty of its fair, the mind
ripens quicker, but is doomed to an earlier decay
than in the temperate zone. Certain it is, that
if the mind of a West Indian expands earlier
than that of a European, it rarely arrives at the
same point of maturity. Few of the former have
given proofs of literary eminence, and those few
have owed that eminence to the influence of a
British education. The truth is, that most of
the children here are vivacious and shrewd; but
this does not always turn out to be the early

indications of genius, for the uneducated classes of whites are deplorably ignorant and simple. The West Indian may, by the culture of education, become as deservedly eminent in his particular walk of life as the native of any other country; but it seldom happens that he has the patience to endure the labour of intense study, or to toil up the steep ascents of science. He is too lively, too volatile, too indolent, and too fond of pleasure, for such application; and this perhaps is one great cause of literary pursuits being in such low estimation in the West Indies, and of the very small number of its natives who have distinguished themselves either in science or literature.

With the exception of some medical tracts, and a very comprehensive Hortus published a few years ago, no work of any note has issued from the press here. Periodical works have been repeatedly tried, but without success. Nine-tenths of the inhabitants never think of reading any thing beyond a newspaper, business and pleasure engrossing too much of their attention to leave much leisure for reading. Six newspapers are published here, viz. four weekly and two daily papers: about half of these are usually filled with advertisements, and the other half with political matter, chiefly copied from the English papers, and literary extracts. In Kingston there is a tolerably good circulating library, but none in any of the parishes that deserve the name. Intellectual pleasures are not so much suited to the taste of the inhabitants as something that will create a bustle, and bring a crowd of well-dressed persons together in pursuit of amusements of a more tangible nature—such, for instance, as the parish races, where, in one week, there is as much money spent as would establish a superb public library.

As a taste for literature is but little cultivated, so neither do the elegant arts meet with encouragement here. In Kingston excepted, where there is a theatre, and concerts occasionally, the only public amusements are monthly or quarterly balls. Occasionally a party of the Kingston performers used to visit the different towns, but they collected little more than would cover the expenses of their journey. The balls are generally well attended, dancing, as has been said, being a favourite amusement of the ladies: whole families will travel thirty or forty miles to attend a ball. In temperate climes people usually lay aside this amusement during the summer months, as being rather fatiguing for such a season; but here there is no such renunciation; dancing continues throughout the year—even during the sultry dog-days the gay throng trip it on the " light fantastic toe" with as much vivacity and

animation as in the cooler months of December
and January. During the races, which continue
for five or six days, there are either balls or private dances every night, which are kept up till
three or four o'clock in the morning. Were an
English female to attend and dance at half of
these, it would inevitably produce fever, and
might even be the cause of her death; but the
native fair will resort to all, join in every dance,
and, at the close of the last, lament that there
were no more. They devote the day to repose,
eat sparingly, and on the return of night are
again prepared for a renewal of their darling
exercise. It rather astonishes a stranger to see,
in a hot room, during one of the most sultry
months of the year—where even the sedentary
spectator pants for the refreshing air—a group of
charming well-dressed young women toiling, as
he thinks, through the fatigue of a long country
dance, yet, animated by gayety and a love of the
amusement, renewing again and again the *grateful toil.*

Country dances, with reels between, are chiefly
in use; quadrilles have not yet been generally
introduced; and waltzing, so fashionable in the
higher circles in Europe, is an exotic which has
not yet found its way here, nor would it be much
relished by the transatlantic fair, by whom a modest demeanour is considered an indispensable

charm in their sex. The music is in general very
indifferent; four or more violins, played by black
or brown fiddlers, a tambarine, drum, and triangle,
form the usual orchestra band, very few having
the more appropriate accompaniment of a violon-
cello. Even if the music of the violins were
better than it is, it would be spoiled by the un-
couth and deafening noise of the drums, which
the negro musicians think indispensable, and
which the dancers strangely continue to tolerate.

When the races take place, there is a sort of carnival in the parish. Every person who can afford
a horse, or a gig or other carriage, hastens to the
principal town where they are held, and crowds
of people from the neighbouring parishes increase
the multitude. Feasting, dancing, and gambling,
are the order of the day. The opulent and the
fashionable of both sexes throng the course, in
carriages and on horseback, regardless of the
oppressive heat, and the clouds of dust with
which they are enveloped, while some take refuge in the booths. The purses to be run for
are an hundred pistoles, or an hundred pounds;
they are all raised by subscription, except the
king's purse, as it is called, which is the first that
is run for. The heats are two, three, and four
miles.

There are few rural sports here: there are
neither deer, hares, nor foxes to pursue, and if

there were, there is but a narrow range of level country for such amusement, and that little but ill adapted to it. The hunting of the wild hog is now relinquished as a too fatiguing and troublesome sport. Shooting various sorts of game is however common; these consist of the different species of the wild pigeon, ducks and teal, quails, coots, snipes, plover, ortolans, and other game birds common in the West Indies. There are no game laws, as has been said, existing in Jamaica to restrain the sportsman and protect the feathered race from slaughter at all seasons of the year. This indiscriminate license has diminished the number of some species of the indigenous game, and would in time probably destroy the whole, were it not for the rugged and difficult retreats which the country affords them.

To make amends for the paucity of public amusements, convivial and social parties are much encouraged here. Wherever there is a meeting of the inhabitants on any public business, there must be a dinner, or something in the shape of one. There are militia dinners, vestry dinners, grand jury and road jury dinners, and dinners commemorative of some favourite hero, and of the patron saints of England, Scotland, and Ireland, &c. On these occasions no expense is spared to render the entertainment costly and splendid: every luxury is catered up for the purpose, and copious libations of various wines and other liquors are poured forth to the jolly god of good fellowship. On these occasions, it is rather to be apprehended that there is a greater risk of the sacrifice of health than a certainty of the enjoyment of rational pleasure; excess is commonly the order of the day, and that may be of serious consequence to those indulging in it in such a climate as that of Jamaica. Hard drinking is not so universally practised now as formerly, when it was conceived by the master of a feast, that he did not treat his guests with a cordial welcome, if he did not deprive them of the use of their reason and their legs before he parted with them; and he was considered as a disaffected person, who, at a public entertainment, did not get most loyally drunk. Many thousands are annually wasted on these extravagant entertainments.

The creoles are not extravagantly expensive in the furniture of their houses; it is generally plain, but genteel. Their sideboards and beaufets, however, display a costly brilliancy, in unison with the plentiful and splendid cheer which is spread on their dinner tables. In a large house, consisting of many apartments, the labour of six or eight female slaves is required for two or three hours every morning in burnishing the floors, which for brilliancy of polish rival the finest furniture. They are formed of mahogany, wild orange, or other hard wood.

About the house of a wealthy proprietor there are usually about twenty-five or thirty black and mulatto servants, including grooms, a gardener, laundresses, and persons attending cows, sheep, hogs, and poultry. Besides the ordinary servants of the family, the ladies have each one, and sometimes two waiting-maids, whose sole employment is to attend on their respective mistresses. The occupation of the other female servants consists in keeping the house in order, making the household linen and servants' apparel, running of errands, attending at table, &c.; while the ladies' maids, squatted down on the floor by their mistresses, are employed in various kinds of needle-work. The equipage of such a family consists of a coach or landau, and one or two covered gigs or chaises, and fifteen or twenty horses and mules, with their proper attendants. The whole may be worth about £2000 currency.

When a private entertainment is to be given, no expense or pains are spared to render it as sumptuous as possible. The table is spread with a costly profusion of all the viands and delicacies which industry or money can procure. The dinner is not generally divided into separate courses, but the table is at once loaded with superabundance; flesh, fish, fowl, game, and various vegetables, appear at once to the view, in a style rather indicative of a liberal display of hospitality than taste and selection. The dessert, consisting of various articles of pastry, and a profusion of sweetmeats, is not less sumptuous; while a variety of wines, kept cool with wet cloths, liqueurs, &c. are handed round to the guests by the black attendants, who, on such occasions, appear in their best apparel. After the dessert a variety of the choicest fruits are put down; and when the ladies withdraw (after a few toasts are given), the gentlemen generally smoke segars and sit over their wine till a late hour. If singing be proposed, which is generally the case in mixed parties, the ladies remain longer at table, and take a pleasure in exerting their vocal powers for the entertainment of the company. It may be supposed that none but the most opulent venture to give such costly entertainments; but every one here is ambitious to make a figure in this respect, and usually treat their guests in a style above, rather than below, their circumstances. Families residing in the country can do this at far less expense than those in the towns, who have every article to purchase. The former raise every necessary for their tables on their respective properties.

As there is little variation in the length of the days, the hours for meals, and of going to bed and rising, continue much the same throughout the year. About nine is the usual breakfast time; what is called second breakfast is introduced between twelve and one, dinner at four, and tea at seven; suppers are not generally in use, unless when there is company. A family, when by themselves, retire to rest about ten, and rise sooner or later in the morning, according to habit and inclination. A few industrious matrons get up at six o'clock, or before it, to attend to their domestic concerns; but in general the ladies are fond of indulging in bed, and thus lose the most delightful time of the day (from six to seven in the morning) in dull and cheerless languor. The gentlemen get up, in common, at about six o'clock. The white people on the plantations are under very different regulations as to meals and hours of repose: they breakfast at seven, dine at half past one, sup at eight, go to bed at nine, and rise at dawn of day. This is the invariable routine throughout the year.

Families living in the country, and on friendly terms, pass much of their time in an interchange of social visits. Two or three families collected together at the house of a mutual friend form a lively party, especially with the assistance of a fiddle. When thus assembled, they are not fond of separating; if it suited the inclination and convenience of their hosts, they would very contentedly remain together for weeks. But long visits of numerous parties of friends are by no means so common as they were. Not many years ago, it was no unusual thing for one or more families to pay a six weeks visit to their relations, for the purpose of shewing the warmth and cordiality of their regard. One family of these visitors might consist of from twenty to thirty, including domestics, for whom a suitable entertainment was to be provided every day during their stay; so that, instead of a visit, this might more properly be termed a *visitation*. The approach of this cavalcade was announced by the arrival of ten or a dozen female slaves, with trunks, bandboxes, and other articles: soon after came the main body—uncles, aunts, and cousins—some in carriages, some on horseback, followed by grooms, waiting-men, and waiting-women,—in fact, the whole household, with a long train of led horses and sumpter mules Feasting and lounging by day, and dancing at night, formed the whole occupation of these visitors and their hosts. Before the term of their visit had expired, not a turkey, pig, fowl, or duck, fit for the kitchen, was left on the place, and even the vegetable substance was almost totally consumed. Such *migrations* now rarely occur. The natives in general have become more attentive to a prudential economy; they see that continual feasting and dissipation have proved ruinous to the most ample fortunes, and reduced families, once great and opulent, to embarrassment and distress. The spirit and taste still remain with many, but motives of self-preservation restrain them. Much hospitality prevails, but it is of a more moderate and rational nature than that above described: the natives have got more enlightened, and the " feast of reason, and the flow of soul" are more valued as a part of the entertainment than heretofore. A genteel family, too, has more resources within itself than formerly; its members, from being educated in England, are more or less intelligent and conversable, and have accomplishments, the exercise of which occupy and enliven their time. About twenty years ago, very few females were taught music, drawing, &c. few of them had any taste for reading, and visiting, feasting, and dancing, became therefore their only and darling amusements.

Travelling in Jamaica is far less pleasant than in Great Britain, and other temperate climes and finely-embellished countries in Europe. Here, at certain times of the year, the sun blazes so fiercely, and the whole atmosphere is so heated with his sultry beams, that travelling on horseback at mid-day is absolutely intolerable even to a person seasoned and accustomed to the cli-

mate; it is even fatiguing and disagreeable in
a carriage. If the weather be dry, suffocating
clouds of dust often envelope the traveller; and
during the rainy seasons he is impeded and an-
noyed by the badness of the roads, and liable to
be drenched to the skin by the sudden torrents
that fall. From November to March is the most
pleasant time for travelling, being the coolest
period of the year, and for the most part fair.
At this season there are neither thunder and
lightning, nor heavy torrents of rain; and the
showers that fall give an additional coolness to
the air, lay the dust, and refresh vegetation—so
that, while the inhabitants of a northern climate
are shivering beneath a bleak and tempestuous
sky, carefully guarding themselves from cold by
pelisses and furs, and regretting the temporary
annihilation of vernal beauty, the people of these
more southern regions are enjoying their sweetest
season, and exulting in the verdure that smiles
around them. But the summer and autumn of
the temperate zone are incomparably more beautiful, more desirable in all respects, than those of
the torrid zone.

Nothing can be more sweet than a fair December morning in this island, just as the
sun has risen, and the traveller, from a commanding eminence, has a wide and diversified
prospect before him. There is a blandness and

vivifying freshness in the air, impregnated as it is with the perfumes of numberless wild flowers and blossoms, that must be felt to be conceived. Hills, valleys, woods, pastures, clusters of trees of all sizes and shades, and a river meandering through them, with the calm unruffled ocean in the distance, are spread beneath him in beautiful variety. The morning mists, which still partially hang over parts of this landscape, have the illusive appearance to the beholder of lakes resting on its bosom. The sun, just emerged into sight, appears as if resting on the crest of a distant rising, and casts a golden light on the higher eminences and on the tops of the trees. Nothing disturbs the stillness of the scene, except the busy officious mosquito, the screeching of the parrots, which pass in large flocks towards their haunts, and the more pleasing note of the mock-bird, and other feathered songsters. Such is a landscape here in December at sunrise ; but in a short time much of its beauty is lost in the wide-spread effulgence of the solar blaze.

But to return to the subject of travelling. The morning is by far the most desirable and healthy time for performing a journey. If a traveller has fifty miles to ride in the course of a day (and more than that he cannot, without great fatigue and risk of health, perform), he should, if possible, travel half of his journey by nine o'clock in the morning—that is, before he breakfasts; and this he may easily do by starting at four. There is no risk of catching cold by travelling thus early, or earlier, in the morning; but one cannot travel with equal impunity at night, in consequence of the unwholesomeness of the dews. If compelled to travel under a vertical sun, an umbrella, or some sort of shade, is necessary,—at least to those unused to exposure to a tropical sun. About nine o'clock in the morning the heat is begun to be felt. Travelling along the sea-side is certainly least unpleasant at mid-day, as the sea-breeze, cooled by the waves over which it passes, tempers the heat and refreshes the traveller. The moonlight is peculiarly brilliant here, and greatly favours the traveller who commences his journey at an early hour of the morning.

There are no stage-coaches or other public vehicles for the conveyance of passengers; but every one who can afford it keeps his gig or chaise. But it is impracticable to travel with these in some of the mountainous roads, being too steep and narrow, so that riding is the most general mode of travelling, and there are consequently at least three saddle-horses in the island for one carriage-horse. It is in the level parts of the country where gigs and chaises are chiefly made use of: one travels with far less fatigue and exposure to the sun in one of these than on horseback. As for palanquins, the inhabitants of the West Indies have not yet arrived at that pitch of effeminacy as to copy this example of it from the Asiatics. A horse here will travel fifty miles in a day; but it would be improper to exact so much labour from an English horse in this climate, he being more liable to surfeits and other diseases, arising from heat and fatigue, than the native-bred horse. Walking is very little practised by the whites; though the negroes, who are hardier, and better accustomed to this kind of exercise, will walk forty miles in a day with ease. In Great Britain, a walk of ten or twelve miles is a pleasant and healthy exercise; in Jamaica it would overpower the stoutest person, if performed in the ordinary time, unless it was during the cool of the morning, or under the shade of trees.

There are many interesting things which the traveller must not expect here. He will not meet with noble and highly-embellished seats and mansions, magnificent castles, and the venerable remains of ancient abbeys and churches, which, perpetually presenting themselves to the British tourist, recall to him the stories, legendary tales, and records of history, with which they are connected. But if he be an admirer of the wild magnificence of nature, he will here have ample room for the gratification of his taste, particularly in traversing the mountainous districts, where many stupendous objects will arrest his attention. In passing to the valleys, he will see a highly-cultivated and diversified country around him, though in general little indebted to the embellishing hand of taste, few improvements being made here except for the mere purposes of interest. There is no such thing in the whole island as what are called pleasure-grounds. Some gentlemen of taste and fortune have gardens judiciously laid out, and stocked with a variety of exotic and indigenous plants; but the generality of the gardens are nothing more than small enclosed pieces of ground, with a few mango, bread-fruit, and other trees, planted round the sides, and the centre laid out into beds of various esculents.

CHAP. XIV.

CONDITION AND TREATMENT OF THE SLAVES—REGIS-
TRY ACT—OPINIONS ON THE SUBJECT OF THE EMAN-
CIPATION OF THE SLAVES.

THE author is now entering upon a subject the
most important and interesting—a subject which
has engaged the attention and interested the
feelings of a considerable portion of civilized
mankind—which has given employment to the
ablest pens, and called forth the eloquence of the
orator. Like most subjects taken up by opposite
parties, it has not been represented with perfect
fairness by either. One party would wish to
make it appear that the slaves are still suffering
under every species of the most revolting tyranny,
injustice, and oppression; while the other would
have us believe that they are a contented and
happy people, uniformly treated with mildness
and humanity, and enjoying comforts beyond
even those of the British peasant. Between these
opposite representations the truth lies,—which it
will be the sincere endeavour of the author fairly
and impartially to state.

And first, as to the provisions of the consoli-

dáted slave-code, or body of laws enacted—
chiefly within the last thirty years—for the protection of the slaves. Of this code it may be
truly said, that, with a few exceptions, it is
fully calculated, if its provisions were universally and duly carried into effect, to render the
slaves as comfortable, and as secure from oppression, as it is possible for slaves to be. And as it
is, the amendments and improvements it has
brought about are great and salutary. By its
principal provisions, the owners of slaves are
obliged, under heavy penalties, duly to clothe
and feed them, to support them when aged and
helpless, and to allow them what is deemed sufficient time* for the cultivating of their provision-
grounds. Owners and overseers are restrained
from inflicting more than thirty-nine lashes at a
time on the slaves, and inferior superintendents
more than ten.† The legal hours for working
the slaves are from sunrise to sunset (the necessary night-work during crop being an exception
to this provision), and a reasonable time is fixed

---

* One day in a fortnight, exclusive of Sundays. Some humane owners allow their slaves two, except during crop.

† It would have been well if the legislature had abolished the
use of the whip altogether, substituting in its place some less
revolting instrument of correction. Some humane owners have
done this without the compulsory obligation of laws, and it has
answered every good purpose.

for meals. The murder of a slave by a white man is punished with death, and any injury inflicted on the person of the former by the latter is punishable by fine and imprisonment; but if the injury extends to the cutting and maiming, with intent to kill, it is to be presumed that the offender now comes under the operation of Lord Ellenborough's act. When a slave makes a complaint to the magistrates against a white man, for personal violence inflicted on him, there are few who do not impartially and zealously investigate the case; and if they can bring home guilt to the offender, they never fail putting the law in force against him. But the great obstacle is the too frequent insufficiency of legal proof on such occasions.

It may truly be said, that the treatment of the slave depends in a great measure upon the character and temper of his master or manager. How ineffectual to the slave are humane and judicious laws, if a barbarous master or overseer has it in his power to evade them in various ways. There can be no hesitation in saying, that the slave who lives under the immediate superintendence of a humane and considerate master enjoys a life of as much comfort and contentment as the condition of a slave is capable of. This perhaps is the utmost that can be said; for though the wants of the slave may be supplied by the beneficent provision of such a master, and he may consequently be said to be so far more desirably situated than many of the poorer peasantry of Great Britain, yet to argue, generally, that he is happier than they—an assertion which one frequently hears—is certainly saying too much. The situation of the two classes can admit of no other comparison than as to the physical wants of our nature. The being who toils by the compulsion of a master, and whose servitude, whether oppressive or otherwise, ceases only with his life, is, on the scale of moral and social happiness, far beneath him who labours voluntarily, and can choose whom he pleases as his master or employer. Yet it may be said, that the slave, accustomed from infancy to his condition, is incapable of appreciating the blessings of liberty, and looks not for more than mild and just treatment, and the supply of all his wants. That situation, which would be terrible to the peasant, is rendered tolerable, through habit, to the negro slave, and becomes, as has been said, a state of comfort and contentment under a just and humane master; so much so indeed, that there have been instances of slaves, so situated, who would have declined the boon of freedom, had it been offered them. This may be easily accounted for: they were treated mildly and justly, not overworked, a reasonable time was allowed them to attend to their own affairs, all their wants were liberally supplied; they had their houses, gardens, provision-grounds, and pigs and poultry, and they were in a degree attached to a spot where they had tasted comforts far beyond those of other slaves. To relinquish these possessions and advantages, and be thrown on their own resources, inclined to indolence and self-indulgence as many of them are, they knew would not be an exchange for the better. But very differently situated is the poor slave who is doomed to toil for a master of a character directly opposite to the foregoing. If oppressed and ill-treated, he may indeed lay his complaints before a magistrate, who of course is bound to listen to, and, if possible, redress them; and if he be a good man, he will actively endeavour to do so. But he cannot *legally* render justice to the slave by the punishment of the master, should the latter decline giving evidence against himself—a very natural proceeding where no other admissible evidence exists: the evidence of the slave, and of his fellow-slaves, is insufficient to convict him. The magistrate then can only admonish the master, and the slave is sent home, perhaps to suffer renewed severities for his audacity in preferring a complaint against his master. Undoubtedly this is a state of grievous hardship. It may be said, that there

are few masters of the character here described.
It were to be wished it were so; but men's
hearts are not likely to be softened by habits of
too uncontrolled dominion over their fellow-men.
With respect to interest prevailing over a disposition to oppress, while we allow all due weight
to this motive in the prudent and judicious
owner, it will not always counteract the petty
injustice to which the slave is subject from ignorant masters and unfeeling overseers. A slave
may complain, and justly complain, that he is
made to labour at unseasonable hours, and on
days which the law allots to him, and that he is
neither fed nor clothed as the law directs; but
who is to prove these transgressions? The slave
cannot; for the law does not recognise the va-
lidity of his testimony against a white man. If
the master were put upon his oath, equally nugatory would be this expedient; for the man who
wants rectitude and feeling to be just to his
slaves will hardly scruple to serve his ends by
perjury. Again, if a slave is punished or beat
with improper and illegal severity, or even cut
and maimed—not to mention the numerous acts
of petty tyranny to which he is subject under a
cruel master—and there is no legal evidence to
prove those enormities, the offender cannot be
convicted of them. He may then go on with
impunity in this system of oppression as long as

he can contrive to keep without the reach of the laws. Extreme cases of this nature, it may be said, seldom occur; but such a supposition is no argument that the law should not provide effectually against them. Even murder may escape condign punishment while this defect in the slave-laws is suffered to exist.

There is only one way of removing this obstacle to the more effectual amelioration of the condition of the slave; and that is, by rendering his evidence, under certain modifications, legally admissible against the whites. Such an innovation would indeed probably raise an outcry among a certain class of persons, who see danger in every boon of kindness extended to the slaves; but a day will arrive when it will be a subject of wonder, even in the West Indies, that human beings should have been precluded the means of procuring legal redress against injury and oppression—that the shadow and mockery of justice should have been held out to them, while an insuperable bar was placed between them and the reality.* That there might be danger

---

* A highly respectable West Indian proprietor, resident in England, thus speaks, in a letter to a friend in Jamaica, on the subject of the admissibility of negro evidence against the whites.

" The admission of negroes to be evidence in courts of law would be a great, and, in my judgment, a *wise, safe,* and *salutary step.* Where is the danger? Objections to negro evidence

in the immediate unqualified admissibility of negro evidence, in all cases, against the whites, will not be denied; but that danger could be easily guarded against. It will not be said that the low and uneducated whites, in most countries, are in intellect and principle greatly superior to the bulk of the negro slaves. One great deficiency of the latter is their general ignorance of the doctrines and principles of the Christian religion. Without some knowledge of its truths and its duties, it is hardly to be expected that the sacredness of an oath can either be understood or respected by an untutored negro; but after a competent instruction in these, his evidence, on oath, could not reasonably be objected to. Besides, is it to be supposed that a jury of white men would suffer themselves to be unduly biassed against one of their own colour, on the oath of a slave, unsupported by other corrobo-

---

would go, as the lawyers say, to the credibility, not to the competency. And surely where judges and juries are both whites, there would be no great danger of too great a disposition to believe the testimony of the inferior race.

" I have often heard the admission of black evidence discussed in conversation; but I should rejoice exceedingly if you could carry that point in Jamaica, before it is agitated in the British parliament. As a weapon of defence against the assailants of us West Indians, you could furnish us with none more effectual than the fact of your having enacted and enforced so *benevolent* and so *wise* a law of your own accord."

rative testimony? There would rather be an opposite leaning. Let the evidence of one slave besides the party complaining be necessary to convict a white man ; let these witnesses be examined separately, and, if, after the ordeal of a strict cross-examination, they are found perfectly consistent and agreeing in their testimony, and a white judge and jury are of opinion that no counter-evidence has been adduced to invalidate it, it is surely fair that justice should take its course. It should, however, be understood that such legal provision should not preclude the complainant from the full benefit of such circumstantial evidence as should be deemed conclusive by the court and jury, in cases where no witness or witnesses should appear. In order to quiet as much as possible all fears of mischief arising from this admissibility of negro evidence, let it be confined to cases of injury and violence inflicted on them by the whites. The efficacy of the laws for the protection of the slave would thus be more fully felt by him, and would be an additional motive to contentment and a cheerful obedience.

The abolition of the slave-trade has perhaps done more towards substantially improving the condition of the slaves than all the laws which have been enacted for that purpose. However beneficent the spirit in which those laws were framed, and however wisely intended to guard against oppression, still, as has been shown, they are liable to be evaded and violated in various ways by persons so disposed.* The excellent provisions they contain would be productive of the happiest effects could a full and unqualified obedience be insured to them. But as this cannot be done, it was desirable that some more powerful motive than a respect for the laws should be brought into operation. This was interest, to which mankind in general pay a more willing homage than to legal enactments. While

---

* Among other instances of this disregard for the laws, the following remarkable one occurred a few years ago. An overseer, well known as a man of violent and tyrannical temper, was employed, by a great attorney, on an estate for which he was receiver. His treatment of the slaves was so cruel and oppressive, that, after reiterated and fruitless complaints, numbers of them absconded from the property, and would not return to it, doubtless from a dread of the punishment that awaited them. At length a party of these fugitive slaves formed the desperate and atrocious design of murdering this man; which purpose they effected, and subsequently suffered death for the crime. This man had been suffered to hold his situation for many years prior to this catastrophe, notwithstanding that his cruelties were notorious to the whole neighbourhood. The assassins neither robbed the house, nor molested the wife and child of their victim, though both were in their power. It is but fair to add, that this case was an unusual one.

individuals, holding estates, could supply the decrease of strength on them at an easy rate, this decrease would not alarm them much; but when the source of supply came to be cut off, it must necessarily be viewed as an irreparable loss and destruction of capital. The man, who wishes to preserve his property unimpaired, or who would improve its value, must now devote his attention to the means of keeping up, if not increasing, the number and efficiency of his slaves; for these constitute his wealth; without them his lands would be but an unproductive waste. And how is this to be done? By improving their condition to the fullest extent of which it is capable—softening their labours, increasing their comforts, and improving their minds by moral and religious instruction. Though this last-mentioned duty has been attended to but by a very few, much has been done towards effecting the other objects, especially on the plantations belonging to opulent proprietors, who anxiously watch over the prosperity and comfort of their slaves. Many, or most of the old abuses, are removed; punishments are more rare, and far less severe; the slaves are not worked at unseasonable hours (excepting the night-work during crop, which will probably continue until methods are devised for expediting the work by day at that period) ; labour is more mild; * the slaves are better fed, clothed, and lodged, and, when sick, experience kinder attention, and are more amply supplied with necessary comforts; and, above all, the breeding women are carefully attended to, and receive every necessary indulgence and assistance. In consequence of these reformations, there are now few plantations who have not an increase of slaves (formerly the decrease was so great that the planters conceived it impossible to

---

* The plantation-slaves are divided into three classes, or *gangs*, as they are called, according to age and condition. The first gang consists of the ablest of both sexes, from sixteen to about fifty years of age, and are employed in the most laborious of the work; the second gang contains the elderly and weakly men and women, and boys and girls of from twelve to sixteen, who have lighter work assigned to them ; and the third, or what is called *small gang*, consists of the children from about six to twelve, attended by a female driver, and are employed in weeding the young plant-canes, and other easy work adapted to their strength. In most of the jobbing-gangs the different classes, with the exception of children, are very improperly blended together. When the slaves are rendered unfit, by age or infirmity, for field-labour, they are employed in occupations that require little bodily exertion; the men are placed as watchmen over the canes and provisions, and the women to take care of the children, or in other light employments. The duty of the former, though not laborious, is certainly arduous : to prevent depredations on that which they are appointed to protect would require more activity and vigour than many of these superannuated slaves possess.

carry on their plantations without a regular importation); atrocious cases of cruelty are rarely heard of; a greater degree of confidence, comfort, and contentment is observable in the looks and appearance of the slaves, and those ill-treated, heart-broken, emaciated beings which the highways once exhibited, are now seldom to be seen.

Such are some of the happy effects of the, at one time, so much deprecated and so much abused abolition law *—that great and important fruit of the labour and perseverance of a man, the proudest wreath of whose fame is that he

---

* It is not a little discreditable to Great Britain, that, while she glories in having interdicted her own subjects from pursuing this unnatural traffic, she should passively have allowed other nations to carry it on to a disgraceful extent, and to the serious injury of her own colonies; nations, too, over whom she had at no distant period a paramount influence—who owe in fact their political existence to her. To strike at the root of this traffic, it would be necessary that it should be declared piracy by the common consent of all civilized nations. Some are of opinion, that the late Marquis of Londonderry had an excellent opportunity, at the congress of the sovereigns, of obtaining their consent to such a measure, had he pressed it on their attention with that zeal and earnestness which so momentous an object deserved. Be this as it may, it appears, by papers lately laid before parliament, that the atrocities of the slave traffic, far from being diminished, have greatly increased since the abolition of the trade by Great Britain!

achieved so beneficent a work—yet of whom it is, even now, the fashion, among some, to speak virulently and contemptuously.* Not that the author would be understood to conceive that there were not, among the proprietors of estates in the West Indies, individuals who sincerely

---

* No unprejudiced person will call in question the purity and goodness of this gentleman's intentions, or withhold the homage of their highest praise of his unwearied labours in the cause of humanity. It must, however, in fairness, be allowed, that, in his allegations against the colonists, he is by no means so impartial and unprejudiced as a public redresser of wrongs should be —who, in doing justice to one party, should beware of any injustice towards the other. Not that the author conceives that Mr Wilberforce would wilfully shut his eyes to the truth because it militated against his favourite opinions; but it is evident that he and other members of the African Institution are more disposed to listen to evil than favourable reports of the West Indians,—carefully treasuring up and recapitulating the former, while they treat the latter as altogether unworthy of credit. They have a heavy list of accusations against them unqualified by any redeeming merit. They are no doubt often misled by false or exaggerated reports, mixed up with statements of real enormities, from which, however, it would be most unfair to draw a sweeping conclusion that cruelty and oppression universally prevailed in the West Indies. If Mr Wilberforce would himself visit the colonies, particularly Jamaica, and personally observe what is going on, he would at least find some things on which to ground a more favourable opinion than he has generally entertained of the colonists; and that opinion would carry far greater weight with it than one formed from the reports of others.

desired, prior to any discussion on the slave-
trade, to carry into effect many humane regulations for the bettering the condition of their
slaves; but how small the number of such characters, and how limited the influence of their example, may readily be conceived from the general
existence of gross abuses at the period spoken of.
It unfortunately happened, too, that few of the
better order of proprietors saw those abuses with
their own eyes. They were content to receive
their revenues, and looked no farther.

The slaves belonging to the smaller settlers,
and what are called jobbers, are not in general
so comfortably situated as those belonging to the
estates. This is in part owing to the situation
and circumstances of the masters. They do not,
in common, possess the means of rendering their
slaves so comfortable as the slaves on the plantations, and the poorer and more ignorant are too
apt to overwork and otherwise ill use them.
Many of the jobbers living in remote parts of
the interior, their slaves have often a considerable
distance to travel, once a week, to the places
where they are to work, and are deprived, while
they remain so far from home, of all the comforts and conveniences of their dwellings; they
are also usually employed in the hardest and
most disagreeable work of the plantations, it being the policy of those who employ them to save

their own slaves as much as possible from such work. The poor jobbing slave, thus often deprived of the comforts of a home, has only to depend on the humanity of an overseer, or the kindness of an acquaintance, for a shelter at night and from the inclemency of the weather. This way of life must necessarily be disheartening; and it is no wonder, therefore, if the jobbing slave has not so healthy and contented a look as the plantation-slave—that he should envy the superior comforts of the latter, and be delighted at the thought of being sold to the owner of an estate, or at least of his master's finding sufficient work for him at home. It may not be because his master is a man inferior in humanity to the owner of the estate, that he would wish to be so transferred, but that he wishes to be at home, that he might have the comforts of his house, and be able to attend to his garden, his poultry, &c. In other respects he may be as well treated as the plantation-slave. The treatment of both mainly depends, as has been said, on the character of the master or manager.

The slave-registry act, when first introduced in parliament, excited a great ferment in the colonies. This measure was indeed brought forward in a way little calculated to conciliate the minds of the people of the West Indies. Ushered in by a publication, in which the colonists were characterized as persons utterly averse to legislate for themselves whenever humanity to their slaves was the object, it is no wonder that the proposed measure should have met with the most prompt, warm, and determined opposition in all the islands. It was viewed as a theoretical and dangerous project of the African Institution, to the carrying of which into effect government had been persuaded to pledge its assistance. Mr Stephen, and the other active members of the African Institution, were, in retaliation, denounced as bitter and determined enemies to the colonies—hypocrites, calumniators, mere pretenders to philanthropy, who made use of the term only to cover their own selfish views and deceive the government. That both parties carried their virulence and abuse too far, all moderate and impartial men will allow. Be this as it may, the mere proposal of a slave-registry would have created much less antipathy and alarm, had it not been thus preceded by Mr Stephen's attack, and had proceeded simply from the government. It would then have been opposed merely on the ground of its being an unwarrantable interference in the internal affairs of the island. But emanating, as it avowedly did, from the African Institution, it came forth in a more than questionable shape. Strongly prepossessed as the minds of the planters are against the leading members of that body, it could not but excite in them fear, distrust, and suspicion. They viewed it—not as a necessary measure of precaution against the illicit traffic in slaves, which did not exist, nor as a preventive of free persons being held in a state of slavery—these they conceived to be only its ostensible objects,—but as a preliminary step to a fearful and dangerous proceeding—the prompt emancipation of the slaves—an object which, they were persuaded, the leading members of the African Institution had even then in view. It was not therefore surprising that the whole of the West Indies was thrown into a state of ferment and alarm when it was made known that the slave-registry bill was to be brought into parliament, under the sanction and countenance of ministers. The merchants who had capital embarked in the islands, and all others who had an interest at stake in them, partook of this alarm ; to calm and allay which, the British government adopted the wisest and safest mode it could of making the measure palatable to the colonial legislatures—namely, by *recommending* to them the keeping, by their own acts, registers of their slaves. This recommendatory measure, with a slight show of opposition in some of the islands, has been carried into effect, and has since been followed by the establishment of a general register of slaves in England. Thus has the object originally contemplated been brought about in a round-about way—that is, by avoiding any direct interference with the authority of the colonial legislatures, and by steering clear of any appearance of falling in with the views of the African Institution.

The avowed objects of the slave-registry measure are, as has been said, to prevent more effectually any illicit traffic in slaves, and the holding of free persons in a state of slavery. With respect to the first of these objects, though the author is not competent to say what may have been going on in the other islands, he can at least assert that, to the best of his knowledge, *not one slave has been illicitly imported into the island of Jamaica since the passing of the abolition act.* He had opportunities of knowing this to be the fact, having been almost constantly resident in the island since the passing of that act.*

The second object is doubtless a humane and proper one. Of late years, however, there has existed no disposition on the part of the magistrates and courts of law to hold any one, justly

---

* On a late occasion, two men were prosecuted, convicted and punished by transportation, under the abolition act, for an attempt to smuggle into the island certain African negroes taken at sea.

entitled to his freedom, in a state of slavery: on the contrary, the utmost readiness is evinced by both to listen to the complaints of all persons on this subject, and to grant them every redress. Mr Stephen erroneously asserts, that the *onus probandi* was, in such cases of complaint, thrown on the person claiming his freedom. Whatever may be the practice in the other islands, or in former times in this island, the uniform practice now is, that the person, claiming a reputed slave as his property, shall clearly establish such claim. Many cases of what is called *homini replegiando* have, within these few years, been tried in the courts, and uniformly with a humane leaning to the weaker party. The alleged slave is generally, before the question of his freedom is decided, taken under the protection of the magistrates of the parish where his supposed master resides; and counsel, much to their honour, are ever ready to offer their services, gratuitously, in his behalf.

A case, which lately occurred in this island, may be mentioned, in proof of the readiness with which the magistrates assist and protect persons unjustly detained as slaves. A gentleman, a member of council, had, it was alleged, held a free woman in slavery for twenty-five years. This woman had been sent, in consequence of some misbehaviour, to the parish workhouse, the overseer of which was directed by her master to inflict a severe punishment on her. The magistrates, by whose order she had been committed, immediately interposed to prevent this illegal severity, and advertised the woman as one claiming her freedom. The privy-counsellor, in not very courteous language, complained, through one of the public prints, of this, as he deemed it, unjustifiable infringement of his right. The magistrates indignantly repelled this attack, and justified what they had done. This was as it should be: one part of their reply might, however, as well have been spared: " *What would they have said in England if we had not acted as we have done ?*" said they—as if a conscientious sense of duty was not a sufficient incentive on such an occasion. Be this as it may, the magistrates did their duty; the oppressed woman was taken under their protection, and ultimately obtained her freedom, no satisfactory proofs of her being a slave having been produced.

With respect to the general effects of the slave-registry law, it is now found to be not merely harmless, but in some respects beneficial —not only to those whose advantage the proposers of it had mainly in view, but to the interests of the whites, individually and collectively. It is doubtless calculated to obviate much fraud, and it has already been productive, in Jamaica, of an increase of the public revenue, which had before been defrauded by false returns.

If this law be merely meant as a measure of regulation and precaution, as its original proposers professed, or if it be intended as a preliminary step towards introducing other gradual improvements in the condition of the slave, that are safe, salutary, and practicable, all is well. But if emancipation be the object in view, let the government and legislature beware how they listen to schemes on that subject. The extinction of slavery in the West Indies can only be contemplated as a work of time, to be brought about by a series of progressive changes and improvements in the minds, habits, and condition of the slaves. Those who have been in the West Indies for a sufficient length of time to be enabled to judge of the character of the negro slaves, in all its bearings, and who will also take into account the vast and complicated interests depending on the state of our dominion in that quarter, can alone form some idea of the difficulties and dangers which would attend such a measure in the present state of the colonies. It would not be advisable on grounds either of humanity or policy. Were freedom to be given to the slaves, in their present moral and intellectual condition, they would neither be made happier, nor even *more free*—paradoxical as this may seem—by the change; for they would only thereby be exchanging white masters for others, of their own colour,* more unprincipled in their tyranny than the worst description of the whites. The slaves themselves are fully aware of this; they are sensible of the existence of laws for their protection, and of a disposition to redress their wrongs in the public authorities and in the more humane class of masters—an order of things they are not quite sure of were they under the dominion of black masters: when oppressed and ill treated by the black drivers or other head men, they usually draw a comparison between blacks and whites, on the score of humanity and justice, favourable to the former.

The great bulk of this emancipated people would in fact become the victims of the tyranny of a few; discord and anarchy would soon produce their usual effects among them—injustice, violence, and mutual slaughter; the country, in short, would be desolated, and the people become

---

* M. de la Croix, in his " Account of the Past and Present State of Hayti," says, that the agricultural labourers there are in a worse state than they were under the dominion of their former masters, the French. This is saying much, for the French planters of St Domingo had the character of being tyrannical to their slaves.

more savage and wretched. The whites would not long be suffered to hold quiet possession of their properties; they would soon have no safety but in flight. This is no imaginary presage of the result of such a change hastily brought about; St Domingo, at the period of its revolution, exhibited a memorable example of the atrocities of which a negro population, suddenly released from the control by which they were held in obedience, are capable.

With respect to the policy of the measure, in a national point of view, it may be reduced to the very momentous questions—first, whether, in such an event, the mother-country would be in a condition to pay nearly one hundred millions of money to her subjects whose capitals were embarked in West-India property, under the guarantee of *British laws*, for the loss of that property?—which she would be as much bound in honour and good faith to do, if she gave freedom to the slaves, as to keep faith with the national creditors;—and, secondly, whether she could afford to suffer a defalcation in her revenue of five millions and a half, derived from her colonial commerce—the loss of a market for her manufactures to the amount of more than three millions and a half per annum—a great nursery for her seamen, and employment for a consider-

able portion of her shipping ? * It is easy to specu-
late on such a subject; but theory and practice
are very different. The warmest rational friends
of humanity would hardly advocate a measure
fraught with so much evil on one side, without
being likely, on the other, to be attended by the
good contemplated.

But though such would be the awful consequences of a too precipitate emancipation of the
slaves, let no one draw from thence an argument
in favour of the perpetuation of slavery. It is
clearly repugnant to the immutable principles of
reason and justice as well as to the mild spirit of
Christianity; and those who endeavour to justify or excuse it, by telling us that it has prevailed from the remotest times, and existed among

---

* It was stated in the House of Commons, that, from the
papers laid before parliament in 1822, it appeared that, on an
average, the exports from Great Britain and Ireland to the
West Indies amounted in value to the sum of £3,560,000 annually—that Great Britain derived from her West-India commerce an annual revenue of £5,500,000,—and that 23,700 seamen, and 438,000 tons of shipping, were employed in that commerce. The average annual amount of revenue in the five
years ending the 5th of January 1813, was £6,585,643. In
1816, the value of exports from the united kingdom to the colonies was £4,155,163: during the war they were sometimes
little short of five millions.

all the great nations of antiquity—the Greeks, Romans, &c., and under the Jewish and Christian dispensations,—merely inform us that a great moral evil was suffered to exist in those times and among those nations. Bryan Edwards, one of the most able and zealous champions of the West Indies, speaking of slavery, abstractedly, says, " After all, I will not conceal that I am no friend to slavery in any shape, or under any modification." If then a West-Indian, holding large properties in one of the islands, makes this candid avowal, what shall we think of those who gravely set up a defence of slavery, and would thus justify its indefinite continuance? Nothing surely can be more revolting than the thought that a state of degrading bondage (for such slavery at best must be considered) shall be handed down from generation to generation—to beings yet unborn, on whom the morn of freedom shall never dawn ! The strong plea of necessity is the only ground, in short, on which the continuance of slavery, for a time, can be defended. The national weal, the incontrovertible right of a large and opulent body of British subjects, whose whole property is embarked in the colonies, under the sanction and faith of acts of the British legislature, and even the welfare of the enslaved themselves,—forbid other than a gradual extinction of slavery, by progressive ameliorations,

The liberal-minded West-Indian himself must look forward, with pleasure, to a period when the boon of rational freedom shall be extended over the American Archipelago—in other words, a just and secure reciprocity of interests and services between the landholder and the labourer, in which the wholesome control of just and impartial laws only shall have force. By what progressive measures such a state of things may be brought about, without danger or substantial injury to the possessors of the soil, and, of consequence, to the parent state, is a question full of difficulty, and involving many considerations of deep interest. Time and a gradual improvement of system can only develop the safest and wisest means of bringing about that effectual change in the moral and political condition of the slaves, which the liberal and enlightened of all parties seem to view as so desirable.

Such are the author's unprejudiced opinions on the question of the abolition of slavery in our West-India colonies—a question surpassed by none in magnitude and importance, whether as it regards the rights, property, and safety of a numerous, opulent, and respectable body of British subjects, or the vital interests of the empire at large. A precipitate emancipation of the slaves is allowed by all parties to be a wild, impolitic, and ruinous scheme. Such a change must be the work of time, and of a preparatory moral and intellectual improvement of the slaves. In the meantime, such improvements in the slave-laws, as can with perfect safety be made at the present moment, should be carried into effect—not by the imperial parliament, as has been strangely recommended, but by the colonial legislatures, to whom belongs the right of regulating all matters connected with their internal policy. The former, and the government, may indeed recommend to the latter such enactments as they conceived would be productive of good; but any attempt to force such enactments on the colonies would most assuredly *be resisted at all hazards.* Those who would persuade the British parliament to legislate for the colonies may be very well-meaning people, but, unquestionably, they are not aware of the consequences of what they recommend. The colonial assemblies have uniformly and strenuously resisted all interference of the British parliament in their internal affairs, even in matters of inferior moment —on the ground that it was a direct violation of their right to legislate.—What, then, would they think of such interference in a matter of vital importance, involving not merely their rights, but their lives and property?—that if they submitted to it their authority would be but a shadow and a mockery. Jamaica, in particular—

an island almost equal in value and importance to all the other colonies—has always been most inflexible on this point. A contention between the imperial parliament and the colonial assemblies, on such a subject, would be pregnant with the most dangerous consequences. The slaves, made acquainted with what was going on, would be incited to disaffection and rebellion, and thus an event would be brought about which would too probably terminate in scenes of havock and bloodshed, and, finally, *in the loss of the colonies to Great Britain.*

CHAP. XV.

CHARACTER OF THE SLAVES—THEIR MAXIMS AND
OPINIONS—THEIR CAPACITY.

THE different tribes or nations of the negroes are, like the different nations of Europe, of various characters and dispositions. Some are mild, docile, and timid—while others are fierce, irascible, and easily roused to revenge. They are in general crafty, artful, and plausible, little ashamed of falsehood, and strangely addicted to theft: to pilfer from their masters they consider as no crime, though to rob a fellow-slave is accounted heinous: when a slave makes free with his master's property, he thus ingeniously argues, —" *What I take from my master, being for my use, who am his slave, or property, he loses nothing by its transfer.*"

The character of the negro slaves are no doubt deteriorated by the nature of their condition. They have, however, good qualities mingled with their bad ones. They are patient, cheerful, and commonly submissive, capable at times of grateful attachments, where uniformly well treated, and generally affectionate towards their friends, kindred, and offspring.* The affection and solicitude of a negro mother towards her infant is ardent even to enthusiasm. The crime of infanticide, so repugnant to nature, is seldom or never heard of among the negro tribes; though it is said, that, prompted by avarice, the African father will sometimes sell his child to the European slave-trader. It is no easy matter to delineate correctly the true character and dispositions of the negro slaves, collectively considered; there will occur examples among them that bid defiance to analogy. The dispositions of some are a disgrace to human nature; while there are others whose good qualities would put many of their white rulers to the blush. This diversity of character is, in part, owing to the different dispositions of the various tribes brought to the island, and which may in some measure pass to their respective descendants, the creole negroes. The Eboc is crafty, artful, disputative in driving a bargain, and suspicious of being over-reached by those with whom he deals; but withal, patient, industrious, saving, and tractable. The Coro-

---

* Between Africans brought together from their country in the same ship, a friendship is formed which usually continues to the end of their lives. *Shipmate,* by which name they address each other, seems synonymous, in their view, with brother or sister.

mantee is, on the contrary, fierce, violent, and revengeful under injury and provocation; but hardy, laborious, and manageable under mild and just treatment. This tribe has generally been at the head of all insurrections, and was the original parent-stock of the Maroons. The Congo, Papaw, Chamba, Mandingo, &c. are of a more mild and peaceable disposition than the Coromantee, but less industrious and provident than the Eboc. The Mandingoes are a sort of Mahomedans, though they are too ignorant to understand any thing of the Alcoran, or of the nature of their religion : some of them, however, can scrawl a few rude Arabic characters, but without understanding or being able to explain much of their meaning. Probably they are scraps from the Alcoran which they have been taught by their imans, or priests. The creole negroes are the descendants of the Africans, and may be said to possess in common the mingled dispositions of their parents or ancestors. But they pretend to a great superiority in intellect and manners over the Africans—boast of their good fortune in being born creoles,—and the farther they are removed from the African blood the more they pride themselves thereon.

The passions and affections of the negroes, not being under the control of reason or religion, sometimes break out with frightful violence; rage, revenge, grief, jealousy, have often been productive of terrible catastrophes; but it is only in their intercourse with each other that this impetuosity prevails; they are so far subdued by a habitual awe of the whites as to have a mastery over their passions, and, if ill treated, they brood in silence over their wrongs, watching for a favourable opportunity of revenge.

Many examples are given us of the gratitude and attachment of the negro race. These are far from being surprising; on the contrary, nothing is more easy than for a humane master to attach to him, by ties of gratitude, a slave of good dispositions, whom he is in the habit of employing near his person, where a reciprocity of kindness, on the one hand, and fidelity on the other, must necessarily produce that effect. But it rarely happens that two such characters shall be associated; more frequently the indulgent master and perverse slave, or the faithful servant and harsh unfeeling master, meet unhappily together. As for the great bulk of the slaves, they are beyond the ken of their master's immediate observation: indeed there are many of the great attorneys who do not personally know a tenth part of the numerous slaves belonging to their constituents. They see them once a-year, collected to receive their annual allowance of clothing, and this is the only opportunity they have of knowing any thing about them, except by report.

Two instances may here be given of uncommon gratitude and attachment in slaves towards their masters, both of which are well authenticated.

Soon after the breaking out of the insurrection in St Domingo, when the unfortunate whites were everywhere hunted and massacred, and their dwellings given up to fire and pillage, a negro, who loved his master, hastened to him with the first intelligence of the revolt, and the imminent danger in which he stood ; " but," said this faithful slave, " I will save you, or perish myself in the attempt." He immediately conveyed his master to a place of safety, where he could be concealed for a while. In the dead of night he put him into a sack, and, placing him across a mule, conveyed him to some distance before dawn of day, and again concealed him in the cavern of a rock : at night he again renewed his journey ; and in this manner did this faithful creature safely conduct his master a distance of an hundred miles, till he brought him to a navigable river, where he procured a canoe, and at night paddled it down with the stream till he came to a post occupied by the whites, to whom he delivered his master in safety and unhurt.

The other instance occurred in Jamaica during the Maroon war, and is well attested by several respectable gentlemen, who were eye-witnesses of the transaction. During the ambuscade-attack of the Maroons on Lieutenant-colonel Sandford's party of dragoons and militia, at a narrow defile leading from the New to Old Trelawny Maroon Town, a gentleman's negro servant, being close to his master, and observing a Maroon's piece levelled at him, he instantly threw himself between him and the danger, and received the shot in his body. Happily it did not prove mortal, and the faithful slave lived to enjoy the well-earned fruits of his master's gratitude.

Numerous instances of the gratitude and attachment of negro slaves towards their masters have come within the author's knowledge; though he has also had occasion to witness the most hardened ingratitude in individuals of this race, not only to their masters and their fellow-slaves, but even to their parents, when age and decripitude had rendered their kindness and assistance doubly necessary and welcome. Filial gratitude is not so powerful an affection as parental love, and among the negro race this is often strikingly exemplified.

Very affecting scenes often occurred of negro sales during the existence of the slave-trade. Groups of slaves were seen with their arms entwined round each other's necks, waiting, with sad and anxious looks, the expected moment of separation. Perhaps they were sisters and friends—perhaps a mother and her children—perhaps a husband and wife. In vain was the endeavour to separate them—they clung closer together, they wept, they shrieked piteously, and, if forcibly torn asunder, the buyer had generally cause to regret his inhumanity; despair often seized on the miserable creatures, and they either sunk into an utter despondency or put a period to their lives.

Though scenes of this kind often occurred, it is yet too true that the unnatural African father, prompted by the love of lucre, will sometimes sell his children, the children trepan their parent, and one friend betray another! This is no groundless allegation; the author has often heard recitals of this savage conduct from their own mouths. He was once an eye-witness of a curious scene arising from a circumstance of this nature. A negro, who had been some years in the country, happening one day to meet an elderly slave who had just been purchased from a slave-trader recently arrived, he recognised him as his father—who, it seems, had sold him to the Europeans. Without explanation or preface, he addressed to him a speech, in his country dialect, which he thus translated to the bystanders.—" *So, you old rogue, dem catch you at last—no.—Buckra* * *do good—you no care for your pickininnic (child)—but they will make you feel work pinch too.*"

The negroes, though so rude and ignorant in their savage state, have a natural shrewdness and genius which is doubtless susceptible of culture and improvement. Those who have been reared among the whites are greatly superior in intellect to the native Africans brought at a mature age to the country. Many are wonderfully ingenious in making a variety of articles for their own use, or to sell; and such as are properly brought up to any trade, show a skill and dexterity in it little inferior to the Europeans.† In reckoning numbers they are somewhat puzzled, being obliged to mark the decimals as they proceed. Some author mentions a nation so extremely stupid that they could not reckon beyond the number five. The negro can go far beyond this—indeed, give him time, and he will, by a mode of combination of his own, make out a pretty round sum; but he is utterly perplexed by the minuter combinations of figures according to the European system of arithmetic.

---

* White men.

† On the plantations there are negro carpenters, masons, coopers, &c. some of whom are as expert as white mechanics.

Their ideas cannot be expected to extend to abstract and metaphysical subjects. Of the existence and attributes of a Deity, of a future state, and of duration and space, they have but very imperfect notions. They cannot dilate and subdivide their conceptions into minuter distinctions and more abstract combinations; yet they will often express, in their own way, a wonderfully acute conception of things. These conceptions they sometimes compress into short and pithy sentences, something like the sententious proverbs of the Europeans, to which many of them bear an analogy. Their sayings often convey much force and meaning, and would, if clothed in a more courtly dress, make no despicable figure even among those precepts of wisdom which are ascribed to wiser nations. When they wish to imply, that a peaceable man is often wise and provident in his conduct, they say, " *Softly water run deep;*" when they would express the oblivion and disregard which follows them after death, they say, " *When man dead grass grow at him door;*" and when they would express the humility which is the usual accompaniment of poverty, they say, " *Poor man never vex.*" Mr Bryan Edwards mentions an instance of sagacious wit in a negro servant of his. He had fallen asleep, and, on one of his fellow-servants awakening him and telling him, somewhat tartly, that

" *Massa heart burn* (angry) *because him de call him—call him, and him de sleep and no hearie,*" he drily observed that, " *Sleep no have massa.*"

The negroes are astonished at the ingenuity of the Europeans, and there are some articles of their manufacture which appear quite unaccountable to them, as watches, telescopes, looking-glasses, gunpowder, &c. The author once amused a party of negroes with the deceptions of a magic-lantern. They gazed with the utmost wonder and astonishment at the hideous figures conjured up by this optical machine, and were of opinion that nothing short of witchcraft could have produced such an instrument. They are also astonished at the means by which the Europeans can find their way to Africa and other remote countries, and guide their vessels, through trackless oceans, with as much certainty as they can travel over a few miles of well-known country. This they can only attribute to some supernatural gift of knowledge. A master of an African trader, travelling in Jamaica, and not knowing his way, inquired of a negro whom he met the road to Mr ——'s house. The negro recognising him to be the captain of the ship in which he had been brought from his native country, eyed him with a look of ineffable contempt, without making any reply: on the question being reiterated, he replied with much indignation, as conceiving himself jested with by one who had injured him so deeply—" *You want for make fool of me—no?—you can find pass go in a Guinea country bring me come here, but you can't find pass go in a massa house.*" —In short, they say, they require no greater proof that the Almighty chose the whites as his favoured people, than that he has communicated to them every useful and curious invention— that he has taught them the use of books—that he has taught them how to make gunpowder, wherewith to defend themselves, or to assail others—that he has taught them the way to make all kinds of merchandise, and pointed out to them the country where slaves were to be bought for such merchandise—and that he has taught them the art of sailing thither to fetch those slaves for the purpose of cultivating their lands,—a task which they themselves could never have performed. Such are the opinions which the negroes have of European invention, arts, learning, and dominion.

They are at a loss what to think of earth-quakes; though often shrewd in their remarks and conjectures, earthquakes and eclipses puzzle them. As to hurricanes, they naturally enough consider them as indications of the Divine wrath, —as punishments inflicted by Heaven on the human race for their crimes and impiety ; they have no idea of their arising from natural causes; the necessary war of the elements is to them an incomprehensible doctrine; and they would smile to hear the philosopher say, that though these visitations inflict evil, they also import benefit, by purifying the atmosphere of those pestilential vapours which would otherwise spread disease and death. They do not look much to natural causes and remote consequences. If the winged lightning which flashes across the fields should strike dead an oppressive overseer under whose tyranny they suffered, they would hail the circumstance as a just judgment of the Almighty; but they are guilty of blasphemy when they arraign him of partiality if, when their day of rest returns, it should prove a tempestuous one, or when any other unforeseen disaster befalls them. But, above all, they cannot reconcile it to fairness that the Supreme Ruler of the universe should have shown so marked a predilection for the whites as to give dominion to them, while he placed the blacks, *who have no wish to offend him,* in a state of perpetual bondage under them. They have not yet learned the doctrine of unrepining submission to the will of Providence; though such among them as boast of being Christians, when they meet with crosses and vexations, usually exclaim, " The Lord's will be done."

The ideas which they entertain on the subject of moral equity are not the most liberal and correct. They are of opinion, in unison with their African habits, that we should, on most occasions, bow to superior power, and be influenced and directed in a great measure by favour, affection, and interest, without reference to moral fitness or principle. It is curious to observe with what avidity they catch at every occasion of enjoying and exerting a petty authority over their fellow-slaves. This propensity shows itself very early in life, and is no doubt generated and nourished by the system of domination around them. When the young negro is *promoted* to an office of superintendence and responsibility, he feels an additional pride and importance; he considers himself as then belonging to a superior *caste*; but, like too many of his white prototyes, he is prone to exercise but little moderation in his new *office*, to domineer with a high hand, and is more solicitous about his own prerogatives than the justice and humanity with which he asserts them. His maxims are—to have no consideration but for himself and his friends, and to retain his situation, at whatever expense of severity to those over whom he is placed. He himself has been domineered over by a driver, or head-man; it is now his turn to domineer over others. If, for instance, a negro is employed as a head wain-man, he has two boys given him as assistants; these boys he compels to perform almost the whole labour; they catch and yoke the cattle, while he looks on, and drive and direct them in the waggon, while he rides at his ease on the shaft, or sleeps in the waggon. The poor boys perform their task with wonderful adroitness, under the terror of the whip of this their unconscionable task-master; but they console themselves with the hope that they will one day be head-men themselves, when they will be just as unreasonable and harsh to others. Thus is a habitual spirit of tyranny and injustice engendered in the blacks, which shows itself when they get invested with a little power. Much of the suffering of the slaves is owing to the hard-heartedness of their black drivers; and *Buckra better* is a common expression among the former when appealing to the whites against the cruelty and injustice of each other.

On many of the estates the head-men erect themselves into a sort of bench of justice, which sits and decides, privately, and without the knowledge of the whites, on all disputes and complaints of their fellow-slaves. The sentences of this court are frequently severe, and sometimes partial and unjust: they consist in pecuniary fines, which often exceed the means of the party. Frequent appeals have been brought

before a manager from one of these courts complaining of enormous *damages and costs of suit,*
which the appellants were utterly unable to
make good. He has reversed or softened these
sentences, always to the great satisfaction of one
party, but to the never-failing discontent of the
other. He has atttempted to abolish these courts
altogether, but without success; still they would
frequently hold their sittings, and were countenanced and desired by the principal negroes and
their adherents. There were no advocates or
pleaders in them; the judges themselves plead-
ed, and, when agreed in opinion, they passed
sentence. Bribery, of course, had great *weight* in
their decisions, and favour and affection were not
unattended to; so that the poorest and most
unfriended of the negroes had the worst chance
of justice from their hands. The opening and
proceedings of this court were curious enough.
On the judges taking their seats (usually three
in number), and the parties appearing, not a
word was spoken on any of the causes, till the
former had half intoxicated themselves by copious
potations of rum, which were presented to them
by the respective plaintiffs and defendants, this
offering being considered as an indispensable
preliminary to the dispensing of justice. It is
wonderful, however, with what patience they
will hear each other's long harangues; though

sometimes, where there was an irreconcilable difference of opinion between the judges, they would break up with much clamour and wrangling.

Although the proverbial sayings of the negroes have often much point and meaning, they, however, no sooner begin to expatiate and enter more minutely into particulars, than they become tedious, verbose, and circumlocutory, beginning their speeches with a tiresome exordium, mingling with them much extraneous matter, and frequently traversing over and over the same ground, and cautioning the hearer to be attentive, as if fearful that some of the particulars and points on which their meaning and argument hinged should escape his attention. So that by the time they arrive at the peroration of their harangue, the listener is heartily fatigued with it, and perceives that the whole which has been said, though it may have taken up half an hour, could have been comprised in half-a-dozen words.

The creole slaves are in general more acute and quicker of apprehension than the Africans. A creole negro boy put to learn a trade acquires a thorough knowledge of it in five or six years, and performs his work with as much neatness as a European workman, though with less despatch. Excellent negro masons, carpenters, coopers, blacksmiths, tailors, sailors, pilots, &c.

abound here;—and there cannot be a doubt but that, by the culture of education, they are capable of the higher attainments of the mind. There have been examples of negroes, who, with but little assistance from education, have displayed astonishing proofs of talent; among these the celebrated Toussaint L'Ouverture, who, though an uneducated slave, acquitted himself as a general and a statesman in a manner that astonished and confounded those who maintained that negroes were incapable of intellectual improvement.

CHAP. XVI.

THE houses of the slaves are in general comfortable. They are built of hard-wood posts, either
boarded or wattled and plastered, and the roof
formed of shingles (wood split and dressed into
the shape of slates, and used as a substitute for
them), or thatched with the leaves of the sugar-
cane, or the branches of the mountain cabbage :*
this latter is of so durable a nature that it will
last for thirty or forty years. The size of the
houses is generally from fifteen to twenty feet
long, and from ten to fifteen wide. They contain
a small hall, and one or two bed-rooms, according to the size of the family. The furniture of
this dwelling is a small table, two or three chairs
or stools, a small cupboard, furnished with a few
articles of crockery-ware, some wooden bowls
and calibashes, a water-jar, a wooden mortar for

---

* A species of the palm.

pounding Indian corn, &c. and various other articles. The beds are seldom more than wooden frames spread with a mat and blanket.

Adjoining to the house is usually a small spot of ground, laid out into a sort of garden, and shaded by various fruit-trees. Here the family deposite their dead, to whose memory they invariably, if they can afford it, erect a rude tomb. Each slave has, besides this spot, a piece of ground (about half an acre) allotted to him as a provision-ground. This is the principal means of his support; and so productive is the soil, where it is good and the seasons regular, that this spot will not only furnish him with sufficient food for his own consumption, but an overplus to carry to market. By means of this ground, and of the hogs and poultry which he may raise (most of which he sells), an industrious negro may not only support himself comfortably, but save something. If he has a family, an additional proportion of ground is allowed him, and all his children from five years upwards assist him in his labours in some way or other. On the sugar plantations the slaves are not allowed to keep horses, cows, sheep, or goats,* and they

---

* On the pens, and coffee and other settlements, they are usually allowed to keep a few goats, but neither horses nor cattle.

are obliged to prevent their hogs from wandering over the estate.

The common food of the slaves is salt meat (commonly pork), or salted fish, boiled along with their yams, cocos, or plantains, mixed up with pulse and other vegetables, and highly seasoned with the native pepper (*capsum Indicus*). Pimento they never use in their food. They receive from their masters seven or eight herrings per week, a food which most of them, who can afford better, despise; and they accordingly sell them in the markets, and purchase salted pork, of which they are exceedingly fond. They also get about eight pounds of salted cod-fish once or twice a-year: this food is more a favourite with them than the herrings, for no reason that can be imagined, but because the former is a greater rarity than the latter. They cannot afford to indulge themselves with a fowl or a duck, except upon particular occasions.*

The common dress of the male slaves is an osnaburgh or check frock, and a pair of osnaburgh or sheeting trowsers, with a coarse hat. That of the women is an osnaburgh or coarse linen shift, a petticoat made of various stuff, according to their taste and circumstances, and a

---

* Some of the Africans eat the cane-field rat, which they regard as a great luxury.

handkerchief tied round their heads. Both men and women are also provided with great-coats (or *croocas*, as they call them) of blue woollen stuff. Neither sex wear shoes in common, these being reserved for particular occasions, such as dances, &c. when all who can afford it appear in very gay apparel—the men in broad-cloth coats, fancy waistcoats, and nankeen or jean trowsers, and the women in white or fancy muslin gowns, beaver or silk hats, and a variety of expensive jewellery. But it is only a small proportion who can afford to dress thus finely. The annual allowance of clothing which they receive from their owners is as much osnaburgh as will make two frocks, and as much woollen stuff as will make a great-coat; with a hat, handkerchief, knife, and needles and thread to make up their clothes. This specific quantity an owner is obliged by law to give to his slaves. But all of them who can afford to buy a finer dress, seldom appear, excepting when at work, in the coarse habiliments given them by their masters.

The slaves have little time to devote to amusement, but such occasions as offer they eagerly embrace. Plays, as they call them, are their principal and favourite one. This is an assemblage of both sexes, dressed out for the occasion, who form a ring round a male and female dancer, who perform to the music of drums and the songs of the other females of the party, one alternately going over the song, while her companions repeat in chorus. Both the singers and dancers shew the exactest precision as to time and measure. This rude music is usually accompanied by a kind of rattles, being small calibashes filled with the seed of a plant called by the negroes *Indian shot.* Near at hand this music is harsh and clamorous, but at a distance it has not an unpleasant sound. When two dancers have fatigued themselves, another couple enter the ring, and thus the amusement continues. So fond are the negroes of this amusement, that they will continue for nights and days enjoying it, when permitted. But their owners find it prudent and necessary to restrain them from it, excepting at Christmas, when they have three days allowed them. This and harvest-home may be considered as their two annual festivals. Little do they consider, and as little do they care, about the origin and occasion of the former of those festivals; suffice it to say, that *Buckra* gives them their three days—though, by the bye, the law allows only two, in consideration of the injury they may sustain by three successive days of unbounded dissipation, and of the danger, at such a time of unrestrained licentiousness, of riots and disorder.

On these occasions the slaves appear an altered

race of beings. They show themselves off to the greatest advantage, by fine clothes and a profusion of trinkets; they affect a more polished behaviour and mode of speech; they address the whites with greater familiarity; they come into their masters' houses, and drink with them; the distance between them appears to be annihilated for the moment, like the familiar footing on which the Roman slaves were with their masters at the feast of the Saturnalia. Pleasure throws a temporary oblivion over their cares and their toils; they seem a people without the consciousness of inferiority or suffering.

Many of them, however, but especially the men, give themselves up to excessive intemperance, which, with their nocturnal dances, often produces sickness, and sometimes even death. Such is the violent exercise they undergo in these dancings, such the heedless manner in which they abandon themselves for successive nights and days to this favourite amusement, even in the open air, during the Christmas holidays, that were this unrestrained indulgence permitted for two or three weeks, instead of as many days, it would probably destroy a great number of these thoughtless people. After their riotous festivity, they experience a degree of lassitude and languor which for some days incapacitates them for much exertion or labour.

Plays, or dances, very frequently take place
on Saturday nights, when the slaves on the
neighbouring plantations assemble together to
enjoy this amusement. It is contrary to the
law for the slaves to beat their drums after ten
o'clock at night; but this law they pay little
regard to. Their music is very rude; it consists
of the *goombay* or drum, several rattles, and the
voices of the female slaves, which, by the bye, is
the best part of the music, though altogether it
is very rude. The drums of the Africans vary
in shape, size, &c. according to the different
countries, as does also their vocal music. In a
few years it is probable that the rude music here
described will be altogether exploded among the
creole negroes, who shew a decided preference
for European music. Its instruments, its tunes,
its dances, are now pretty generally adopted by
the young creoles, who indeed sedulously copy
their masters and mistresses in every thing. A
sort of subscription balls are set on foot, and parties of both sexes assemble and dance country
dances to the music of a violin, tambarine, &c.
But this improvement of taste is in a great measure confined to those who are, or have been,
domestics about the houses of the whites, and
have in consequence imbibed a fondness for their
amusements, and some skill in the performance.
They affect, too, the language, manners, and

conversation of the whites: those who have it in their power have at times their convivial parties, when they will endeavour to mimic their masters in their drinking, their songs, and their toasts; and it is laughable to see with what awkward minuteness they aim at such imitations. They have also caught a spirit of gambling from their masters, and often assemble and play at games of hazard with the dice, though there is a law against such species of gambling, and such slaves as are found assembled for this purpose are liable to punishment. At horse-races, betting goes on among the negro servants who are present as regularly as among their masters.

On new-year's-day, it is customary for the creole negro girls of the towns, who conceive themselves superior to those on the plantations, to exhibit themselves in all the pride of gaudy finery, under the denomination of *Blues* and *Reds*—parties in rivalship and opposition to each other. They are generally dressed with much taste, sometimes at the expense of their white and brown mistresses, who take a pride in shewing them off to the greatest advantage. Their gowns are of the finest muslin, with blue or pink satin spencers, trimmed with gold or silver, according to their party; and gold necklaces, ear-rings, and other expensive trinkets, shine to advantage on their jet black skins. The most comely young negresses are selected, and such as have a fine and tutored voice; they parade through the streets, two and two, in the most exact order, with appropriate flags and instrumental music, accompanied by their voices, the songs being for the most part such as they have caught from the whites, and which they previously practise for the occasion. Each party has its *queen*, who eclipses all the rest in the splendour of her dress. Their appearance, upon the whole, is tasteful and elegant, and would somewhat astonish a stranger who had associated with the idea of slavery other images than those of gayety and costly display.

These exhibitions are not so frequent as they used to be. The mistresses of the slaves, who were the patronesses of them, and at whose expense much of the requisite finery was provided, find that they cost more money and trouble than they can well spare. The negresses must, however, have their annual display of fine clothes and suitable ornaments, if they should go in filth and raggedness all the rest of the year.

At their funerals, the African negroes use various ceremonies, among which is the practice of pouring libations, and sacrificing a fowl on the grave of the deceased—a tribute of respect they afterwards occasionally repeat. During the whole of the ceremony, many fantastic motions and wild gesticulations are practised, accompanied with a suitable beat of their drums and other rude instruments, while a melancholy dirge is sung by a female, the chorus of which is performed by the whole of the other females, with admirable precision, and full-toned and not unmelodious voices. When the deceased is interred, the plaintive notes of sympathy are no longer heard, the drums resound with a livelier beat, the song grows more animated, dancing and apparent merriment commence, and the remainder of the night is usually spent in feasting and riotous debauchery.

Previous to the interment of the corpse it is sometimes pretended that it is endowed with the gift of speech; and the friends and relatives alternately place their ears to the lid of the coffin, to hear what the deceased has to say. This generally consists of complaints and upbraidings for various injuries,—treachery, ingratitude, injustice, slander, and, in particular, the non-payment of debts due to the deceased. This last complaint is sometimes shewn by the deceased in a more *cogent* way than by mere words; for, on coming opposite the door of the negro debtor, the coffin makes a full stop, and no persuasion nor strength can induce the deceased to go forward peaceably to his grave till the money is paid; so that the unhappy debtor has no alternative but to comply with this demand, or have his creditor palmed upon him, as a lodger, for some time. Sometimes, however, the deceased is a little unconscionable, by claiming a fictitious debt. In short, this superstitious practice is often made subservient to fraudulent extortion. A negro, who was to be interred in one of the towns, had, it was pretended by some of his friends, a claim on another negro for a sum of money. The latter denied any such claim; and accordingly, at the funeral of the deceased, the accustomed ceremonies took place opposite to the door of his supposed debtor; and this mummery was continued for hours, till the magistrates thought proper to interfere, and compelled the defunct to forego his claim, and proceed quietly on to his place of rest.

The most dangerous practice, arising from a superstitious credulity, prevailing among the negroes is, what is called *obeah*,* a pretended sort of witchcraft. One negro who desires to be revenged on another, and is afraid to make an open and manly attack on his adversary, has usually recourse to *obeah*. This is considered as a potent and irresistible spell, withering and palsying, by undescribable terrors and unwonted sensations, the unhappy victim. Like the witches'

* This practice is less common at present than it used to be.

caldron in Macbeth, it is a combination of many strange and ominous things—earth gathered from a grave, human blood, a piece of wood fashioned in the shape of a coffin, the feathers of the carrion-crow, a snake's or alligator's tooth, pieces of egg-shell, and other nameless ingredients, compose the fatal mixture. The whole of these articles may not be considered as absolutely necessary to complete the charm, but two or three are at least indispensable. It will of course be conceived, that the practice of *obeah* can have little effect, unless a negro is conscious that it is practised upon him, or thinks so; for as the whole evil consists in the terrors of a superstitious imagination, it is of little consequence whether it be really practised or not, if he only imagines that it is. But if the *charm* fails to take hold of the mind of the proscribed person, another and more certain expedient is resorted to—the secretly administering of poison to him. This saves the reputation of the sorcerer, and effects the purpose he had in view.* An *obeah* man or woman (for it is practised by both sexes) is a very wicked and dangerous person on a plantation; and the practice of it is made felony by the law, punishable with death where poison has been administer-

---

* The negroes practising *obeah* are acquainted with some very powerful vegetable poisons, which they use on these occasions.

ed, and with transportation where only the charm is used. But numbers may be swept off by its infatuation before the crime is detected; for, strange as it may appear, so much do the negroes stand in awe of those *obeah* professors, so much do they dread their malice and their power, that, though knowing the havock they have made, and are still making, they are afraid to discover them to the whites; and others, perhaps, are in league with them for sinister purposes of mischief and revenge. A negro under this infatuation can only be cured of his terrors by being made a Christian: refuse him this boon, and he sinks a martyr to imagined evils. The author knew an instance of a negro, who, being reduced by the fatal influence of *obeah* to the lowest state of dejection and debility, from which there were little hopes of his recovery, was surprisingly and rapidly restored to health and cheerfulness by being baptized a Christian. A negro, in short, considers himself as no longer under the influence of this sorcery when he becomes a Christian.

But, though so liable to be perverted into a deadly instrument of malice and revenge, *obeah* —at least a species of it—may be said to have its uses. When placed in the gardens and grounds of the negroes, it becomes an excellent guard or watch, scaring away the predatory runaway and midnight plunderer with more effective terror than gins and spring-guns. It loses its power, however, when put to protect the gardens and plantain-walks of the *Buckras*. When an oath is taken by a negro, according to a certain *obeah* process, it binds by ties the most sacred. This ceremony is usually performed over a grave. The creoles, however, think it equally binding to swear on *Buckra book*—the Bible.

The negroes believe in apparitions, and stand in great dread of them, conceiving that they forebode death or some other great evil to those whom they visit; in short, that the spirits of the dead come upon earth to be revenged on those who did them evil when in life.

CHAP. XVII.

THE African negroes of the West Indies, whatever superstitious notions they may bring with them from their native country, agree in believing the existence of an omnipotent Being, who will reward or punish us in a future life for our good or evil actions in this. But their ideas in other respects are peculiar and fanciful. They think that, for some unexpiated guilt, or through some unaccountable folly of the primitive blacks, servitude was the unfortunate lot assigned to them, while dominion was given to the more favoured whites. Their superstitious reverence for certain animals, common in their own country, they retain in some degree. Some tribes are far more rational than others in their religious opinions. By intercourse with each other, and with the Europeans, the absurdity of many of their native superstitions is gradually laid aside—at least in practice. One opinion they all agree in, and that is the expectation that, after death, they shall first return to their native country, and enjoy again the society of kindred and friends, from whom they have been torn away in an evil hour. This idea, combined with their terrors, used to prompt numbers, on their first arrival, to acts of suicide. As an example to deter others from this crime, the head of the unhappy wretch who thus, from a delusive hope, laid violent hands on his life, used to be cut off and fixed on a pole by the side of some public road, a dismal and disgusting spectacle, while the body was sometimes consumed by fire. This, it was thought by some, would induce a belief in the survivors, that the body, thus annihilated, could not again be restored to life and liberty, as the wretched victims fondly imagined. This horrible practice has long since been discontinued. After a term of years, the Africans, however, become more reconciled to their new situation, particularly if they have the good fortune to fall into the hands of a humane master, and are industrious and get families; in which case they retain, as has been said, but little of their primitive superstition, and experience no wish to return, had they it even in their power, to their original wild life and savage state of precarious liberty. As to the creole slaves, they have no particular superstition which they have not adopted from their African forefathers, and that they have now in a great measure cast off.

Little heretofore has been done towards instructing the slaves in Christianity, and that little chiefly through the efforts of dissenting missionaries. Some of these were low ignorant men, who perhaps did more harm than good by their instructions, if they might be so called. Instead of inculcating the plain practical duties which Christianity enjoins, they expatiated on topics altogether incomprehensible by their ignorant auditors,—as the new birth, grace, election, and the utter inefficacy of mere good works to recommend them to the favour of the Almighty. These doctrines were too subtle for their understandings: they were told that they were in a perilous state, while the way by which alone they were instructed they could escape from it was so full of intricacy and mystery, that they became utterly perplexed, and gave up the pursuit in despair. In short, the negroes who attended these ignorant fanatic preachers, who would discuss doctrines which they themselves did not clearly understand, were only Christians by halves: they were reduced to a worse condition than that in which they were found, both with respect to mental comfort and a true sense of the proper duties of religion and morality.

They became, in consequence of the fanatical
cant of these pretended teachers, more hypocri-
tical, more cunning and cautious in their actions,
more regardful of outward appearances and ob-
servances of religion, without improvement of
its genuine duties—less cheerful and lively, full
of a fanatic gloom bordering on settled melancholy, and, in many respects, less attentive either
to the affairs of their families or the interest of
their owners. Like their instructors, they conceived, or affected to think, that canting, whining,
and psalm-singing, were more acceptable in the
sight of Heaven than honesty, sobriety, charity,
and forgiveness. The author knew a poor elderly
negro woman, who had always been remarkable
for cheerfulness, alacrity, and an animated attention to herself and her family, suddenly, from an
over-zealous attendance on a mulatto preacher,
sink into a gloomy listlessness and despondency :
she neglected herself, she neglected her family,
she would not even exert herself to provide for
the most obvious and urgent wants ; and when
reproved for it, the poor creature would reply,
with a piteous look and whining tone, " The
Lord would help his servant."

Among the different sects at present in this
island, perhaps the Moravians and Wesleyan
Methodists are the most useful, rational, and
unwearied instructors of the slaves. These are

a far superior order of men to the ignorant itinerant fanatics above described. Still even they, but especially the Methodists, however sincere and well-meaning in their endeavours, are not sufficiently simple and practical in their doctrines to be understood by their sable congregations. But surely it is better to have such instructors of the slaves than none. The more civilized and better instructed they are, the more capable they will become of appreciating benefits and making a good use of them. Duly instruct a negro, for example, in the nature and awful obligation of an oath, and you may with safety administer it to him as the test of his veracity; but leave him in ignorance, and he will treat it as a jest. Convince him that crimes will inevitably be punished in the next world, if they should escape punishment in this, and you have a stronger hold of him on the score of moral duty. Make his mind more capable of a sense of gratitude for what good you may render him, and he will labour more cheerfully in your service. Christianity would place the slave beyond the reach of *obeah* and other superstitions; and it would lessen polygamy, that impediment to population. As far as the author has observed, he must say, that the slaves who are Christians are generally more sober, steady, peaceable, and obedient, than those who are not. But it were useless to enlarge farther on so obvious a topic. Suffice it to say, that there is no man of information and liberal views, even in the West Indies, who does not acknowledge the humanity as well as good policy of rescuing the slaves from heathenism, ignorance, and superstition. The assembly of this island have given a pledge of the sincerity of their opinions on this subject in the very liberal provision they have made for the lately appointed curates. But of what use are wise and salutary laws, if the petty interests and prejudices of individuals are suffered to interpose so as to render them abortive?

It will be worth while to take a view of the progress which has been made in the religious instruction of the slaves in this island, and what remains yet to be done therein.

Not many years ago it was the prevailing opinion here that it was highly preposterous to think of instructing the slaves in Christianity— that they were too stupid and barbarous, and too much attached to their own superstitions and opinions, to be effectually so instructed—that if it were even possible so to instruct them, it would answer no good end, for that it would tend to produce among them ideas and opinions unfavourable to the dominion of their masters, would unnerve and unfit them for their labours, occupy too much of their time, and ultimately render them sullen, disaffected, and even seditious. These were alarming anticipations; that they were well-founded is questionable. One would suppose that the excellence of the Christian precepts was calculated to produce very different effects, and every liberal-minded man in the island was doubtless of that opinion. But interest and prejudice dictated this repugnance to what was at the time deemed an injurious and unnecessary innovation.

At that period the very name of Methodist or other sectarian missionary created suspicion, hostility, and alarm. His motions were strictly watched, he was opposed, abused, and insulted. He was viewed as a dangerous intruder, and even incendiary, who had come, under pretence of instructing the slaves, to poison their minds with notions hurtful to themselves and injurious to their masters. There were, however, a few individuals who entertained different ideas on the subject—who thought that the religious instruction of their slaves an object of some importance, and a duty they owed to them, and who, finding that little could be expected from the exertions of the regular clergy, encouraged and employed Moravian and other missionaries to impart that instruction to them. A hue and cry was raised against this novel and very unpopular conduct, and the slaves in the neighbourhood were interdicted by their masters, under threats of punishment, from attending the preachings of those missionaries.

These prejudices at length began to wear away, and at the present day few openly avow them. Still, however, the missionaries are restrained from going on the estates to preach, without the express permission of the proprietors or attorneys—a favour which very few are disposed to grant, though the attendance of she slaves on the preachings is not now considered as a matter of serious consequence, and the magistrates in most of the towns readily grant a license, *to preach and teach,* to such missionaries, of decent and peaceable character, as apply for it. The corporation of Kingston were, however, extremely tenacious on this subject; it was only to a few that they would grant a license ; and they have interdicted the preaching without it, under severe penalties. It may indeed with some reason be alleged, that the granting an indiscriminate permission to missionaries of all characters and descriptions to hold meetings in such a populous city as Kingston would be only multiplying resorts to idle and disorderly negroes, and thus endangering the peace and security of the inhabitants. There was, however, a spirit of hostility in this city, some years ago, to one sect in particular, the Methodists, arising in a great measure from an absurd opinion that the missionaries of this sect were a dangerous class of persons, from their supposed connexion with the African Institution, or some of its active leaders, by whom it was suspected they were tutored to no good purpose. That this opinion was quite unfounded, and that the views of the missionaries were purely of a religious nature, individuals among them offered to adduce irrefragable proofs. But this would not satisfy the minds or allay the suspicions of some of the rulers of Kingston. How far this intolerant spirit was worthy of a respectable and opulent city like Kingston, or in unison with the liberal ideas of the times, the reader is left to judge. One thing is certain, that in a country where nine-tenths of the people are in a state of utter ignorance of all religion, the gratuitous labours of any sect of Christians should at least be tolerated until it appears that they are productive of public mischief. The corporation of Kingston have for some years past acted with a far more tolerant spirit; Methodist missionaries, as well as others, are now licensed to preach in the city.

When it came to be pretty generally acknowledged—at least tacitly—by all classes of persons in Jamaica, that the religious instruction of the slaves would confer an important benefit on them, the question arose, how this was to be effected. Heretofore little had been done in that work by the established clergy. It is true, a law existed, enjoining the rectors to set apart a certain portion of each Sunday to instruct such slaves as might attend for that purpose. But this law was well known to be, with a few exceptions, little better than a dead letter. A few slaves were annually baptized in the different parishes; but the mere ceremony of baptism was of little use without the necessary ground-work of instruction. It was not to be expected that the rectors would go out of their way to promote any extra duty of their calling; at least few of them had given any proofs of a disposition to devote any part of their leisure time to the instruction of their heathen parishioners.*

In this state of matters, an act was passed by the legislature (in 1818) for the appointment of twenty-one curates (one for each parish), for the express purpose of imparting religious instruction to the slaves. On the passing of this bill in the house of assembly, an intelligent and independent member somewhat prophetically observed, that " he conceived that the duties of the curate were

---

* One gentleman, the Rev. Mr Trew, shewed, as has been mentioned in a former chapter, a highly praiseworthy example of zeal and diligence in his pastoral office, which it would have been well if his brethren had followed.

not clearly defined: he may dwindle into the
mere assistant of the rector, and the country may
be put to the expense of £10,500 per annum, to
relieve incumbents who are the least active in
the observance of their spiritual duties. We well
know the object of the legislature, and that it is
expected from the curates that a sense of duty
to their sacred calling will supersede the necessity
of positive enactments. We hope it may be so;
we hope to see the reproach of indifference to
the eternal welfare of the greater part of their
flocks no longer attach to the established clergy.
We shall be most happy to see the new pastors
toiling in their vocation among the class that
most requires instruction: to the rector they
must leave the affluent; the condition of their
appointment is to preach to the unconnected
multitude, and to be seen in the cabin rather
than in the church. When Jesus washed his
disciples' feet, he said, ' I have given you as an
example, that you should do as I have done to
you.'—' The servant is not greater than his Lord;
neither he that is sent greater than he that sent
him.' "

By this act, the salaries of the curates were
fixed at £300 currency ; but this being deemed
an insufficient stipend, it was subsequently augmented to £500. They had also the prospect
of being promoted in time to vacant rectories.

Thus were they placed in a situation far more encouraging than that of many of their brethren in England, who, after half a life of laborious exertion in their callings, have neither so comfortable a livelihood nor such animating prospects,—and easy and independent compared with the condition of the dissenting missionary. The Moravian is supported, miserably enough at the best, by the fortuitous fruits of his labour, or eleemosynary donations of those who employ him; for from the impoverished funds of his brethren he can expect to draw little or nothing. The Wesleyan missionary is in the receipt of just £45 currency, together with an allowance of £2 per week for board and lodging—in all £149 currency,—a sum hardly sufficient to support him with as much comfort, in Jamaica, as a third part of the amount would in England. Yet these men manage to get through their laborious duties with a zeal, diligence, and fidelity worthy of a better reward: they must imitate the patience and self-denial of the first followers of their heavenly Master, and be content at times to satisfy their hunger with the humble crust, and slake their thirst with the water of the brook.

What then has been done by this newly-established order of clergy in Jamaica, in return for the generous encouragement of the legislature? Little more than, as was predicted, to assist the rectors in the performance of those duties which they were well able to discharge without such assistance. The curates have in fact been publicly accused of utter neglect and inefficiency in their offices, as far as regards the duties for which they were expressly appointed by the legislature. It is but fair, however, to state what has been said in exculpation of them, which, if true, shifts much of the blame from them, and fixes it elsewhere. A writer in one of the public prints of this island (1820) complained that " the curates had done nothing in the way of their calling, except saving the rectors the trouble of performing the whole of *their proper and exclusive duties,*—in other words, doing that which *is not,* and neglecting to do that which *is,* expressly required of them by the legislature, namely, visiting the plantations, at stated times, for the purpose of baptizing and instructing the slaves in the Christian faith,—*provided,* however, it is with the consent of their owners." In reply to this charge, another writer (supposed to be a clergyman) says, " Has he" (the first-named writer) " allowed the curate of his parish an opportunity of discharging the functions of his office towards his negro servants, agreeably to the tenor of the act on which he lays so much stress? If not, he has no reason to complain of neglect. If he has, *he is almost a solitary instance;* as, to my knowledge, some curates have applied to many proprietors, trustees, and managers of properties, expressing not only their willingness, but their desire to be called upon to discharge the active duties of their office in the instruction of the ignorant slaves, *but in no single instance have their services been accepted;* and surely it cannot be expected that any man, who has a proper regard for himself, would intrude on the property of another, though for the most praiseworthy purposes, with the apprehension in view of being turned off it."

The allegation thus publicly brought forward by this apologist has not been satisfactorily replied to; and we must therefore conclude that there is a general disinclination on the part of the planters to have their slaves instructed in Christianity. There are, it is true, some enlightened men who have different ideas and feelings on this important subject; but their number is too small to be productive of any good beyond the boundary lines of their respective properties. What then is to be done? Either a positive law must be enacted, obliging proprietors and others to have their slaves baptized and instructed, or those slaves must be abandoned to the probability of indefinitely remaining in their present

state of intellectual barbarism; and while they
so remain, little more can be attempted towards
still further improving their condition; a progressive improvement in their moral and in their
political condition must go hand in hand.*

The author cannot better conclude this chapter
than by quoting the very praiseworthy circular
address of the Rev. Mr Trew to his parishioners,
while rector of Manchester.

" At a period when the Gospel-light seems to
dawn with increasing glory upon the heathen
world, and the minds of men are better fitted
for receiving those truths which it unfolds, I
trust that, while I address you upon a subject of
much importance, you will be more ready to ap-
prove than condemn the motives which impel
me to solicit your attention. Sensible, however,
that in making the instruction of your slaves the
subject of a circular communication, I may be
thought to deviate from the regular course of
my professional duty, I shall, in the first place,
state my reasons for thus publicly addressing
you. By the late act of assembly, which so
strongly recommends the instruction of the slave
population by the ministers of the established

---

* Since the author quitted the island (in 1821), it appears
that, in a few of the parishes, the work of instruction has made
some progress.

church, a duty is hereby imposed upon the clergy of earnestly calling upon their parishioners for their co-operation in carrying into effect the salutary measures which the act proposes, a duty, also, which I feel the more impelled to perform, from a firm conviction of its beneficial tendency. The variety of opinion which has of late prevailed will, I hope, warrant the length of my address, while I endeavour to impress upon your mind, not only the practicability, but also the necessity, of this undertaking, which must, in the opinion of every reflecting man, be productive of the greatest good, and tend to dispel that mist of heathenism which lowers throughout the land. Formed, as you have been, into a new district, and denied hitherto the benefits arising from the public institutions of religion, the field before me appears no less extensive than interesting; and while I am instigated to the discharge of my duty, by disseminating more widely the word and spirit of the Gospel, to you I naturally look up as the blessed patron, under whose auspices I may be permitted to convey the benefits of redemption to that portion of slaves committed to your care—to that portion of God's creatures over whom you have received the most absolute authority, and for whose wellbeing you will be strictly called to account hereafter. Would the majority of planters consider the importance of that situation in which they are placed, and the responsibility incumbent upon them to provide for the spiritual as well as the temporal necessities of their slaves, they would make it the subject not only of their earnest but frequent contemplations. They would consider them as their fellow-creatures, partaking of the same nature, liable to the same passions, the same infirmities, and, consequently, to the same fate. They would consider them as talents, the due account of which will hereafter be required, whilst, with the ready hand of Christian charity, they would relieve their spiritual necessities, and turn the hearts of the disobedient to the wisdom of the just. But, sir, in thus presuming to address you, I appeal not to your liberality as a man, but to your charity as a Christian. Strange it is that the received opinion of the present day should prove so detrimental to an object, which embraces alike the spiritual comfort of the slave, with the security of the master,—conducive, at the same time, to the happiness of the one, and the eternal interests of the other. Let us candidly inquire what those tenets are which the Gospel so strongly inculcates : doubtless, amongst others, humility, obedience, and submission to every ordinance of man, for the Lord's sake.

" Experience tells us, that instruction, so far

from rendering the slave insolent or disobedient, fits him, on the contrary, by a sense of that duty which religion impresses, for his daily toil, and enables him to bear the load of life with patience, —qualifies him for a more pure and intimate union with his God, and teaches him to regard his fellow-labourers around him as children of the same parent, and sheep of the same sheep-fold. From the works of creation he learns to adore the wisdom and power of the Almighty, while from his providence he is taught to fear that retributive justice, which stays the fiercer passions of his soul, and tells him that there is a God above, who regardeth the meanest of his creatures, and who will not so much inquire *what part* they have acted in this life, as *how* they have acted the part assigned them. An acquaintance with his laws will also lead to an obedience to his will, while his daily task will be lightened by this cheering reflection, that his obedience and fidelity on earth will be rewarded in heaven by a life of glory, which shall be interminable.

" Such, sir, are the views which this subject holds out, and how far they accord with the language of truth let conscience testify. That it will be objected by some that instruction will raise the slave above the level of his station, and render him less satisfied with his condition, I am well aware. Let us however look to other countries where the light of the Gospel hath shone with undivided lustre; let us turn our eyes to every portion of the habitable globe, from the dreary regions of the north, even to the western hemisphere which we inhabit; let us search the historian's instructive page; and never will we find that the pure religion of the holy Jesus, which proclaims '*peace on earth, and good will towards men,*' hath been subversive of those ends which lead to social order and good government. Of late years fanatics have instilled a deadly poison into the minds of men : to guard against an evil so baneful in its consequences, be it your peculiar care. Since then other countries have assisted in that glorious work, the conversion of the heathen to Christianity, surely it is a duty becoming you also to follow an example which has for its object the instruction of your slaves, through that safest of all channels, the ministers of the established church. I therefore, sir, address myself to you in behalf of the negro and other slaves under your authority, and I implore you, as their guide, to whom they look up for every temporal enjoyment, that you withhold not from them the benefits of religious instruction. I shall be ready to attend them upon your own property at such seasons as shall be best suited for your and their convenience; and I trust that you will devote at least a part of one week-day in every month for the purposes of their improvement in the fundamental truths of our holy religion. In saying, however, thus much, I shall be happy to attend to any other plan which you may suggest, or which you may deem better calculated to promote this salutary measure with regard to the slaves under your immediate care; and, as a still farther call upon your most serious consideration, I shall conclude this letter in the words of that learned and pious prelate, the late Dr Porteous, as expressed in his letter to the governors and proprietors of plantations in the British West India islands."

The following extract from the letter here mentioned is an impressive appeal. " But you must allow me, gentlemen, to add, that I by no means rest this great question" (the instruction of the slaves in the Christian religion) "on the grounds either of public utility, but on much higher and nobler principles,—on the principles of justice, of humanity, of religion, of duty,—by which most sacred ties you are bound, as men and Christians, to take care of the souls, as well as of the bodies, of that numerous race of men over whom you have obtained the most absolute dominion. They are

ave made yourselves responsible for theme made yourselves responsible for themtty ; their welfare
is placed exclusively in your hands ; their happi-
ness or misery depends absolutely upon your
care of them ; and, by taking possession of them,
you have made yourselves responsible for them
both here and hereafter."

CHAP. XVIII.

IT is not a little remarkable, that some of the
diseases to which the white people in this island
are subject, seldom or never affect the negroes;
while the former are totally exempt from the
disorders peculiar to the negroes, unless communicated by infection. But there are diseases,
also, which are common to both, as pulmonary
complaints, liver disease, bowel disorders, dropsy,
common intermittent fever, &c. That dreadful
scourge of the whites, malignant epidemic fever,
does not, as has been said, attack the negroes :
while raging with the greatest violence among
the former, the latter may be perfectly healthy.
Consumptions are very rare among them, nor
are they subject to gout, and some other chronic
disorders known to the Europeans. They are,
however, liable to rheumatic affections, and to a
disorder of the bones, which seems peculiar to
them, appearing in round swellings about the
joints. They are also more frequently subject

to obstructions and inflammations of the bowels than the whites.

The small-pox and the measles seem not to be common diseases of that part of Africa inhabited by most of the tribes who have been brought hither, neither are some other diseases to which they are subject in the West Indies. But there are diseases, peculiar to the Africans, of a more terrible nature. One of these is called by the slaves *cocobay*, a distemper the most horrible in its nature, and the more so as it is utterly incurable: it is peculiarly infectious among the slaves, but the whites are not liable to catch it except by cohabitation.* There is no doubt of its being a hereditary disease, as whole families are usually infected with it. The unhappy patient infected with it becomes soon changed in appearance, different parts of his body swell, he is covered with a leprous scurf, he sinks into deep dejection, he loathes his food, and yet his miserable existence is prolonged for years. When a slave is infected with this loathsome disorder, he is re-

---

* One instance only of a white man's being infected with this distemper comes within the author's recollection. This unhappy man caught it from a negress who was secretly infected with it. After lingering for six or seven years an object of misery and dejection, he was at length relieved by the welcome hand of death.

moved, on the first appearance of the symptoms, to some sequestered spot, where a hut is built for him, and the rest of the slaves are interdicted from all intercourse with him. Some are of opinion that this distemper is the leprosy, and there is certainly some foundation for the supposition. No instance ever was known of a negro recovering from it; indeed the medical men do not attempt a cure, conceiving all attempts to extirpate it as ineffectual.

Another loathsome disease among the negroes is the *yaws :* this, however, is curable in six or eight months, with proper care and attention. Alterative medicines, cleanliness, and nourishing diet, are the means resorted to for effecting a cure. But if a white man is infected with this disease, he does not so easily recover, and some have fallen victims to it : it is too severe and dreadful a trial for him to endure. Patients afflicted with it are usually covered over with loathsome and painful ulcers.

Both the above diseases are of African origin. Since the abolition of the slave-trade, they have become less common; indeed on some plantations they are altogether unknown; and it is probable that in a few years they will totally disappear. There is no doubt that negro mothers wilfully infected their children with *yaws*, that they might be released for a time from labour, and were thus instrumental in perpetuating the disease; but the introduction of a milder system will obviate the temptation to so unnatural an act, and all classes of the slaves will come at last to dread and abhor this disease so much as to take every precaution against infection.

Another disorder common to the slaves is the *elephantiasis;* it consists in a very great and indurated swelling of the feet and legs, which continues and is seldom cured: negroes affected by it are rendered unfit for much labour. This disease is frequently brought on by *chigoes.* These are very small insects, almost indeed invisible, which, burying themselves in the fleshy parts of the feet, soon increase in size, and deposite, if suffered to remain in their usurped abode, a numerous progeny; these spread into other parts; and this annoyance, though not a disease in itself, soon becomes the parent of diseases, such as inveterate ulcers, *elephantiasis*, &c. Nothing more however is necessary to guard against this mischief than cleanliness, and taking care to extract these intruders as soon as possible. But so indolent and negligent are some of the slaves in this respect, that they will sometimes suffer these insects to remain till they have ate away the flesh from their toes, and brought, as frequently happens, incurable lameness on them. The entrance of this animal into the flesh is easily perceptible by a sharp pain, resembling the puncture of a fine needle, and its subsequent presence is known by an incessant and troublesome itching around the part. Either the negroes are not so susceptible of this sensation as the whites, or it is not so unpleasant to them.

One of the most curious diseases to which the Africans are subject, is the *Guinea-worm*, as it is called, being a worm of great length, which breeds in the flesh, commonly the leg: few or none of the creole negroes are attacked with this disease. Hernia and hydrocele are very common among the negroes. It is remarkable that the Barbadians are peculiarly subject to the former of these affections, the cause of which the author has never heard satisfactorily explained.

The disorders that are most fatal among the slaves are pleurisies and other affections of the lungs, inflammations of the bowels, dysenteries, and influenza. The dysentery and influenza rage at times over whole districts. The author has known the tenth part of the population of some estates carried off by the latter disease, while few escaped considerable loss. It was attended with a violent cough, and hot consuming fever; in two days the patient was reduced to a state of the most helpless debility, and, unless a favourable turn took place, he seldom survived beyond that time. In the rapidity of its progress it resembled the yellow, or malignant bilious fever among the whites : but as the negroes are exempt from the attacks of this latter disorder, so are the whites not at all liable to influenza during its prevalence among the negroes.

The appearance of dysentery among the slaves is most to be apprehended in August, when the new yams are begun to be got in, and the avagata pear (a favourite article in the meals of the negroes) still remains too green for use, but which they will yet eat. This is a contagious disease, and frequently very fatal. Rhubarb is commonly administered in it; but small dozes of castor oil, frequently repeated, and, as a nourishment, Indian arrow-root pap, mixed with a little port wine, given in the intervals, are considered as the most sovereign remedies.

The negro children are subject to a variety of disorders, some of which are of a fatal tendency. The most formidable of these is locked-jaw. Grown negroes are also sometimes seized with this terrible affection, and suddenly expire under it, unless relief be soon given : the jaw-bones become fixed in their sockets, the upper and lower teeth adhere closely and strongly to each other, so that even a pin can hardly at times be introduced between them, and the silent and wild looks of the afflicted patient show the agony he endures and the danger he is in. This dreadful affection sometimes seizes infants without any apparent cause, but it is more frequently the concomitant of some other disorder. Numbers of the negro children die of it; but it seldom visits a white child. The other fatal disorders to which the negro infants are liable, are sore throats, hooping-coughs, convulsion fits, &c. The hooping-cough is an epidemic complaint among the children here, and frequently carries off great numbers: both white and negro children are liable to it, but chiefly the latter. Sore throats are however most fatal to the white children; but liver complaints, by which they are often dangerously attacked, do not often seize the negro children—as if the bodily system, as well as habits of the two races, were of an opposite nature.

The most peculiar disease to which the negroes are subject is *mal de stomach*, being a strong and irresistible craving of the stomach for earth. Earth-eaters are common upon almost every plantation. This strange propensity, or craving, is as common among the children as among the grown negroes. If this practice originates in a diseased stomach, as it no doubt does, it must of course be in a great measure involuntary, and the harsh means which are often used to reclaim the negroes from it are doubtless improper and barbarous. The true remedy would be found in mild treatment, and a plentiful supply of wholesome and nourishing food; these, and a necessary restraint, would answer every purpose. Many of the whites, and some even of the negroes themselves, are of a different opinion; they treat this wretched craving, not as a disease, but as a *crime*. When a negro mother discovers her child indulging this strange appetite, she has recourse to correction; she storms, threatens, and chastises by turns, and it would be in vain to persuade her that this unfortunate appetite is the inevitable effect of disease. The effects which it produces on the system, are nausea, bloated swellings over the body, a corruption of the whole mass of the blood, shortness of breath, reachings, &c. These, if the practice be not discontinued, reduce the infatuated negro to the lowest state of debility, and must inevitably end in death. In general this diseased appetite proceeds from an insufficiency of wholesome and nourishing food : it is commonly the poorer class of negroes who are subject to it. When of long standing it becomes very obstinate and difficult to be cured.

Formerly there was a regular natural decrease of the slaves, in this island, which was deemed unavoidable, and therefore only to be supplied by importation from Africa. This delusion has now vanished, as, at the present day, on every well-regulated plantation, where the slaves are humanely treated and duly taken care of, there is generally an increase. Still on the whole the increase is inconsiderable. This is owing to various causes. The numerous and fatal disorders to which the negro children are liable have justly been assigned as one cause. Another which has been given, is the state of polygamy in which the negroes live. This, doubtless, is a very obvious cause. To enter into a discussion of the question, why polygamy should thus operate, were superfluous; it is sufficient that experience shows that it is inimical to population. But the question is, how is it to be remedied among the negroes? The negro, who does not profess himself a Christian, smiles at the idea of confining himself to one female, when his circumstances enable him, and his passions and taste for variety instigate him to have half-a-dozen. He would consider a restraint in this respect, so hostile to his habits and the practice of his forefathers, as the most arbitrary of all proceedings, and it would require a thousand Arguses to watch and circumvent him in these illicit indulgences. Such as are baptized as Christians are more scrupulous; some of these have a form of marriage, and seem to lay aside all thoughts of other women than the one to whom they are thus united. But in general this is little better than form. Imbued as they are with strong passions, and witnessing as they do the licentiousness of their more enlightened rulers, it is not likely that the slaves will relinquish the pleasures or resist the temptations of an unrestrained sexual intercourse. Were they, however, duly instructed in the Christian religion, there can be no doubt that it would at least give a check to polygamy among them, if it did not altogether do away with it.

The mortality among the grown negroes may be ascribed to various causes ;—to intemperance and irregularity, night exposure, violent exercise at their *plays*, sudden transitions of the weather, and, at particular seasons, disorders brought on by green roots, unripe fruits, &c. The lives of a proportion of the slaves, who belong to or are under the care of improvident or unfeeling persons, are no doubt shortened by an insufficiency of wholesome food : on all or most of the plantations there is a proportion of the slaves so indolent, improvident, and careless, that they would literally starve were they not regularly and duly fed by their masters; while the more active and industrious amply provide for themselves and their families out of their grounds, their small stock, &c. As to the labour they are made to perform on most of the estates, it is seldom more than they can go through, with ease and without injury to their health. The health of the slaves upon a plantation or settlement depends much upon the situation of the place: their houses should be built in dry airy situations, and they generally are so situated; but on the mountain estates and other properties, they are liable, in spite of every precaution, to severe colds, and various complaints originating in these, in consequence of the heavy and frequent rains, which in those parts prevail to a much greater degree than in the low country.

Much of the decrease of the slaves which formerly took place was owing to a want of care for the breeding women, and an inattention to the rearing of the children. The former were made to labour at improper times, and were frequently treated with a harshness unsuited to their situation; and the children were in a great measure left to the care and management of the parents, who in fact had not time, if they had inclination and prudence, to take proper care of them. The case is at present very different. On every well-regulated plantation there are now lying-in houses, and rearing houses, each with their necessary attendants; the women are treated with every proper indulgence, and have every comfort and assistance which their situation

requires ; * and the children, when weaned, are
placed in the rearing hospital, where they are
kept and carefully attended to until old enough
to be useful to their parents. It were to be
wished that these humane and judicious regulations were universal throughout the island; but
that is not the case. The hospitals for the sick,
with some exceptions, are not yet so assiduously
attended to as could be wished ; nor will they
be so attended, until the plantation practice is
so apportioned among the medical attendants
as that each hospital should be visited at least
once a-day. As it is, there are some properties
on which the medical attendant does not come
above once or twice a-week to visit patients. A
more frequent attendance were necessary if only
to see 'that the prescriptions were duly attended to.

The negroes are acquainted with the use of
many simples for the cure of certain disorders—
as yaws, ulcers, bone-ache, &c. ; and the care and
management of negroes afflicted with these disorders is generally confided to an elderly negro
woman who professes a knowledge of this branch
of physic.

---

* By the law, a female slave is released from hard labour
after having given birth to and reared six children.

CHAP. XIX.

THE original Maroons were, as has been said, fugitive slaves who had absconded from the first English settlers, and joined a body of slaves belonging to the Spaniards, who, at the time of the expulsion of their masters, fled into the woods and refused to surrender themselves. Their subsequent history has already been detailed. Nothing therefore remains but to give some account of their character, customs, and mode of life.

After their treaty with the whites, in 1739, they built towns for themselves on the lands assigned to them. The principal of these, as containing the greatest number of inhabitants, and the chief leaders of the Maroons, was Trelawny Town, in the parish of Trelawny, situated in the mountains, and about equidistant from Montego Bay and Falmouth.

They led a wild and roving sort of life. The women were chiefly employed in cultivating the grounds, and attending to the wants of their families; while the men were exploring the woods for runaway slaves, hunting the wild hog, or shooting the ringtail. Their arms were a light fusee and powder-horn, a *machette* or short sabre, and sometimes a lance made of the hardest wood ; and, in war, a horn, by its various modulations, directed their movements. With these the Maroon climbed, with the nimbleness and celerity of the roebuck, the precipitous rocks and rugged mountains, while traversing them in quest of his prey. He patiently explored the deepest retreats of the forest, lived in them for whole weeks, found everywhere abundance of materials wherewith to erect his hut, or kindle a fire to dress his game; and, if unsuccessful in procuring it, he could easily subsist on the mountain-cabbage, while he assuaged his thirst with the water from the wild pine,* the *water-withe*, or the excavations of the rocks, should no rivulet be near. He was wonderfully adroit in the management of his fusee ; he could load and fire with celerity in almost any position, and his aim was unerring. Out of a party of ten regular soldiers who were cut off by an ambuscade of the Maroons, six were shot through the head.

It is no wonder, therefore, that in the contest between these people and the whites, they should avail themselves, so fatally to the latter, of those advantages and qualifications ; nor can there be

---

* Tillandsia maxima.

a doubt that the terror of the Spanish dogs alone operated, as has been said, more powerfully to induce them to surrender, than all the troops and military talent in the country. Not that there was a deficiency of either; but what could a body of gallant troops, headed by the bravest and most skilful officers, do against an enemy who was invisible to them,—who, lurking behind rocks and trees, were so placed as to be unassailable, while they enfiladed the narrow and rugged defiles through which the former were obliged to pass?

It would be painful to dwell on the shocking barbarities exercised on the unfortunate white men who fell, in those encounters, alive into the hands of this savage enemy, who gloried in such opportunities of glutting their blood-thirsty vengeance. Many of the fugitive slaves who accompanied the Maroons were eye-witnesses of these atrocious barbarities. There is something inconceivably appalling, even to the bravest heart, in the dread of such a fate; and the general sentiment among the troops employed in this rebellion was, *If we are wounded and cannot be carried off, put us to death, rather than let us fall alive into the hands of the savages.*

The Maroons, however successful they were in their surprises, skirmishes, and ambuscades, were certainly deficient in one of the first qua-

lities of a soldier—courage. Confident of their
security in their fastnesses and retreats, the
marches and movements of the whites gave
them little concern as to their safety ; yet in the
open field they were perfectly aware that they
were no match for the regulars and militia, nor
was their mode of warfare at all calculated for
an open and champaign country. While they
remained in the vicinity of their town, which, as
a preliminary to war, they burnt, some shells
were thrown, during the night, from the post
there into the surrounding woods, in order to
scour them and prevent night surprises. These,
blazing through the darkness, terrified and
amazed them for a while ; but at length, keeping a little beyond their reach, they were wont
to gaze on them merely as an amusing spectacle.
The brigands of St Domingo have often openly
skirmished with the European troops, and have
indeed at times fought pretty obstinately, and
even come to the charge of the bayonet: they
were partly trained to European tactics, and
were supplied with artillery, to the use of which
they were by no means novices.—The Maroons
neither knew, nor desired to know, any thing of
artillery or the bayonet.

At the outset of this contest there was too
much of the " pomp and circumstance of war."
The troops marched in their proper regimentals,

as if they were going to fight a regular and civilized enemy, and sometimes had even the absurdity to traverse the mountainous roads with drums beating. Nothing could be more ill-judged in such a contest, nor more subservient to the views of their savage and artful foe. The sound of these instruments could answer no other end than to warn the Maroons to *keep out of the way*, or to throw themselves into a convenient ambush, from whence they could cut off their assailants, without danger of annoyance to themselves. The customary accoutrements were too clumsy and burdensome for traversing the woods and clambering over the rocks, and the red coats were too conspicuous an object to the Maroon marksmen, who seldom missed their aim. These encumbrances were at length felt and laid aside; light-green or blue jackets and trowsers were adopted, and, instead of cross belts, &c. a light cartouch-box round the middle, without a bayonet, this instrument being useless here. This, and a fusee and canteen, formed the military equipment of the militia; and the dress of the regulars was also considerably lightened. Baggage negroes followed in the rear of the detachments, carrying provisions, &c. for the troops; and thus they traversed the deepest woods, crossed over mountains, clambered up high, rugged, and precipitous rocks, or defiled along glades impervious to the rays of the sun, or through ravines darkened by impending woods. Here they were often encountered by the Maroons, who hardly ever were seen, nor could the troops know where to direct their fire, except by the flashes of their adversaries' pieces. On these occasions the regular soldiers were less adroit than the militia: having never been trained to this sort of bush-fighting, they disdained for a time to have recourse to rocks and trees as a shield against their enemies' fire, accounting it base and unmanly in a soldier thus to shrink from danger; nor was it till they had repeatedly experienced the fatal effects of their temerity that they overcame this prejudice, and reluctantly consented to put themselves on a footing with their savage enemy, by availing themselves of these natural entrenchments.

A considerable number of the whites were killed in this contest, while it was never positively ascertained that any Maroons had been slain in action; though it is probable some had fallen, from the recent graves which had been discovered in their retreats.* So superior were

---

* A few negroes were killed in some of the skirmishes with the Maroons; but it afterwards appeared that they were runaway slaves, the Maroons prudently giving them the post of honour on all occasions.

the Maroons, by their agility, their hardihood, and knowledge of the woods, in this species of warfare, that if their courage had been equal to these, the whites would have been still less able to cope with them, and many more would have perished in the unequal conflict. But they carried their caution and their fears, luckily for the whites, to an unnecessary extreme, only venturing on an attack when they were certain they could make it with impunity. They generally procured intelligence of the motions of the whites from the fugitive slaves, who were employed by them in getting this information from the other slaves. They once received notice that a considerable quantity of provisions, &c. was to pass forward to one of the posts occupied by the whites, on a certain day, under the escort of a party of regulars, commanded by a sergeant. They sent a party to waylay this escort. On receiving the first volley from the Maroons, which killed the half of the soldiers, the sergeant drew up the remainder, and told them to stand *openly and manfully* and fight these cowardly miscreants : they did so, and not one of them escaped. The provisions, &c. carried by slaves, fell into the hands of the assailants.

During this contest, only one instance occurred of mercy having been shown to a white man who had fallen into the hands of the Ma-

roons. This man had led a solitary life in the
midst of the woods, and was actually ignorant
that the Maroons were in rebellion against the
whites. He had at one time resided among
them, and was useful to them in a medical capacity, having been bred as a surgeon. The leader
of this party had become a Christian, and had
retired from the other Maroons to live with his
family on a small retired spot which he had cultivated, and on which he had erected a small
dwelling. On coming up to the white man's
house, he restrained his banditti from putting
him to death,* which some of them were about
to do. "No," said he, "we must not kill this
poor Buckra; him never do we harm, but him
sometimes do we good when he been live with
we." Then addressing himself to the astonished
and trembling white man, he said, "No be
afraid, we won't hurt you, we won't burn your
house; but give we key, we want what you

---

* Another Maroon leader, whose name was Parkinson, wished
to spare the life of a white settler who had fallen into his hands,
in return for some hospitality he had received from him; but,
through the persuasions of a woman who was his mistress, his
savage heart was turned from its purpose, and he shot the unfortunate white man while in the act of supplicating mercy.
This woman had formerly been the mistress of the white man,
and acted thus in revenge for some slight or contemptuous usage
she had received from him.

have in your house to eat and drink. When we
gone, no stay here; go to Buckra, and tell them
say, Johnston" (this was the Maroon's name)
" no been want for trouble them—him been
want for keep himself to himself; but Buckra
come and burn him house—them *root out him
ground*—them say they want for kill me—my
wife and *pickininnie* no have house, no have
victual. Well, so long as Buckra trouble me
first, I will show them something too." This
Maroon did not want generous and grateful
feelings, though now bent on deadly purposes
of revenge. A party of militia had destroyed
his property prior to his joining his rebellious
brethren, and this unprovoked aggression instigated him to take up arms and assume a command in the war against the whites. He became one of the most formidable and daring
leaders of the rebels, taking a dreadful revenge
for the outrage he had suffered. It must indeed
be confessed, that the white parties sometimes
committed acts, during this rebellion, which
could answer no other end than to exasperate
the Maroons, and render them more desperate
and blood-thirsty. On taking possession of the
forsaken haunts of the rebels, it would have
been well had they always stopped at burning
the huts and destroying the provisions; but instances occurred of their opening the graves,

and cutting off the heads from the putrid carcasses of the Maroons who had been there interred. What were the survivors to think of this, but that those who could thus extend their hatred to the dead would wreak a horrible vengeance on the living, if they had them in their power?

The Maroons that now remain in the island amount to about 1200. In 1810 the number was as follows :—Accompong Town 238; Moore Town 348; Charlestown 256 ; Scotshall 51 : total 893. In 1816 there were in Accompong Town 286; in Moore Town 393; in Charlestown 306; in Scotshall 70: total 1055: being an increase of 162. Though neither of these tribes were engaged in the rebellion of the Trelawny Town Maroons, it was thought prudent to take their fire-arms from them. They are in general peaceable in their conduct, less ferocious than the Trelawny Town Maroons, and ready to assist the whites, when paid for their trouble, in taking up the hordes of runaway slaves who collect in the woods. In 1820, a numerous and formidable body of those runaways was taken up and dispersed, with their assistance, in the Healthshire Hills. This horde became a focus for all discontented slaves, and had increased to such a degree as to be alarming to the neighbourhood. On a representation being made to the governor on the subject, he ordered an armed force, consisting partly of Maroons, to be sent against the fugitives: the Maroons, from their superior activity and knowledge of the woods, were of very essential service on the occasion. The runaways were completely surrounded, and most of them taken, with but very little bloodshed on either side.

CHAP. XX.

THE PEOPLE OF COLOUR—THEIR CHARACTER, MANNERS, AND AMUSEMENTS—THEIR POLITICAL SITUATION.

BETWEEN the whites and the blacks, in the West Indies, a numerous race has sprung up, which goes by the general appellation of *people of colour*. These are subdivided into mulattoes, the offspring of a white and a black; samboes, the offspring of a black and a mulatto; quadroons, the offspring of a white and a mulatto; and mestees, the offspring of a white and a quadroon. Below this last-mentioned grade the distinction of colour is hardly perceptible; and those who are thus far removed from the original negro stock are considered in law as whites, on obtaining their manumission if born slaves, and competent of course to enjoy every privilege as such. Between these particular *castes* an endless variety of non-descript shades exist, descending from the deep jet to the faintest tinge of the olive, by gradations which it would be difficult to trace and designate.

The people of colour may be supposed to possess the mingled natures of the two original stocks from whence they spring; and the more or less they are removed from one or the other, they seem to be imbued in proportion with their particular qualities. The sambo differs little in manners, habits, &c. from the negro; while the mestee and his descendants approximate as near in these particulars to the white as it is possible for a mingled race to do; and when polished by a genteel education, that little distinction ceases to exist.

It is remarked of the people of colour, that they are peculiarly hardy, and far less subject to disease than either the whites or the negroes; of course a considerably less proportion of them are swept off by the general mortality of the country than of the two other classes. They feel a kind of pride in being removed some degrees from the negro race, and affect as much as possible the manners and customs of the whites. Few marriages take place among them. Most of the females of colour think it more genteel and reputable to be the kept mistress of a white man, if he is in opulent circumstances, and can afford to indulge their taste for finery and parade, than to be united in wedlock with the most respectable individual of their own class. They view marriage, indeed, as an unnecessary and unnatural restraint. On one occasion, a female of colour consented to be united to a person of her own class, a decent industrious man, but of limited means. For a few years she bore her fate without repining or regret; after which, however, she became uneasy and discontented, and often lamented the evil hour in which she had sacrificed at the altar of Hymen. Her husband, who gained an honest livelihood by the trade he professed, wished her to stay at home and attend to her children and household affairs; but the lady was of a pleasurable turn, and had, like most of her colour, a longing to enjoy a life of freedom and voluptuousness. She had been accustomed, prior to her marriage, to balls, parties, and jaunts, and she could therefore but ill brook this life of restraint and drudgery. She beheld with envy the gay, showy, and dissipated life which many of the companions of her youth led; who, being the *housekeepers* of men of fortune, were enabled to dress finely, and dash about in style in their carriages, attended by servants in livery; while she, poor woman, was obliged to toil from morning to night in dirty drudging occupations, without one faint ray of hope that she would ever be liberated from this sad state of thraldom, and enjoy again the dear delights of freedom and variety.

These are the sentiments of nine-tenths of the females of colour in this island, and accordingly at least that proportion are in the situation of *housekeepers,* as they are here styled, to white men; while the males console themselves in the same way either with one of their own colour, or with a sable companion. Though some of the females of colour are possessed of considerable property, given them by their white parents, or amassed by their own industry, they never aspire to a conjugal union with a white man; nor, if such a union were sanctioned by the custom of the country, is it probable they would desire to enter into it. A white man, indeed, according to the ideas of distinction which here prevail, would be considered as degrading himself by a matrimonial alliance with a woman of colour, however favoured by fortune or accomplished by education. But the latter gives herself little concern about this, while the most distinguished and opulent of the whites pay an illicit homage to her charms, and even the man of family shall openly and unblushingly forsake his wife and abandon his children to hold dalliance in her company.

If the females of colour are asked, why they do not more generally intermarry with men of their own class, their reply is, that the greater number of the brown men are either too poor or too indolent to support a wife and family, and that, moreover, as husbands they are very prone to be jealous and tyrannical. But the truth is,

it is not the custom of the country for these females to marry, and their own inclination and
convenience are, as has been said, in unison with
the prevailing usage.

Among the more favourable traits in the character of the women of colour are, their great attachment and devotedness to the white men who
choose them as companions, their general fidelity
in the discharge of any trust reposed in them,
their extreme attention to cleanliness and neatness
in their persons and houses, and their unwearied
solicitude and usefulness in nursing the sick—an
office in which they are frequently employed.

The brown children of the more opulent of
the whites are either educated in the island, or
sent to Great Britain for that purpose. Such as
have received a liberal education, and do not
follow the immoral examples around them, are
for the most part well-behaved, respectable people. Notwithstanding which, they are excluded
the society of the whites, and exposed to many
other mortifications, in consequence of the line
of distinction which custom and the laws draw
between the whites and the browns. A white
man, though he lives on a footing of the most
perfect familiarity with his brown *housekeeper*,
never sets her down at his table, nor introduces
either her or his children to his respectable acquaintance. If a white and a brown child should

be sent to Europe at the same time, and educated together at the same school, though they
may be in habits of the greatest intimacy while
there, they discontinue that intimacy on their
return to the West Indies, however much on a
footing on the score of accomplishments and
mental culture. The white Miss no longer re-
cognises her quondam companion and school-
fellow as an equal, because born with a darker
tinge of skin, and the customs and distinctions
of the country forbid her cultivating such acquaintance. Some such distinctions are doubtless necessary, constituted as society is in the
West Indies. It is, therefore, a pity that a parent, after having bestowed on his offspring a
genteel and liberal education, in a country where
at least they experience a respect and attention
equivalent to their merits, should suffer them to
be brought back to one where their feelings—of
which it must be supposed they have acquired a
suitable portion along with their mental culture
—are perpetually liable to be wounded by con-
tumely and neglect.

The more independent people of colour, shut
out from the general society of the whites, form
a separate society of themselves. They have
their own amusements, their parties, their visit-
ings, and their balls. The latter are fully as gay
and as expensive as those of the whites; and as

the brown females are the chief planners and sup-
porters of these, the young and dissipated of the
white men, their admirers, form a distinguished
part of those meetings of pleasure. On these
occasions the men of colour—the brothers, uncles,
cousins, and other relations of the women, are excluded; though sometimes the brown ladies condescend to attend a ball given by the men of
their own colour. The practice of white men
giving dances to the women of colour is thought
a matter of little consequence, except by the
brown men, who, being contemptuously excluded
from these entertainments, must feel the indig-
nity; in fact, it is calculated to excite feelings
not the most amicable between the two classes.
The white gentleman, who to-night leads out the
fair creole as a partner in the dance, may to-
morrow give his hand, on a similar occasion, to
the beauty of a darker shade, who dresses as well,
and thinks herself as lovely and attractive as the
other. The white ladies sometimes resent this
behaviour in their male acquaintance with a becoming spirit; but in general it is not thought
of much consequence.

The females of colour emulate, and even strive
to excel, the white ladies in splendour, taste, and
expensiveness of dress, equipage, and entertainment. At races, and on other public occasions,
they spare no pains or expense to make an im-

posing display, as if anxious to outstrip the whites in the race of fashion, gayety, and pleasure. The latter are often outdone in gaudy exhibition by these extravagant females; but the truth is, they do not aim at a competition with them; to be surpassed in costly finery by a woman of colour excites no uneasiness in a white female, though she would not wish to be eclipsed by one of her own class.

Many of the quadroon and mestee females are comely, if not beautiful, as they partake chiefly of the European features; but the mulattoes and samboes, being less removed from the negro stock, retain more or less of their thick lips and flat noses. Many of them, however, as well as of the negroes, have agreeable features. As for the Africans, their ideas of beauty in the human countenance are almost the reverse of those of an European. They have no idea that the finest Grecian contour is more beautiful than their large and gross features, and the jet-black Venus from the banks of the Bonni or of the Rio Grande prefers her sooty Adonis to the handsomest European.

The people of colour in general are not so mild towards their slaves as the white people; indeed, too many of them are exceedingly harsh and tyrannical; and the negroes, aware of this, are wont to say, " *If me for have massa or misses, give me Buckra one—no give me mulatto, dem no use neega well.*" Such of the brown people as receive European educations are however more humane and considerate.

The free people of colour are excluded from many of the privileges of the whites; they are not competent to serve as jurors, and they are excluded from all offices, civil, military, and ecclesiastical. These disqualifications are thought necessary for political purposes. About ten years ago they were in a much worse state than they are at present; their testimony, on oath, was not then admissible in the courts of law, and they were not permitted to inherit property beyond a limited amount. Awakened at length to a sense of these unjust grievances, they petitioned the legislature for redress, and accordingly the right of giving evidence, and of inheriting property, was acceded to them.* A few years afterwards they again petitioned the legislature for a removal of the remaining disqualifications under which they lay ; but their petition was rejected, with an admonition as to the unreasonableness of their demand.

But it is in vain that such laws and provisions are thrown in the way of this people's acquiring

---

* All free persons of colour, serving in the militia, are also competent *to save deficiency.*

an ascendency in the country, while other productive causes exist for bringing this about.
While the number of the whites remain station-
ary, or nearly so, the people of colour are rapidly
increasing. In 1788 it was computed that there
were 10,000 free people of colour in the island;
there are now upwards of three times that number.* That a population should be trebled in
thirty-four years, by natural increase within itself, were physically impossible; but this vast
increase arises out of the whole mass of the population, white, black, and brown. It is probable
that nineteen-twentieths of the white males have
their brown or black mistresses, either free or
otherwise, by whom they generally have children, who, if born slaves, are often manumitted.
This will account for the vast increase above
stated. A respectable clergyman in the island
assured the author, some years ago, that he
usually had occasion to baptize about fifteen
brown children for one white child. The male
part of this population may be divided into three
classes—namely, the offspring of men of fortune
and station (some of the most distinguished in

---

* Though this estimate of the number of the free people of
colour is not taken from any specific data, no regular census
having been lately taken of them, it may, at a moderate com-
putation, be set down at 35,000.

the island have families of this class), who are sent to Great Britain to be liberally educated, and are destined to inherit independent fortunes—the offspring of men in moderate circumstances, who generally give them a plain education, and leave the bulk of their property among them at their death—and, lastly, the offspring of men who either have not the means or the inclination to provide for them. This last is probably the most numerous class: many of them live in idleness and vice, a burden to themselves and to the community. Into the hands of the first and second class much of the property of the country is fast falling.—So that there can be little doubt that the time is not far distant when the free people of colour, feeling their own weight in numbers, property, and information, will not rest content with any qualifications short of what the whites enjoy; nor will the latter be in a condition to refuse this boon. Though this equalization, and blending as it were, of the two classes, be regarded by the whites as a great political evil, it will nevertheless unquestionably be brought about, at no distant period, *through their own agency*. A change in the morals and manners of the latter—not feeble and partial laws and regulations—can alone secure the respect and obedience of this growing class to their dominion.

The free men of colour are enrolled with the

militia of the country; they are embodied in separate companies, and commanded by white officers. The free blacks are also formed into separate companies, under white officers.

Many of the free men of colour are decent and respectable characters, and some are men of education and talents; but the bulk of the uneducated portion are indolent, dishonest, and vicious, leading a wretched and precarious sort of life, unless possessed of some property for their support, or brought up to some trade, to which necessity alone can induce them to apply.

A few men of colour have been so far elevated above their *caste* by the advantages of fortune and a liberal education, as to be received into white society; but it very rarely happens that a brown female is so admitted, whatever her merit or acquired advantages. If she has one drop of African blood in her veins, however remotely derived, it operates as effectually to shut her out from the society of the white ladies, as a moral stain in her character would do in European society.

APPENDIX.

APPENDIX

No I.

REMARKS ON THE VARIOUS MEANS PROPOSED FOR IM-
PROVING THE MINDS AND INCREASING THE COMFORTS
OF THE SLAVES—AND ON THE ABOLITION OF SLAVERY
IN THE COLONIES.

MUCH having been said, since this work was written, on
the further improvement of the moral and physical condition of the slaves, as a preliminary step towards the
abolition of slavery in the colonies, some additional remarks on this subject may not be uninteresting.

The principal desiderata of this improvement are—

I. The moral and religious instruction of the slaves.

II. The making Sunday a day of rest and religious
instruction to the slaves, and allowing them another day
in each week for cultivating their provision-grounds, &c.

III. The rendering the testimony of slaves, against
white persons, valid in courts of law.

IV. The abolishing the use of the whip as an instrument of punishment.

V. The enabling slaves legally to hold, dispose of, and bequeath property.

VI. The effectually preventing the holding of free persons in a state of slavery.

VII. The removal of all obstacles to the manumitting of slaves.

VIII. The attaching of slaves to the soil.

In discussing these points, the author will avoid all merely speculative opinions, and confine himself to facts, and plain and practical reasonings from them. He will candidly and fairly state, to the best of his judgment and experience, both the arguments in favour of the changes and improvements proposed, and the obstacles and dangers which may attend them, by which the reader may draw his own inferences and opinions.

On the benefits of the moral and religious instruction of the slaves, the author has already stated his opinions. With respect to the means of bringing this about, many things are required.

First, then, as to baptism: All slaves arrived at years of maturity should, if they desired it, be entitled to baptism; for the performance of which duty the clergy should not be entitled to any fee from the parties, but be remunerated, if necessary, by their owners, or the public. It would, however, be unreasonable to force a slave, against his inclination, into the pale of Christianity; but infants, and adults incapable of judging for themselves, should be baptized as a matter of course. With respect to the plan of instruction, it would not be advisable, perhaps, for reasons which will hereafter be mentioned, that every Sunday should immediately be allotted exclusively as a day of rest and religious observance to the slaves. But, as a preliminary step to such a proceeding, the following regulations, (in which are embodied the ideas and wishes of many highly-respectable proprietors) might be carried into effect in Jamaica, which has generally taken the lead in every liberal and humane improvement.

1st, A law should be enacted, in lieu of the one now in force, directing that all slaves should be instructed in the Christian religion at least once a month ; such periodical instruction not to be left to the option of the slave-owners, but be made obligatory, and a day to be given to the slaves expressly for this purpose, independent of the other days ordered by law to be given them.

2dly, The rectors should perform divine service not only in their parish-churches, as heretofore, but in all the towns, hamlets, and villages in their respective parishes, at least once a fortnight. This they could easily do, there being not more than two or three of these in any of the parishes. This arrangement would leave the exclusive duty of instructing the slaves to the curates.

3dly, For the purpose of facilitating the duties of the curates, each parish should be divided into certain central points of meeting, where the slaves of two, three, or more contiguous properties, according to local circumstances, should assemble and form one congregation—the slaves to be instructed by their overseers to appear decently clad on such occasions, and one white person at least from each property to accompany them, to note down the absentees, and to assist in preserving a proper order and decorum. By this arrangement all the slaves in the larger parishes would have the benefit of being instructed at least once a month, and those in the smaller ones once in three weeks, or even once a fortnight. In the larger parishes it would be desirable that the curates should be assisted by church missionaries, who might officiate in the remoter parts of those parishes, and thus enable the curates to perform their pastoral rounds within the space of three weeks. At all events, a regular monthly instruction of all the slaves in the duties of religion would be a most desirable beginning in the work of improvement.

4*thly*, As an encouragement to the curates, whose duties, if duly performed, would be laborious, they should be entitled to all fees allowed by law for the baptizing and marrying of slaves (to be paid either by their owners or the public), in addition to their stipends; and they should, besides, have the preference to all vacant livings, according to the term of their services in the island.

5*thly*, The Bishop of London, the diocesan, should appoint ecclesiastical commissioners, not holding any living or other place of emolument in the West Indies, for the purpose of inquiring into all clerical abuses in the colonies—such commissioners to transmit to him an annual account of the state of the church, and the progress of religious instruction among the slaves.

6*thly*, The rectors should transmit to the colonial ecclesiastical commissioners a quarterly account of baptisms and marriages among the slaves, also a particular account of the pastoral labours of the curates—namely, the number of preachings, and of separate congregations, together with the names of the properties to whom the slaves of each congregation belonged ; an annual account of which particulars should be forwarded by the said commissioners to their diocesan.

7thly, An exposition, drawn up from the documents furnished both by the general and colonial commissioners, of the state and progress of religion in the West Indies, might be published annually.

8thly, A full and free toleration should be granted to all sects in the colonies, on the same principle as in the mother-country; their missionaries and preachers to be amenable to the laws for any conduct or doctrine tending to disturb the public peace, or excite the slaves to disaffection and insubordination.

There are doubtless many who, either on the score of interest or from habitual prejudice, will find fault with some of these arrangements. This is to be expected. But until some systematic plan of this nature be established, the slaves will still have in a great measure to depend for religious instruction on the fortuitous labours of the Methodist and Sectarian missionaries, seconded by such liberal-minded proprietors as are of opinion that this instruction will prove a blessing to their slaves, and that it is a duty they owe to them not to withhold that blessing. The assembly of Jamaica, actuated by similar feelings, lament that so little has been done towards fulfilling the object for which they made so liberal a provision for the curates. Excepting in three of the parishes, the intention of the legislature seems to have been lost sight of by the curates.

The instruction of the negro children in reading and writing, as a means of accelerating moral and religious instruction, though a desirable and rational improvement, is generally viewed as a dangerous experiment : it is conceived that by such a medium of communication the slaves would soon begin to feel their strength, and that the safety of the whites would from that moment be placed in jeopardy. There are certainly just grounds for such an apprehension, were this plan forthwith carried into effect ; and extreme caution is necessary as to the proper season for its introduction.

The second improvement proposed would be a most humane and beneficent one, and would be still more so were it likely to be attended by the good proposed by it. But that is doubtful. The minds and habits of the slaves must undergo a great change ere a proper use of the Sabbath is made by them. Hitherto they have been accustomed to regard it as a day of which they were to make the most available use for mere temporal purposes ; to the industrious it is a day of labour, and to the idle, of sport and recreation. Thousands meet on this day in the public markets to sell their poultry and provisions, and to purchase various articles of luxury or convenience : it is a sort of hebdomadal carnival, where friends and acquaintance congregate, merriment prevails, and dissipation is indulged. Tell a slave that he is to get a day, weekly, in lieu of Sunday, on condition that he devotes that day to religious observance, and home-staying sobriety, and he would decline entering into any such compact—at least the generality of them would do so. But though such is the use which habit inclines the slaves to make of Sunday, no one will say that it is not just that they should have one day in the week to themselves for labour and another for rest. Some humane proprietors grant this boon of kindness to their slaves—except during crop—though the law only requires that one day in each fortnight, exclusive of Sundays, should be allowed. The truth is, trifling as the additional boon of one day in a fortnight may appear, it would be incompatible with the means of many proprietors whose estates are burdened with debt—(there are few which are not so burdened)—and of the small settlers. A proprietor of a tolerably fertile sugar-estate, yielding two hundred hogsheads, may receive from it, after all expenses are paid, the sum of £1200 currency : * if then he owes £10,000, the interest † on that sum will reduce his income to £600—being barely sufficient to enable him to keep up a decent establishment. But if from that amount £364 (the hire of 140 working slaves, of all descriptions, for twenty-six days, averaging them at 2s. each per day) were taken, the pittance remaining would be utterly insufficient for his support. The poor settlers would be still less able to afford this curtailment of the labour of their slaves. But the independent proprietors of large estates cannot make a more beneficent use of their wealth and power than by such an act of justice and humanity to their slaves.

The subject of admitting the evidence of slaves against white persons, by whom they have been maltreated, has already been considered. In the opinion, that no danger whatever would attend such a measure, the author is confident he is borne out by the conviction of every enlightened West-Indian who has ever bestowed a thought

---

* There were many estates of that size, even of the better class, which did not, some time ago, net half that amount. As to those of inferior description, they are not worth the cultivating. According to a statement published in 1822, it appeared that the crop of a sugar-estate, yielding 160 hogsheads, produced a greater sum to the merchant who disposed of it than to the proprietor.

† At six per cent., the legal rate of interest in Jamaica.

on the subject. A few years ago it was indeed openly and candidly discussed in Jamaica in a literary journal, conducted by a society of gentlemen, some of whom were members of the assembly.

The continuance of that long-standing opprobrium of West Indies, the cart-whip, as an instrument of punishment, has been condemned by every enlightened colonial proprietor, and no voice is now raised to defend it. In Jamaica the use of it is fast wearing away. On many plantations it has been abolished for many years past, and some less revolting instrument of correction adopted in its place.* However averse a proprietor may be to the too free use of the whip, abuses will prevail while it is suffered to be used at all: even an overseer cannot, if he was so disposed, effectually control the unjust and arbitrary exercise of it by the drivers, who are too generally hard-hearted and partial in the distribution of the minor punishments they are authorised to inflict. A driver may maltreat and persecute, in a petty way, the unfriended slave against whom he has a grudge, while he connives at the faults of those whom he wishes to favour. He makes a show, by way of saving appearances, of equal

---

* An opulent proprietor of estates in the parishes of Saint James and Trelawny has adopted the cat-o'-nine-tails as a substitute for the whip; while others conceive the twigs of the lance-wood tree (resembling the birch used in schools,) to be a still less harsh instrument of correction. The time is probably not far distant when corporal punishments will cease to be inflicted on slaves by other authority than that of the sentence of a court, or the order of a magistrate. The delegating the power of inflicting such punishments to inferior superintendents, must, however modified, be productive of abuses.

severity to both; but, by the dexterous command he has of the whip, he has it in his power to inflict either a very slight or a very severe punishment. On such occasions the ill-treated slave is too often afraid to complain to his master, thinking it would lead to renewed persecutions; and though there are doubtless men in the situation of overseers who would not permit such barbarities were they aware of them, it is equally true that there are others who will support the authority of their drivers however iniquitously exercised. It is absurd to suppose that the whip is necessary to maintain obedience and subordination among the slaves. Experience has shown that this is a groundless pretence. Some years ago a gentleman who had the management of a sugar-plantation, on which were three hundred slaves, tried the effect of interdicting the use of the whip upon it. So wedded were the neighbours to the use of it, that this proceeding was denounced as a *silly* and *dangerous* experiment, inevitably leading to insubordination among the slaves and the ruin of the property. The reverse of these presages was however the result; the slaves were orderly, obedient, and grateful for this act of lenity; they performed their labour with cheerfulness and alacrity, and the crops were increased *far beyond their former average amount.*

Slaves are not permitted to hold certain descriptions of property—as land and other freehold property, slaves, horses, mules, and cattle. Their owners are obliged, by law, either to give them the use of as much land for raising provisions as is sufficient for the support of them and their families, or to purchase food for them; and such slaves as, from age or infirmity, are incapable of

labour, the owners are bound to feed and clothe. Masters are also obliged to build houses for their slaves,
which, however, the latter cannot dispose of or bequeath.
But if a slave builds a house at his own expense, he can
either sell or bequeath it : it is as much his property, by
universal usage, as his pigs, poultry, goods and chattels.
No master is permitted to seize any property lawfully
possessed by his slave ; nor has ever an instance occurred, within the author's knowledge, of a master's seizing
for his own use even unlawful property claimed by his
slave—fire-arms and gunpowder excepted ; but he can
compel him forthwith to dispose of it, should it be injurious to his interests—as a cow or a horse pastured on his
plantation. Were the slaves permitted to keep and breed
horses and cattle, their masters' properties would soon be
overrun by these animals, to the serious injury of their
own stock. In short, the right of a slave to hold and
dispose of his property as he pleases, though not secured
by legal formalities, is, with the exceptions mentioned, as
universally recognised and held as inviolable as that of a
white man.

On the subject of the means adopted to prevent free
persons from being held in a state of slavery, little need
here be added to what has already been said. If a negro
makes complaint that he is unjustly held in slavery, the
magistrates (two of whom regularly sit in rotation to hear
and redress the grievances of slaves) take an account of
the particulars of his complaint ; and if there appears to
be any foundation for it, he is taken under their special
protection until a formal inquiry is made into the affair.
The application of the complainant is advertised for a
certain time ; after which a bench of magistrates is

formed, before whom the reputed master appears to endeavour to substantiate his claim: if he cannot produce
satisfactory documents in proof of his right to the negro,
the latter is of course declared free. But if the claimant,
dissatisfied with this decision, chooses to carry the matter
before a superior court, no expense or difficulty is thereby
thrown on the slave; counsel is appointed to plead for
him, the judges deal impartially, and if the claimant
again fails to prove that the negro is his property, judgment is pronounced in favour of the latter, and he obtains
his freedom.

The removal of all unnecessary obstacles to the manumitting of slaves is unquestionably a just measure. No
fees should be demanded from a master manumitting his
slave, beyond a moderate sum for the trouble of drawing
out the instrument. But the public good requires that
some security should be given that the freed slave shall
not become a burden on the community. Were not such
security demanded, many abuses might ensue. An avaricious and unfeeling master might manumit his slaves
after they had become unfit for labour, that he might
avoid the expense of feeding, clothing, and paying taxes
for them,—a duty which the law makes imperative while
they remain his property, but from which he would be
exonerated were they manumitted. Agreeably to a law
in the slave-code, if a master abandons or neglects his
slave because he is rendered incapable of labour, it is the
duty of the magistrates to place that slave in the parish
workhouse, to be there fed and clothed at the expense of
the master. The intention, therefore, of the law requiring
a deposite from the master manumitting his slave is to
obviate such probable abuses; but instead of a sum of

money being demanded, the bond or recognisance of a respectable freeholder ought to be deemed sufficient security against his freed slave becoming burdensome to the parish, especially if such slave is in a condition to support himself.

The existing laws relating to property in slaves are a bar to their being attached to the soil. Slaves are subject by law to be levied and sold on writs of *venditione exponas*, for satisfaction of judgment debts. This law could not well be disturbed ; an *ex post facto* law rendering it nugatory would be a direct interference with the rights of creditors. Were all the smaller properties merged in the larger, such a measure would be more practicable. On the larger plantations there is little probability of a removal of the slaves ; and from many of the small settlements a removal to a more permanent and comfortable home would be a desirable change to them. It is, however, a most grievous hardship to a poor slave, to be dragged away from a home to which he is attached, and a master from whom he experiences kindness. This liability of the slave to be seized and sold for the debts of his master is, in short, one of those evils for which the only remedy would involve much confusion and no little injustice.

In the late discussions on the momentous question of the abolition of slavery in the colonies, the mode most generally recommended is—that all the children born of slaves, after a certain period, shall be free; and some have suggested that the owners of the mothers of those children should be obliged to support them until they attained a certain age ; but the proposers do not say any thing of compensation to be made to the owners for the loss they would thereby sustain. It certainly must appear strange to those unacquainted with slavery and its details, that a law should be deemed unjust which declared a child, hereafter to be born—in fact a nonentity—free, without the consent of, or any compensation to, the owner of its mother. But the fact is, that a female with a healthy infant is held to be at least twenty per cent. more valuable than she was before it was born; and at five years of age that child is computed to be worth half the price of an able field-slave : so that if such a measure were resorted to, the least the owner would expect would be compensation in full for what he considered to be *bona fide* his property. Were this the only obstacle to the measure, there would be little difficulty attending it : compensation would be made, and there would be an end of the matter. But there are other and more weighty objections to such a proceeding. In twenty years after the adoption of this measure, the bulk of the young and vigorous portion of the negro population would be free persons, while the remainder would be slaves—a state of things inconceivably mortifying and disheartening to the latter, and calculated to excite a dangerous spirit of discontent and disaffection. There would be a favoured and free community of blacks in the midst of another doomed to slavery for life—and for no other reason but because the latter had the misfortune of being born a few years, months, or days, sooner than the former. It would, in fact, be the spectacle of a chosen and a condemned *caste*, formed from people of the same race and lineage—the one exalted, the other degraded, by a mere accidental cause, over which neither had any control ! The slave who had spent the flower of his days in faithful service to his master would have no cheering prospect of enjoying that freedom which had been gratuitously extended to the rising generation. The contrast of his condition with that of the favoured race—who had not earned, as he had done, the reward of freedom by a life of toil—would convey to his mind an impression of the most flagrant injustice. But it is not probable that such an unnatural state of things would long exist without producing a convulsion, in which the liberated race themselves would probably be aiding and assisting. The ties and sympathy of kindred and connexion would powerfully dispose them in favour of their enslaved brethren. Instead of resting satisfied with the liberty they enjoyed, they would, from the moment they began to feel their strength, look with longing eyes to the possessions of the whites, and, in concert with their enslaved brethren, meditate plans for their expulsion. They would regard the boon they had received, not as the voluntary act of the colonists, but as one flowing from the parent country, as the friend of universal freedom. They would behold the spectacle of a negro empire in their immediate neighbourhood—of the history of which they would be fully informed;* they would see other revolutions, either matured or in progress, in the condition of the negro race; and they would be incited by the example to throw off all subjection to European dominion.

---

* So completely has all intercourse with Hayti been heretofore guarded against, that the slaves of Jamaica know no more of the events which have been passing there for the last thirty years than the inhabitants of China—though the two islands are but a day's sail distant from each other.

In what manner this free black population was to be governed and employed—whether they were to mix as agricultural labourers with the slaves, or to form a separate community for the cultivation of lands assigned to them by government—whether they were to be compelled to labour, or to be suffered to lead idle and vagrant lives, like the Maroons and many of the other free blacks and people of colour,—and, if the former, by what laws and regulations,—are subjects · which the proposers of this plan of emancipation have probably not contemplated. They are subjects, however, of the greatest import, and involving many difficulties. If the emancipated race were not compelled to labour, they would soon become —at least the bulk of them—a burden and a pest to the country, a band of vagrants and plunderers: if compelled to labour—a no very easy matter—they would be exempt from the harsh treatment to which the slaves of unfeeling masters are exposed, but their physical comforts would probably be far inferior to those of the better-treated slaves.

The abolition of slavery, in whatever light viewed, is a measure pregnant with danger and encompassed with difficulties. One thing is certain—and that is, that no scheme of emancipation can safely be attempted until a great improvement has been produced in the minds and habits of the slaves. When this has been effected, it would, in the opinion of the author, be more prudent and practicable, as a first step towards the desired change, to extend the boon of freedom to all slaves after a certain period of service, than to declare the children free—the value of such slaves being paid by the government to their respective owners; every liberated slave to engage himself in the service of some employer, either his former master or other proprietor, at a stipulated rate of wages, under pain of being dealt with as a vagrant. By this plan a cheering prospect would be held out to the slave, by which his labours would be lightened and his mind soothed and encouraged; while the master would have an additional inducement for treating his faithful slave with kindness, namely, that he might retain him in his employment when the period of his service had expired. In the meantime, asylums in each parish, established by government, would be required for the reception of such of those emancipated slaves as age, infirmity, or accident, rendered incapable of supporting themselves. If such a beginning proved successful, there would no longer be danger in educating the children of the slaves; and other improvements would naturally follow those preliminary ones.

The author offers these remarks with great deference; they are the result of a most attentive consideration of the very important question to which they relate: still they are but opinions, and, as such, liable to error. No one can with certainty anticipate what the precise results would be of the great change proposed to be introduced in the colonies; but all agree that it is one of extreme difficulty and hazard.

No II.

REMARKS SUGGESTED BY THE GREAT MORTALITY AMONG
THE TROOPS IN 1821.

A DREADFUL epidemic fever broke out in the above year
among the troops in Jamaica, particularly in the 50th
and 92d regiments, which in two months lost nearly two-
thirds of their number: all the field-officers, and the
greater part of the captains and subalterns, fell victims to
this terrible visitation. Its ravages were also severely
felt in Kingston.

The following remarks, suggested by that event, were
published in Jamaica.

The late mortality which has prevailed in Kingston
and its neighbourhood, but particularly at Up Park
Camp, among the troops stationed there, is truly deplorable. It is painful to think that so many brave men,
who have so often faced danger and death in fighting
the battles of their country, should be thus cut off by a
cruel disease, far from their homes—the hope of revisit-
ing which and enjoying an honourable repose had often
cheered them in the hour of peril and privation.

To guard against a malady so direful, so unsparing in
its ravages, is doubtless an object of infinite importance;
and those who can offer any useful thoughts or hints on
such a subject, derived from experience and observation,
are at least rendering a well-meant service to the cause of

humanity. Under this impression, the writer ventures to offer the following remarks; which, though they may not be new to persons some time resident in the country, may at least not be without their use to those who are strangers to the climate.

The degree of virulence attending a malignant epidemic fever, prevailing in a camp, in this island, must depend, the writer conceives,—first, on the predisposition in the habits and constitutions of the men to febrile affection; secondly, on the nature of the situation in which the camp is placed; and, thirdly, on the manner of life the soldiers lead.

When troops first arrive here from England, they are generally full of health and vigour, and many of them are of gross habits. This is precisely that state of body, in new-comers, which fever attacks with the most fatal virulence. To effect an alteration in the system, some preparation, previously to or immediately on their arrival, is, therefore, highly advisable;—namely, by cooling, laxative, and antibilious medicines, and, where the habit is very full, by bleeding. This latter practice is not generally resorted to; but the writer has known it productive of very beneficial effects.

The second point is one of very great moment. There is an inconceivable variation in the temperature and salubrity of different parts of this island. In low situations, near the sea, and especially if they be in the neighbourhood of stagnant marshes, persons live in a very different climate and breathe a very different air from what they would do in the mountainous parts of the interior, about fifteen or twenty miles from the coast. In the former, the atmosphere is not only heated to an extent of twelve or fifteen degrees beyond that of the latter, but is often loaded with miasmata from the stagnant water, if there be any, in their neighbourhood. In the mountains, a pure, uncontaminated, and comparatively cool air is breathed, and all that is required is to guard against improper exposure, or what is called *catching cold*—the fruitful parent of disease in hot as well as other climates. Such situations as the first-named cannot but be highly unfavourable to the health of new-comers; though such portion of the inhabitants as are inured to the climate may be uninjured by them.

Now, what the writer would propose is, that troops just arrived, and unaccustomed to the climate, should be marched, in a day or two after disembarking, to barracks in a healthy situation in the interior, for the purpose of a *seasoning* to the climate. Here they should remain at least ten or twelve months; and if, after that period, they were brought down to the low country, they should, during the hot months, or when sickness began to prevail, be marched back to their healthy quarters, should their services not be urgently required elsewhere. These barracks would also, at all times, be an excellent spot for the recovery of convalescents, or the restoration of the sickly and infirm. Stony Hill barracks must be a more healthy situation than Up Park Camp; but a situation still further back, as a seasoning barracks, would be far more desirable, as possessing a cooler climate, more congenial to a European constitution. To illustrate what is here said, let it be supposed that troops, lately arrived from England, and stationed at Montego Bay, or Falmouth, were seized with malignant fever: remove those troops ten miles up into the interior, and they would doubtless suffer much less from this attack than if they were to remain in the towns: remove them ten miles farther back, that is, to the site of Trelawny Maroon Town, and there would be a still greater probability of their escaping its ravages. But if those troops had been marched thither immediately on their arrival, it is more than probable that they would not have experienced this attack at all. This reasoning is drawn—not merely from a comparative view of the temperature and salubrity of the two climates—that of the sea-side and that of the Maroon Town,—but from facts which have come within the writer's observation.

Some short time prior to the breaking out of the Maroon war, the 16th regiment, stationed at Montego Bay, lost in one year nearly three hundred men, chiefly by malignant fever. At the termination of the Maroon war, the Maroon Town became the head-quarters for the regiments stationed on the north side of the island, and continued as such until 1813, during which period the troops placed there suffered very little from sickness of any kind; and as to malignant fever, *it never made its appearance among them.* The proportion of men, which the regiments lost while stationed there, was very trifling. The first battalion of the 60th regiment, consisting of from five to six hundred men, lost thirty-five men in five years, chiefly by dysentery, which, with intermittent fever (which rarely proves fatal), were the only diseases they experienced. Such a mortality was hardly greater than what they might have suffered in the heart of England; besides, the regiment was in a sickly state when it arrived at Maroon Town. The 55th regiment was still more healthy while stationed at Maroon Town. During seven months not a man had died out of seven hundred which the regiment mustered, and at one time there was not a sick man in the hospital—a rare proof of the salubrity of a spot not often paralleled even in climates deemed far more healthy than that of Jamaica. It would be a waste of words to say more in proof of the superior salubrity of this and other elevated parts of the interior of this island, compared with the intensely-heated atmosphere and impure air of the low lands near the sea. Falmouth and Montego Bay, and their vicinities, are far more healthy than Kingston and the level country around it ; but there is little difference in point of salubrity between the mountainous parts of the north side and the most healthy parts of Liguanea, &c. of the same elevation, on the south.

The third point is of equal importance with the second. In all countries health greatly depends on the mode of life men lead, but more particularly in hot climates. Undue exposure to the mid-day heat of the sun, or to wettings from rain, often prove fatal to Europeans not inured to the climate ; and men cannot here indulge in dissipation with the same impunity as in a colder region : even a single debauch may prove fatal. Conviviality of spirit is natural to men, in a degree endeared to each other by habits of intimacy and mutually-shared dangers, when met at the festive board ; but it should not be suffered to carry them far beyond that point at which a prudent self-regard should stop. In the towns and their vicinity, the gentlemen of the army are more exposed to the temptations of what is called a free life— in other words, the hurry and bustle of convivial and other parties, unusual sacrifices to Bacchus, late hours, exposure to night air, and their usual concomitants, broken rest, headaches, and sickness—than if they occupied the more recluse and tranquil scene of a camp in the interior. It is true, in this retired station they must feel the want of that mixed society which the towns afford— of balls, routs, and other amusements ; but, on the other hand, they would enjoy the inestimable blessing of health ; they would breathe a pure and refreshing air ; they would be delighted with the view of Nature in all her simplicity and grandeur, and have leisure for that most rational and profitable of all amusements, the improvement of the mind in science and literature.

With respect to the privates, their way of life depends much on certain regulations in the regiments to which they belong, and on the strictness with which those regulations are enforced. There is indeed one crying evil, which cannot always be duly corrected under the best regulations, namely, the excessive use of spirituous liquors—a practice which has perhaps destroyed more men, in hot climates, than all other causes whatsoever. In the towns, it is almost impossible to prevent soldiers from having free access to spirits ; and a license to the keepers of canteens to sell rum must be productive of equally bad consequences. Some of the soldiers may have the good sense to use this rum in moderation, and properly diluted ; but others will think this precaution quite superfluous. There is no habit which takes a stronger hold of men of the lower order than dram-drinking ; and the poor fellow who has been accustomed, in his own country, to *take off* his *noggin* or his *gill-stoup* of whisky, does not always consider how much more pernicious such a draught must be in a hot climate.

Next to a temperate use of spirituous liquors, the most

essential requisites for the preservation of health, in a tropical climate, are cleanliness and adequate exercise. Nowhere is cleanliness in apparel more rigidly enforced than in the army. But to be effectually conducive to health, it must be duly attended to in the apartments, the beds, &c. of the soldiers, the latter of which should be very frequently aired. With respect to exercise, nothing can be more beneficial to health than early morning parades, say from dawn of day till about seven o'clock. That marching and practising of evolutions, which would be most oppressive and hurtful during the mid-day heat, is, at an early hour of the morning, not only not fatiguing, but highly salutary and healthful. It is doubtful whether the keeping of their arms and accoutrements in order affords a sufficient degree of active employment to the soldiers within doors. It would, therefore, be an excellent plan, where troops are stationed in the interior, to have a public garden (from which both officers and privates, as well as the hospital, might be supplied with vegetables), in which the soldiers should in turns, at proper times of the day, perform a certain quantum of labour. An establishment of this sort would thus prove a benefit in two essential respects.

Sea-bathing (before sunrise) twice or thrice a-week, in a hot climate, where troops are stationed near the sea, is equally conducive to cleanliness and health.

Persons lately arrived in this island, and unhappily witnessing the wide-spread ravages of malignant fever, and the frightful rapidity with which it hurries its victims to the grave, must naturally be prone, in consequence, not only to conceive a most unfavourable opinion of the climate, but an idea that there is little or no hope of a recovery from this malady. Under this impression, should they unfortunately, in their turn, be seized by it, they give themselves up to a fatal despondency, which, co-operating with the disease, too frequently verifies their presages.* This is a deplorable case; for where both the body and mind sink together in utter prostration, there can indeed be little hope. The writer has known an unhappy panic of this kind produce the most fatal effects in a district of this island where malignant bilious fever, or, as it is called, yellow fever, prevailed. From the fangs of this disease it became a prevailing opinion that there was little chance of escape. This unhappy and mistaken opinion was productive of infinite mischief, for there can hardly be a doubt that terror did as much execution as the disease. Men, who, in full health one day, had been ministering at the bed-side of a dying friend, fell sick the next, and on the following was a corpse. Much about the same time (about twenty-five years ago), the same terror of the yellow fever produced in America, particularly in New York and Philadelphia, far more desolating effects than even in the West Indies. In these cities, but especially in the last-mentioned, not even famine and plague could have destroyed more numerous victims in so short a space of time. Philadelphia was at one time forsaken by all but those who were unable to fly, or by such as felt it a duty to remain to watch the last moments of their friends; and its streets exhibited a dismal scene of deso-

---

* The general sentiment among the troops, when the fever had spread to an alarming extent among them, was, that they would infinitely sooner fight all their battles over again than encounter so terrible an enemy.

lation, with no sound but that of wo, and no sight but that of the dead, and the agonized friends who mourned over them. Since that dreadful period, both those cities have in general been as healthy as any in the world of their size. The government saw the necessity of having recourse to some measure for tranquillizing the public mind at times when malignant fever might be more than usually prevalent. Accordingly health-officers were appointed, whose duty it is to watch over the public health, to guard against the introduction of disease from foreign parts, and to publish periodical bills of health, or, to adopt a lately-introduced phrase, bulletins of the state of the public health. This plan has been attended with the most salutary effects.

These facts are mentioned to shew how fatally an undue prejudice against a climate, or an unhappy persuasion of the hopelessness of a recovery from any certain disease, may operate. The suffering patient should beware of resigning himself to despair, under any such presentiment; it is perhaps more fatal than the disease itself; it gives it strength, it heightens its virulence; while a hope and persuasion that he will recover is, to use a familiar phrase, *almost half the cure.* Experience has proved that the malignant epidemic fever of the West Indies is by no means, under proper treatment, so deadly a malady as was once supposed; and with respect to the climate, it need only be repeated, that, in the interior and more salubrious parts of the island, Europeans may, by a regular and temperate life, enjoy as good health, and live to as great an age, as in Great Britain.

THE END.